CHINESE POWER ANIMALS

CHINESE
POWER
ANIMALS

Archetypes
of Transformation

PAMELA LEIGH POWERS

SAMUEL WEISER, INC.

York Beach, Maine

First published in 2000 by
Samuel Weiser, Inc.
P.O. Box 612
York Beach, ME 03910-0612
www.weiserbooks.com

Library of Congress Cataloging-in-Publication Data
Powers, Pamela Leigh.
    Chinese power animals : archetypes of transformation / Pamela Leigh Powers.
      p. cm.
    Includes bibliographical references and index.
    ISBN 1-57863-147-5 (pbk. : alk. paper)
    1. Astrology, Chinese.   I. Title.
BF1714.C5 P69 2000
133.5'9251—dc21   99–087142

EB

Typeset in 11/13 Galliard

Cover art and interior illustrations © 2000 Caroline Patrick
Photograph of cover art by Jon McNally, Benicia, California
"The Waiting Room," based on Kevin Skaritt illustration by Virginia B. Deans.

Printed in the United States of America

07 06 05 04 03 02 01 00
8   7   6   5   4   3   2   1

The paper used in this publication meets the minimum requirements of the
American National Standard for Information Sciences—Permanence of Paper for
Printed Library Materials Z39.48-1992 (R1997).

To James, Dawn, and David
for being my inspiration
to find sense in this world and
to raise my children in a healthier manner

To H. B.
for the intangible gifts that kept me going

and to Charlie
The Woodsman who saved
this Little Red Riding Hood

Contents

Preface

In 1990, I had an intuitive reading with Pamela Galadrial (who wrote the Bach Flower chapter herein). At the time she said, "You are going to do something new with astrology." I certainly wasn't going to doubt her, but I thought at the time, "What could I possibly bring to astrology that is new?" About the same time, my friend, actress Veleka Gray (who has appeared in numerous soap operas), introduced me to Chinese Astrology. I thought it was interesting, but there were too many things on my plate at the time to pursue it.

I had published a holistic newspaper, *Aquarius Rising,* from 1988–1991 and I had interviewed numerous people about their healing modalities. At one juncture, I interviewed Robert Waldon and Betty Lue Lieber about "Touch for Health." Muscle testing seemed fascinating and I became accredited in the practice. "Touch for Health" is based on the Chinese five-element system, into which the twelve meridians are integrated.

As an astrologer of some twenty years by that time, I noticed the Chinese had a "Time of Day Wheel" that related the Chinese astrology animals to two-hour increments during the day.

My friend, Kya Coté, and I wondered what it would reveal if we looked at the rising sign of a person's birth in relation to the Time of Day Wheel . . . and that was the beginning. I introduced her to the idea of using the meridians as pathways to use in her Reiki healing. It was a magic time frame and we enjoyed giving each other priceless gifts.

At first, I just used the planet and its associated meridian/organ in hypnotherapy, but as the work revealed itself, it grew and grew until it reached its current form.

Chinese Power Animals synthesizes Chinese Astrology with Western principles of astrology. In most instances, these dovetail very well. There are a few areas, though, that are unique to the work.

Chinese Astrology indicates one shouldn't marry the person on the opposite side of the wheel to your animal. Yet, in Western astrology, that's exactly what we do, to face our "shadow" issues and integrate them. So, too, did I find the Chinese animal opposite the animal at the time of your birth to be the type of personality you marry. Your mate may or may not be the actual power animal, but s/he will exhibit these qualities to you in your relationship.

In Chinese astrology, every twelve years, when the animal pops up again, it is assigned a different element; i.e., Wood Rat, Fire Rat, Earth Rat, Metal Rat, Water Rat, etc. In this work, which correlates the animals to the meridian system, because they each "rule" the same two-hour period during the day, we are assigning the meridian element to the animal. When you expand this to look at the dis-ease probabilities and personalities of the people in your life, it is very accurate.

When I looked to find how the Western astrological Sun signs related to the Chinese animals, I found there were different lists available.

I asked a number of Chinese astrology authorities. Gahle Atherton told me the creation of personality for the animal signs is the bane of Chinese astrologers throughout Asia, but they have learned to go along with the people in the West because they want it. Behind closed doors, however, they definitely do not acknowledge it (in a personality way). Instead they read the dynamic that exists within the individual astrology chart from their perspective.

Another authority gave me these assignments:

> Tiger month begins on 15 degrees Aquarius and ends on 15 degrees Pisces
>
> Cat (Rabbit) month begins on 15 degrees Pisces and ends on 15 degrees Aries
>
> Dragon month begins on 15 degrees Aries and ends on 15 degrees Taurus
>
> Snake month begins on 15 degrees Taurus and ends on 15 degrees Gemini
>
> Horse month begins on 15 degrees Gemini and ends on 15 degrees Cancer
>
> Sheep month begins on 15 degrees Cancer and ends on 15 degrees Leo
>
> Monkey month begins on 15 degrees Leo and ends on 15 degrees Virgo
>
> Rooster month begins on 15 degrees Virgo and ends on 15 degrees Libra
>
> Dog month begins on 15 degrees Libra and ends on 15 degrees Scorpio
>
> Boar month begins on 15 degrees Scorpio and ends on 15 degrees Sagittarius

Rat month begins on 15 degrees Sagittarius and ends
　　on 15 degrees Capricorn
Ox month begins on 15 degrees Capricorn and ends
　　on 15 degrees Aquarius

So, this is the "official" designation, and the one you are probably most familiar with if you are a devotee of Chinese astrology.

A third expert said the animal astrology available on the market now is akin to newspaper astrology in the West.

So, taking all this into consideration, I took the emotions of the meridians and applied them to the animals according to the Time of Day Wheel. Establishing that, I applied them to the Sun signs in Western astrology, and found that they lined up very well, using the Rat to equate with Aries and following around the wheel, since when the Buddha called the animals in ancient Chinese lore, the Rat came first . . . and Aries is the first sign of our zodiac and likes to be first. Try it out and see how it works for you.

Also, in Chinese astrology, they give an animal for the day you were born. This became too cumbersome to add to this book, but if you know the animal for the day you were born, you can incorporate that energy into your profile.

As an astrologer, I utilize this information in my readings. It adds a new dimension to the standard reading to be able to look at the emotions behind a planet, and see how the planet reacts differently from one chart to another as the meridian/organ is overlaid from the Time of Day Wheel (i.e., Pluto was in Leo from 1939–1957. The house position reveals a lot, but when you see what a person needs to heal in this lifetime, because of meridian emotions connected with it, it adds a whole new perspective).

As a hypnotherapist, I can read the chart, see what the potentials are from natal aspects to transiting aspects, see what meridians/organs are involved, and use the animals in guided visualization to tap into archetypal energies and enlist healing. A recent addition is to assign an apostle to each meridian, and use the animal to see the state of health of the organ in question and access the ancient wisdom of the apostle to find healing.

As a "Touch for Health" muscle-testing teacher through ELB, and a devotee of the practice, I have used the principles of applied kinesiology to muscle test many of these ideas and concepts to find the veracity of the material and to enhance the process from ancient wisdom to modern practice.

As a Reiki Master Teacher, I use spiritual healing as part of the whole process to create "Body-Mind Synergetics™".

Chinese Power Animals accesses ancient Chinese wisdom and the five-element system upon which acupuncture and acupressure are based, and synthesizes it with Western astrology, to bring you a new way to look at your world. I hope you enjoy it.

—Pamela Leigh Powers, 2000

A Chinese Power Animals Fairy Tale

Once upon a time, there lived a Boar who would be king. He had reached adulthood and had not yet taken a bride. His mother, the queen (who was a Tiger), decreed for the sake of the kingdom, that the Boar would marry. The Boar was morose and depressed and was not interested in finding a mate, so the Tiger took it upon herself to find one for him.

In the nearby meadow, a spirited lady Horse, full of life, was prancing about. The Tiger observed the Horse and decided that she would be just the mate for her dour son. The Horse was introduced to the Boar, who was only mildly amused. The family, however, decided that she would be the perfect mate for the Boar and declared a royal wedding.

It was a grand affair, and the Boar dutifully went through the motions; but even this beautiful bride and this gala wedding could not shake the Boar out of his doldrums.

Unfortunately, the story does not have a happy ending. The Boar was known to have cheated with a cute little Snake, and preferred her company to that of the Horse. The Horse gave him two sons, and attempted to live her life, determined not to be pulled down into the bog with the Boar. After a decade or so of marriage, the Horse decided that being married to the future king was not worth living this loveless life and left the Boar to find true love. She met up with a rich, powerful Snake of her own . . . a path that led to her untimely demise.

Part 1

Introduction to Your Power Animals

Chinese Power Animals: Archetypes of Transformation

Ah! The richness of the fairy tale! How better to understand the life of Prince Charles than through metaphor and symbol; to "see" him through his power animals in the fable on page xiii.

What are power animals? They are the Chinese animals that you are familiar with from year to year. In January or February of each year, we hear that now we are in the "Year of the ____" Boar . . . Ox . . . Rooster . . . Horse, etc. We have read about the characteristics and traits of being born in any given year of an animal. But there is more to it than that.

Being a Western astrologer, I didn't give Chinese astrology much attention for a long time, because I thought it was too vague. How could a system, where everyone born in any given year were alike have any validity?

I came to find out that we are not only born in the year of an animal, but also the month, hour, and minute as well. We have a "totem" of four animals who represent who we are (conceivably, you can be born in the year, month, hour, and minute of the same animal, but that doesn't happen too frequently), and define us more completely. When we keep refining it from the general to the specific, we start to sculpt a human being and learn some very valuable truths.

In ancient Chinese parables, it is written that, when the Buddha called the animals, the Rat came first. Then followed, in order, the Ox, Tiger, Cat, Dragon, Snake, Horse, Sheep, Monkey, Rooster, Dog, and Boar. They became the twelve archetypes upon which the Chinese astrology system is based.

But the animals are more than just characteristics of a large group of people who are born every 12 years. They are archetypes of healing.

You will find, in the pages of this book, that you can use their energy in myriad ways that will help and support you in your efforts to know yourself and others better.

Right now, if you don't know the animal for the year in which you were born, turn to page 306 and look it up. Then use the companion tables to find the month, hour, and minute of your birth.

The animals relate to the astrology signs, so find the sign you were born under:

Aries: Rat	Leo: Dragon	Sagittarius: Monkey
Taurus: Ox	Virgo: Snake	Capricorn: Rooster
Gemini: Tiger	Libra: Horse	Aquarius: Dog
Cancer: Cat	Scorpio: Sheep	Pisces: Boar

This system of relating the astrological Sun signs to the animals is based on the five-element system and the meridians and is different from the astrological correlations you may read elsewhere.

By finding your time of birth, you'll discover the power animal that is most personally yours. You'll find they are listed in two-hour timeframes:

11 P.M.–1 A.M. Rat	7 A.M.–9 A.M. Dragon	3 P.M.–5 P.M. Monkey
1 A.M.–3 A.M. Ox	9 A.M.–11 A.M. Snake	5 P.M.–7 P.M. Rooster
3 A.M.–5 A.M. Tiger	11 A.M.–1 P.M. Horse	7 P.M.–9 P.M. Dog
5 A.M.–7 A.M. Cat	1 P.M.–3 P.M. Sheep	9 P.M.–11 P.M. Boar

Finally, turn to page 310 to find the timeframe for the minute you were born and the animal that rules it.

Now, read up on your totem and see what truths it reveals to you in the following pages. Then, read on to discover how you can use them to heal.

I was born in the Year of the _____

Month of the _____ Hour of the _____

Minute of the _____

I Am Adored

Mr. Rat is a charming romantic and a bonvivant. He enjoys the good things of life. He knows he's adored. People flock to him and he accepts it as a matter of course.

One of his most sterling qualities is that he is very altruistic when it comes to others. He will be there for you, no strings attached, if he sees you are in need of some TLC.

In studies of rats, it has been noted that, if a rat goes to its food bowl and steps on a metal plate that sends a charge of electricity over to another rat . . . who jumps in the air because of it . . . the first rat will put two and two together eventually and realize it has something to do with his actions. At that point, the rat will cease going to the bowl and will not eat in order that the other rat will not be hurt.

So, too, do Rat people do what needs to be done without thought of any return. They are the proverbial gentlemen who toss their coats into the puddle so their lady faire can step across without getting wet.

But, Mr. Rat has his moments. He can also be a scavenger, living off the garbage left behind by others. Mr. Rat is small and feels vulnerable. He has lost touch with his natural surroundings. What would he do without the cast-offs of others? This Rat is hard to adore. It carries disease—or, more accurately, dis-ease; being uncomfortable, not being in harmony. He is abandoned by society, which loses sight of his charm.

Mr. Rat can become very subjective about people, places, and things and no one can change his mind. His likes are either black or white; there isn't much gray area in between. He has strong, ingrained opinions that cannot be budged. This rat can feel betrayed and lash out at those he feels have abandoned him.

The Gallbladder is the organ and acupuncture meridian that takes the focus of this energy. The Rat is a master strategist and planner when the energy is healthy and directed correctly. But if out of balance, the Rat energy can cause a

Born in the Year, Month, Hour, Minute of the

Rat

person to "lose it" and strike out with rage, because rage is the acting out of anger. Rat people build up to an explosive point and then, all of a sudden, let it go with an intensity and detonation that surprises even them.

The Rat's affirmation is **"I am adored"** . . . as in, blessed by God. He needs to feel the unconditional love of God as expressed through his personal relationships. When that is not forthcoming, he can feel abandoned and betrayed on a deep, subconscious level. Beneath and beyond the betrayal he may feel from others, there is a sense that he has been betrayed by God.

People born in 1900, 1912, 1924, 1936, 1948, 1960, 1972, 1984, and 1996 share the **Year of the Rat.**

Aries-born have the **Rat** as the power animal for their sign.

Those born between **11 P.M. and 1 A.M.** incorporate this energy into their personality.

During the late 80s and for most of the 90s, **Virgos** focused on Rat/Gallbladder issues and learned that they have a lot of subconscious anger that has come to the surface and surprisingly, it leaked out in sudden bursts of rage they didn't even know they had. If you take notice, you'll realize many of your Virgo friends (and those with late Leo birthdays) had gallstones, migraines, or sciatica during that period.

Where does this energy work in your life?

Everyone has Rat energy somewhere in his/her chart. Wherever this energy is concentrated, due to the time of your birth, you will be very subjective about the people and places it represents. There is no objectivity here. Other people can wonder why you are so close-minded in this area, and sometimes you do, too. If you're going to get angry, this is where, and with whom, you'll do it. It also shows where you will draw in Rat-type people to mirror this energy back to you.

Born 11 A.M.–1 A.M.: The Rat's energies are yours. You have issues with abandonment and betrayal . . . and your search is for unconditional love. When expressed positively, you are adored by those around you and feel loved by God and the universe. You have a natural ability to make clear plans, and are an excellent judge of character.

Born 1 A.M.–3 A.M.: The Ox carries out the orders of the Rat, who dwells in its subconscious. It needs the Rat to be motivated from positive energy in order to get clear directions. When the Rat is running amuck, emotionally upset in its subconscious, the Ox tends to get irritable and impatient and can't follow through.

Born 3 A.M.–5 A.M.: The Tiger can be adored or betrayed by her friends. She needs to be careful of whom she draws in. She may be left out of an inheritance from father and feel abandoned in favor of other siblings. The Tiger can be totally adored by her mate or find that his love leaves something to be desired.

Born 5 A.M.–7 A.M.: The Cat and the Rat are natural enemies, but here, the Cat is dominated by the Rat, because it reflects the personality of the Cat's father. The Cat may stalk the Rat because of the Rat's treatment of it when it was small. In the corporate world, the Cat can be a Rat when dealing with subordinates and needs to remember that adoration, in the guise of positive strokes, does more than keeping them off guard with the threat of firing (abandonment). The Cat has very subjective feelings about the Rat father that other people don't understand.

Born 7 A.M.–9 A.M.: The Dragon breathes fire when it comes to religion. It will never be a topic of idle conversation. The Dragon can get headstrong when it comes to religious principles. The Dragon can have a Rat type for a priest or sports coach and can seethe with anger if the treatment isn't correct.

Born 9 A.M.–11 A.M.: The Snake finds the Rat energy expressed in the bedroom. The Snake is never neutral about sex. If she feels betrayed, she will have a single-minded purpose to get even. Positively, the Snake can feel truly adored sexually. The Snake's mate can treat her like a queen, but she may shy away from Prince Charming and never experience this true love because of previous relationships where she was dumped abruptly, thus creating the "rejector" knee-jerk-type reactions.

Born 11 A.M.–1 P.M.: The Horse has the Rat as its mate. The Horse can overpower the Rat with its size. The Horse, though, has a big heart, and the Rat can be altruistic, so it has the potential of a good relationship. There's no middle ground here, the two either love each other deeply or engender volatile emotions. The Horse can feel totally adored by its mate, or draw in someone who is afraid of betrayal, so keeps her at bay.

Born 1 P.M.–3 P.M.: The Sheep can be the darling of the office to whom everyone turns, or be "hung out to dry" by an employer or another employee. The Sheep will not let this rest and can get into real grudge matches periodically.

Born 3 P.M.–5 P.M.: The Monkey is attracted to Rats. It may not become a committed relationship, but there is a definite chemistry. The Monkey can have a Rat as a first child (or second sibling after him) and the feeling between them will always be intense.

Born 5 P.M.–7 P.M.: The Rooster may have been abandoned by its mother, or can feel the full adoration of God through the love of its mother. Again, there is no objectivity here; the relationship is fraught with emotion no matter which way it goes.

Born 7 P.M.–9 P.M.: The Dog has siblings with Rat traits. They either get along well with their sibs or thay can have intense anger between them. In grade school they can have Rats as pivotal teachers in their lives, who will either make them teacher's pet or be volatile and subjective in their expression.

Born 9 P.M.–11 P.M.: The Boar hoards his money for a rainy day. Don't think he'll be objective about his finances or share with anyone else. Cut into his profits and you'll get him out of his bog when nothing else will.

I Am Independent and Free

The Ox often has a yoke around its neck. It plows the fields at the direction of its master. The Ox looks neither left nor right, but stares straight ahead and keeps its eye on the task that lays ahead.

The Ox is a beast of burden. It bulks up in order to carry the heavy load. The Ox can be content in its lot, never looking for anything more, or it can become frustrated at its lackluster life.

The Ox needs to take the yoke off of in order to be free. The Ox seeks independence and freedom, and can't do it when she's behind the plow (for the Ox is a yin energy in this study and will be referred to as "she"). She develops a deep anger that will eventually surface, a resentment for having been denied her destiny.

Being behind the plow for so long, the Ox can be immature. Not the wild, crazy kind of immaturity, or the self-centered type—but, because she has been single-focused and staring straight ahead for so long, she has missed out on a lot along the way. Being essentially stifled and held back, there is a sense of being naive, of not being exposed to life, not having experienced enough variables to make quality decisions.

The Ox is competitive and wants to win. This archetype will not shirk from the task. The Ox can become frustrated and angry when things don't go her way. She can lash out at others when she's held back from accomplishing what she wants. But support her in growing into her full potential, and you'll have a contented Ox who glories in the creative process.

The Liver is the organ and acupuncture meridian that is the focus of the Ox energy. It takes the feelings of repression and turns them into anger. The Liver meridian not only controls the function of the organ, but also rules the autonomic nervous system. "Liver people" can be rash and impatient and not think things through. They can have one

Born in the Year, Month, Hour, Minute of the Ox

course of action one day and another the next. They chafe at being kept from living their lives to the fullest and yet sabotage their best efforts at getting ahead.

The Ox affirmation is **"I am independent and free."** It deals with being open, free, and autonomous. The Ox needs to go beyond the mundane and reach the stars. The Ox needs to grow to its full potential and not be stunted in its growth. To be creative is to have infinite possibilities, to be bounded by nothing. To be stifled and repressed leads the Ox to be morose and angry, snorting and pawing the earth over its frustration.

People born in 1901, 1913, 1925, 1937, 1949, 1961, 1973, 1985, and 1997 share the **Year of the Ox.**

Taureans have the **Ox** as the power animal for their sign.

Those born between 1 A.M. and 3 A.M. incorporate this energy into their personality.

During the late 80s and for most of the 90s, **Leos** focused on Ox/Liver issues and learned that they have been held back in some area of their life, not living it to its full potential. Anger has simmered beneath the surface, to rise up occasionally and snort!

Where does this energy work in your life?

Everyone has Ox energy somewhere in his/her chart. Wherever this energy is concentrated, due to the time of your birth, you will find yourself stifled in this area and will seek to break free and grow to your highest potential. You will also draw people in these areas who will be mirrors of how intense this desire is and how stifled you may be.

Born 1 A.M.–3 A.M.: The Ox is your primary animal. It defines who you are. You are extremely creative and need to be allowed to follow your bliss. Your parents may have tried to make life too safe for you, and hence, there is a type of immaturity because you haven't experienced a lot of life. When imbalanced, you can be irritable and impatient and not be able to handle refined motor skills. You have a fierce independent streak that often is not allowed to express itself . . . which makes you angry. At some point in your life, you need to throw off the yoke and experience life.

Born 3 A.M.–5 A.M.: The Tiger's anger is beneath the surface. She doesn't show it often, but it's there. The Tiger tends to get frustrated at the slow pace of her spiritual growth.

Born 5 A.M.–7 A.M.: The Cat has sturdy, dependable friends. He can be surprised that they are hotheaded at times. Father could have controlled the Cat by threatening to withhold his rightful inheritance. The Cat's self-esteem issues can be bound up in Father's threat of abandonment over money.

Born 7 A.M.–9 A.M.: The Dragon has an Ox for a male authority figure. Dad probably plowed through life, nose to the grindstone, and perhaps didn't appreciate the Dragon's magical imagination. The Dragon can use the same approach in his career and feel thwarted if he isn't careful. The Dragon needs to play to win rather than playing not to lose.

Born 9 A.M.–11 A.M.: The Snake is traditional in spiritual values. She goes by the book and follows the orthodox view. The Snake must break from this upbringing in order to transform. Religious teachers and coaches in the Snake's life can be Ox types.

Born 11 A.M.–1 P.M.: The Horse finds her mate is very conventional in bed. There may not be much romance in the relationship. The Horse may also be fiercely independent and become morose if she cannot throw off her yoke and explore her sexuality.

Born 1 P.M.–3 P.M.: The Sheep has an Ox for a mate. If the Sheep is in victor mode, and the Ox is free to grow to "her" full potential, then they can go far. If the Sheep feels victimized and the Ox is repressed, they can bring each other down.

Born 3 P.M.–5 P.M.: The Monkey works for an Ox type. If the Ox allows the Monkey full expression, so that the Monkey can climb high in the trees and get a full perspective, they can be very successful. However, if the Ox is overbearing and suppresses the Monkey, the primate can make the Ox pay in many subtle ways.

Born 5 P.M.–7 P.M.: The Rooster is attracted to the Ox. The Ox likes having the Rooster tell her when to get up and what to do.

An independent Ox may become frustrated with the Rooster's henpecking.

Born 7 P.M.–9 P.M.: The Dog has an Ox for a mom. The Dog's foundation tends to be one of smothering love, so the Dog tends to be territorial, because she hasn't been socialized a lot as a child. The Dog has a fierce independent streak that is not often acknowledged and needs to be fostered.

Born 9 P.M.–11 P.M.: The Boar can be bored in school unless properly challenged. Teachers can be Ox types. Some can inspire to the heights of greatness. Others will be pedantic and just go through the paces, much like the Ox plowing a row.

Born 11 P.M.–1 A.M.: The Rat is very serious when it comes to money. He tends to take the conventional route and not take risks when it comes to investment. He'd rather see a small, safe return than speculate.

I Am Recognized

The Tiger is formidable. She has a substantial ego. She enjoys her status in the jungle. As a symbol, she is known for being a go-getter, a "fast cat." She has stamina, strength, and a power for overcoming. She can also be a "paper tiger" without much weight or substance, if her ego has been denied.

Ignore the Tiger and you have the proverbial, "tiger by the tail." You know you are in for a tussle.

She's a presence to be reckoned with. You will not ignore her lightly. If you want to tame her, "handle her," ignoring her will cause her to act in one of two ways. She will roar and demand the attention due her, or she'll sulk and get depressed.

The Tiger is proud and displays leadership in the jungle. If the ego is not acknowledged and the Tiger not granted its status, it has little reason for living. It tends to be sad and melancholy. It's days are gray no matter how brightly the Sun is shining.

The Tiger needs the limelight. She needs to be the center of attention. She enjoys having everyone pay court and tell her how wonderful she is. But she gives as much as she receives. She has a tremendous capacity to open up the largesse within her and give to her adoring throng.

When she's in her element, the Tiger feels alive and the Sun shines brightly. When she's being ignored, or her ego has been stepped on and her natural talents not appreciated, she can feel dead inside—whereupon she puts on a mask of compliance and slowly fades away. . . .

The Lung is the organ and acupuncture meridian that takes the focus of the Tiger's energy. The Tiger needs to have a healthy ego and feel inspired and enthusiastic about life. When that is not happening, the Tiger can feel dead inside and depression can ensue. Some Tigers have a low-grade depression continually that is hard for them to shake.

Born in the Year, Month, Hour, Minute of the

Tiger

They never seem to be able to get "up" for anything, no matter how exciting it is. It is natural for the lungs to expand, and this is where we feel proud about ourselves and excited about the future. When we are depressed, we tend to breathe shallowly and the lungs get used to being in this shallow state.

"**I am alive**" is the Tiger's affirmation. The Tiger can close down and become grief-stricken over life's challenges. The depression that results can lead the Tiger down a long, lonely road. To find a reason for living again—to feel the life surging back into the body—is the Tiger's quest.

People born in 1902, 1914, 1926, 1938, 1950, 1962, 1974, 1986, and 1998 share the **Year of the Tiger.**

Geminis have the **Tiger** as the power animal for their sign.

Those born between **3 A.M. and 5 A.M.** incorporate this energy into their personality as their personal power animal.

During the late 80s and most of the 90s, **Cancerians** focused on Tiger/Lung issues and brought their grief up to the surface to be processed and healed.

Where does this energy work in your life?

Everyone has Tiger energy somewhere in his/her chart. Wherever this energy is concentrated, due to the time of your birth, you will feel sadness when you think about the people and places it represents. You'll tend to get depressed over matters in this area, and look for recognition here.

Born 3 A.M.–5 A.M.: The Tiger is your personal power animal. You wear a mask to the world, which rarely knows who you truly are. When sad, there is a certain heaviness that pervades your personality. When happy, you are full of spirit and joy and exude it to the world. You puff out your chest and are truly proud. You will not be ignored! You command attention.

Born 5 A.M.–7 A.M.: The domestic Cat has its ego energy reposed in its subconscious. It's hard for the Cat to tap into this sense of self. He tends to have self-esteem problems, and needs to tap into his rich unconscious to find his worth.

Born 7 A.M.–9 A.M.: The Dragon attracts Tigers as friends. This can be a magical attraction if the two are in balance. Otherwise, the Tiger's melancholy could bring the Dragon down. Dad may need to feel like the "Top Cat" and be ostentatious in his displays of money. The Dragon's mate can make him feel as if he's the most royal of men . . . or pop his balloon.

Born 9 A.M.–11 A.M.: The Snake can be a "tiger" in the office, constantly looking for the adulation . . . seeking a career that will bring her attention. Dad was a Tiger, who may have tried to steal the spotlight from the Snake. He expected his word to be law.

Born 11 A.M.–1 P.M.: The Horse will put her whole heart into any athletic competition. She has the lung capacity to be heard from the stands as well, if she's not a participant. The Horse loves pageantry and ritual in religious experiences. She can have Tigers as religious leaders or coaches who delight in giving her "breathing" exercises!

Born 1 P.M.–3 P.M.: The Sheep can be a real "tiger" in bed. His mate can get morose over finances and be a drag. The Sheep tends to grieve longer over the death of those close to him and may be hard to pull out of it. He can also mourn over money lost in a divorce.

Born 3 P.M.–5 P.M.: The Monkey has a Tiger for a mate. There can be a tug of war as the Monkey seeks to control and the Tiger seeks to retain a healthy ego. The Monkey must respect the Tiger's need to be the center of attention . . . and glory in the knowledge that the Tiger chose him for a mate above all the others who would gladly take the Monkey's place.

Born 5 P.M.–7 P.M.: The Rooster takes work seriously, and of course, is the one doing "cock-a-doodle-doo" as the day dawns to get everyone up and at 'em. The Rooster may be a good worker, but wants everyone to appreciate the effort, and to be recognized for it! The Rooster can have Tigers as superiors in the workplace.

Born 7 P.M.–9 P.M.: The Dog is attracted to Tigers. The Tiger has a natural ego energy that the Dog likes, because neither allows anyone to come in too close unless they give permission. The Dog has Tiger-type children.

Born 9 P.M.–11 P.M.: The Boar has a Tiger for a mom. She may have worn a mask and the Boar may never have been sure who she was. The Boar's foundation, and hence its depression, comes from how depressed his Tiger mom was during his childhood. If she was positive, it helps the Boar to get out of the bog.

Born 11 P.M.–1 A.M.: The Rat has Tiger types for teachers and can have his ego attacked or crushed by dominating Tigers. The Rat can have a Tiger as the next sibling after him and be continually trying to get out of his shadow.

Born 1 A.M.–3 A.M.: The Ox gets into Tiger mode over money. He can be open and giving, or he can constantly feel a heaviness on his chest from the struggle with money over the years—a heaviness that leaves him depressed over the in-come and out-go of money all the time, never seeming to make ends meet.

I Am Sacred Space

Mr. Cat will make you think he needs no one. He's self-sufficient, thank you very much, and he'll saunter in and out of your life without so much as a "by your leave" . . . but hey! Hasn't he been hanging around a lot lately? Does it seem as if he disappears for a while, but all of sudden, he's back again and ensconced for the duration?

Mr. Cat always knows the way home. Oh sure, he'll take off periodically and seem to be above it all, but he has an inner magnet that directs him back to his roots. You can rest assured he won't be gone for very long. At the center of his personality, he's not quite so sure of himself as he'd like you to believe, and home is always a safe haven.

Mr. Cat is usually one of two varieties: the first is the preening house cat who sits in regal splendor, knowing who he is and not needing anyone. And then there is the cat who continually preens and cleans himself, seemingly never getting clean enough.

Cats are always dealing with self-esteem issues—either they have it or they don't, and no one can tell them any differently. They can be overachievers, always seeking to prove they deserve their position.

Cats can feel defective, as if they came in as defective merchandise and nothing is going to change it. This is different from the Snake, who may feel shame, which is a temporary thing.

In the negative, Cats are often made to feel guilty or can do a good job of making you feel guilty. They tend to sacrifice for the sake of others and, at the extreme can be martyrs. Some Cats have neuroses about cleanliness.

The Large Intestine is the organ/meridian that contains the focus of this energy. The intestines are the elimination system of the body. Unfortunately, as children, we are taught that our bowel movements are "yukky"—that something that comes from us is not good. Hence, wherever we

Born in the Year, Month, Hour, Minute of the

Cat

find the Large Intestine/Cat energy in our lives is where we feel dirty or unclean about ourselves—a defectiveness that seemingly cannot be corrected.

The Cat's affirmation is **"I am sacred space."** The Cat needs to know that, as a drop of water in the ocean contains all the elements of the ocean, so too, does the Cat contain the energy of God, and God could not totally express unless the Cat person was alive.

People born in 1903, 1915, 1927, 1939, 1951, 1963, 1975, 1987, and 1999 share the Year of the Cat.

Cancers have the **Cat** as the power animal for their sign.

Those born between 5 A.M. and 7 A.M. incorporate this energy into their personality.

During the late 80s and most of the 90s, **Geminis** focused on Cat/Large Intestine issues and learned they have to stand up for themselves and not sacrifice for the sake of others. They needed to recognize their true value and worth and not give way to anyone.

Where does this energy work in your life?

Everyone has Cat energy somewhere in his/her chart. Wherever this energy is concentrated, due to the time of your birth, you will tend to have self-esteem issues crop up. Are you good enough? Can you do the job? Sometimes this is where you will sacrifice for others . . . it's also where you can be put down royally by the people in your life who represent this area and where you can have neuroses or have people mirror this to you.

Born 5 A.M.–7 A.M.: The Cat is your personal power animal. If your childhood was one that honored who you were and encouraged you to be your own person, you have a strong sense of who you are, and feel clean about yourself. But if you were continually told you were less and inferior, you have real issues about your own worth, and can develop neuroses.

Born 7 A.M.–9 A.M.: The Dragon has secret issues regarding his worth, which may be why he displays such bravado on the surface. He may breathe fire and try to intimidate you, but underneath, he has real issues about how worthy he is to have this grand position.

Born 9 A.M.–11 A.M.: The Snake has Cats for friends. The Snake can have a vituperative tongue and cause the Cat to question his cleanliness. The Snake may wonder at times why the Cat seems to skitter off from time to time, licking its wounds. The Snake's dad may not have been good with monetary affairs.

Born 11 A.M.–1 P.M.: The Horse has a Cat for a dad or an employer. The Horse may feel that the boss is just as critical as Dad in assessing his worthiness. Dad Cat could also sacrifice himself for the sake of his family. The Horse can get really irritated by the neuroses of his dad or employer.

Born 1 P.M.–3 P.M.: The Sheep has Cats for college professors or ministers. The Sheep may not seek an athletic career because his self-esteem may suffer. The Sheep can feel victimized if forced to grow up in a damning religion.

Born 3 P.M.–5 P.M.: The Monkey is a "cat" in bed. He can have real anxiety over his performance and feel he never measures up. Or he can have a true sense of his worth and be quite the "top cat" in the bedroom. He may also exhibit idiosyncracies in the bedroom.

Born 5 P.M.–7 P.M.: The Rooster has a Cat for a mate. The Rooster can be a workaholic and the Cat can be a martyr. If the Rooster is at peace and the Cat is confident in who he is, they can work well together. The Cat, however, may sit back and clean himself incessantly while the Rooster is up early, heralding the break of day and rushing off to work. The Rooster also has a Cat type as a second child.

Born 7 P.M.–9 P.M.: The Dog can overcompensate on the job. Never feeling quite good enough, she can overextend and take on every job that she's told to do in order to impress. The Dog really needs to get a sense of her worth and draw some boundaries.

Born 9 P.M.–11 P.M.: The Boar is attracted to the Cat. It finds its litheness appealing. The Boar wishes it could move with the cat's alacrity. The Boar often has Cat types as children, who tend to have intestinal problems. The Boar needs to be positive with these children and learn to lighten up.

Born 11 P.M.–1 A.M.: The Rat has a Cat for a mom. This can be a real cat-and-mouse combination if they aren't careful. Mom can keep a spotless house, and the Rat may feel mother-love is tied up in how neat he is. The Rat's father-in-law is also a Cat, and can either be playful or pounce. The Rat has real self-esteem problems as his foundation.

Born 1 A.M.–3 A.M.: The Ox has siblings that are Cats, as well as teachers in grade school. Cats are mercurial and jump around, which can be disconcerting to the Ox who is plowing straight ahead. Cat teachers need to convince their Ox students that they can reach the heights. The parents of Ox children need to make sure their teachers are expressing the positive and not affecting their child's self-esteem.

Born 3 A.M.–5 A.M.: The Tiger is catlike with its money. She can spend it all on others, thinking nothing of herself; or she can be quite the clothes horse, indulging herself. She tends to spend a lot of money on the home, making it a warm place to retreat to at night.

I Am Fulfilled

Mr. Dragon is wound up in his identity. He struts and puffs and is proud to be known as . . . parent . . . child . . . employer . . . employee . . . spouse . . . breadwinner . . . coach . . . grandparent. When the spotlight moves on, and he's been dispossessed from that role, he mopes around and feels as if his right arm has just been cut off. Mr. Dragon is what he does, and when he doesn't do it anymore, he is adrift. He has assiduously carved this identity for himself, and it defines who he is. He can be bereft when changes occur and he has to look at himself, without the role, and see just who he really is.

Mr. Dragon is a mythical animal of magic and fantasy. Or the Dragon can be a fire-breathing reptile, full of bravado and steam. Whichever role he decides to assume, he is always someone with whom to be reckoned. He huffs and puffs and calls us to look at our deepest issues of power and the hunger for it.

Mr. Dragon can be found in our solar plexus—right in the gut. Mr. Dragon has gut issues over getting his needs met, and can become obsessive when he feels "empty;" covering his emptiness by being a shopaholic, alcoholic, foodaholic, sexaholic, etc. He can be greedy and covet whatever he can get his hands on or his mouth around in order to calm his "inner dragons."

There is a fire burning in the pit of Mr. Dragon's stomach that needs to be extinguished. The Dragon needs to be content, to do work that is fulfilling, and be compensated royally for it. The Dragon likes the good life, to be larger than life, and have all his tactile needs met . . . immediately, now. He doesn't want to hunger for long. That fire needs to be quenched frequently. And what does water symbolize? Why, emotions of course. Mr. Dragon needs to be emotionally fulfilled to quiet down and feel content.

Born in the Year, Month, Hour, Minute of the

Dragon

The Stomach is the organ/meridian that takes the focus of the Dragon energy. When the energy is positive, the Dragon's belly is full, and the fires are quenched. When it is not, the Dragon feels empty, and the gnawing causes him to seek to assuage it by most any means. The Dragon can have addictions to hide the ache in his belly. His expectations never seem to be realized, and he is often disappointed and feels deprived because of this.

The Dragon's affirmation is **"I am fulfilled."** The Dragon needs to have his expectations realized, to be fulfilled, in order to find a contentment that will keep him from going from one thing to another, and never really being satisfied.

People born in 1904, 1916, 1928, 1940, 1952, 1964, 1976, 1988, and 2000 share the **Year of the Dragon.**

Leos have the **Dragon** as the power animal for their sign.

Those born between 7 A.M. and 9 A.M. in the morning incorporate this energy into their personality as their personal power animal.

During the late 80s and for most of the 90s, **Taureans** focused on Dragon/Stomach issues and learned that their hunger is dependent on their needs being met and their expectations realized. They held on to their identity and had a hard time changing roles. They went through a period of obsessiveness that they hadn't expressed before. They were more intent on attaining what they wanted.

Where does this energy work in your life?

Everyone has Dragon energy somewhere in his/her chart. Wherever this energy is concentrated, due to the time of your birth, you have a hunger and need to actualize it in your life. This is where you will seek to be identified. It shows where you might have addictions and/or obsessions and the people who express this energy in your life will show you how balanced you are in this area, by their degree of addiction, positive or negative.

Born 7 A.M.–9 A.M.: The Dragon has an insatiable appetite. It is your personal power animal and because of it you deal with quelling this inner hunger on a daily basis. Some of you are partially full, so you don't notice it all the time, but it is there. You have identity crises periodically in your life, losing your role as child— and then, when you are grown, as spouse, parent, and when you marry, divorce, the kids move out (and then back in!), etc. We all experience them, but you take them in and ponder the shift more deeply. You need to know you are a spirit evolving—you are not the roles you play in a lifetime.

Born 9 A.M.–11 A.M.: The Snake has suppressed feelings about his expectations being met. Thay are always just beneath the surface. The Snake hungers for spirituality and the truths of higher understanding. She may have hidden obsessions or addictions.

Born 11 A.M.–1 P.M.: The Horse may find that her father is greedy when it comes to money. He finds contentment in material possessions. The Horse seeks fulfillment through her friends and sometimes her expectations aren't met. The Horse hungers after a sense of belonging. Her mate may feel that money and possessions are adequate compensation and demonstrate the way he loves her, but the Horse may not feel the same way about it, preferring "togetherness" instead.

Born 1 P.M.-3 P.M.: The Sheep can be dominated by the Dragon father, or he can show him the magic of life. The more he can show the Sheep fantasy and magic, the less likely he'll be to follow the herd or be victimized. The Dragon father can be a scion of industry who's preoccupied with filling his own personal fire in the belly, or he can have open—or closeted—addictions.

Born 3 P.M.–5 P.M.: The Monkey can have the Dragon energy as a minister or coach or scholarly professor who would hold high expectations for him. The Dragon helps the Monkey define himself in contrast to others and leads him to be his own person. The Monkey has a hunger for religion or higher education and is a perpetual student.

Born 5 P.M.–7 P.M.: The Rooster finds that her mate has a deep-seated hunger that she continually tries to fill. He can be a big spender, causing havoc with their bank account, or he can be comfortably well-off and still feel that he doesn't have enough.

Born 7 P.M.–9 P.M.: The Dog has a Dragon for its mate. The Dragon can be overwhelming for the smaller dog, regardless of its size. The Dragon can draw out the Dog and help her to be more intimate if he is into the magic of the mythical animal. If he is overbearing, though, she can retreat into her shell, and hide in her modesty. She can become inhibited because the Dragon moves in on her too fast with an untethered sexuality, in the manner of Robert Preston and Shirley Jones as the Music Man and Librarian Marian in the Broadway musical.

Born 9 P.M.–11 P.M.: The Boar finds Dragons in the workplace: larger-than-life Dragons who encourage him to get out of his doldrums and find the magic of life . . . which he may balk at if the Dragon is too upbeat and pushy.

Born 11 P.M.–1 A.M.: The Rat can love a Dragon, but will marry a Horse. The Rat's kids will reflect the Dragon energy. These are large animals for the little Rat to handle. The Rat can feel overwhelmed by such offspring and they can be a handful. The Rat needs to watch out for overindulgence in his Dragon children.

Born 1 A.M.–3 A.M.: The Ox has a Dragon for a mother. There is a deep hunger at the base of his psyche that needs to be filled. The Dragon mom may have had high expectations for the little Ox; expectations that were hard to live up to. The Ox has a bedrock philosophy around identity issues, and Mom may have had an obsessive personality.

Born 3 A.M.–5 A.M.: The Tiger has Dragons for siblings, particularly the one after him. They probably get along pretty well, since each respects the other's power. The Tiger also has Dragons for teachers, who need to be magical and bring education to life.

Born 5 A.M.–7 A.M.: The Cat needs to amass a lot of cash. Money fulfills a need when the real issues won't surface. The Dragon energy can compensate for a lot of self-esteem issues, but one must face his own Dragon at some point, and find his self-worth.

I Am Self-Love

Ms. Snake has to be right. It's not that her ego demands it, it's just that she tries so hard to do everything right, that it affects her so deeply when she's challenged. "Didn't I cover all the bases?" . . . "Didn't I check it all out?" she worries. Yes, the Snake is a worrywart and frets when everything isn't just perfect. It's a lack of self-love, of course, and when Ms. Snake has found her sense of self, no one outside can assail her. She's constantly learning and widening her frame of knowledge. She works constantly on how she dresses, wanting to make a good impression. She can slither into a group and out of one with amazing ease. She's very intuitive, and when she feels her skin crawl, she knows the other person is up to no good.

Serenity is the quest for this Snake. She fears rejection and will often rise up and hiss (reject) first before she's rejected. Sometimes, she misreads the signals and can sever a very good relationship without realizing it . . . but better to sacrifice that, than to take the chance of being the "dumpee" instead of the "dumpor." There can also be bonding issues in childhood.

. . . And, oh, yes . . . The Snake has to have the last word. When she feels rejected, she will make sure that her word is the final one. You might as well just let her have it, because she won't stop until she gets it. Ms. Snake is always testing. Testing . . . testing . . . to see where your tolerance line is. She worries and frets and . . . pushes and pushes; subtly, covertly at times, but she pushes nonetheless, trying to find where your line is. The Snake is testing your loyalty, testing your stamina. Will you put up with all of the Snake's hissing, and shedding skin, and her occasional strike to bite???

In the process, relationships are strained to their breaking point at times. When you react, "That's enough!" and stalk away, the Snake has one of two options. She'll either shrug and say, "I knew that would happen. It always does."

Born in the Year, Month, Hour, Minute of the

Snake

Or, if the Snake values the relationship, she will have succeeded in her quest . . . she has found the line she must not trespass again to keep the relationship. And, content that she knows the perimeters, she will stay within them. Her relationships become much easier when the other party subconsciously realizes that underlying testing is no longer there.

Somewhere in the Snake's childhood, a lie was established. Either something was misperceived and the Snake built a whole scenario around it that wasn't true . . . or she was told a lie on purpose or by omission by someone that she constructed her life around. Part of the Snake's healing is to go back and find that lie and remove the curse that has followed her life ever since. Seeing the event from an adult perspective can often do wonders.

The Spleen/Pancreas is the organ/meridian that takes the focus of the Snake energy. The spleen transforms food into energy and thus is a transforming agent in our lives. Sugar is a downfall for the Snake, who can become numb in the warmness of the sugar in order to cover feelings of rejection.

The affirmation for the Snake is **"I am self-love."** The Snake needs to find acceptance for who she is. Even though she looks for it in other people, she must first love herself. She abhors being rejected and can be the true codependent making everything right so no one will leave. At some point, she needs to know that she is acceptable simply for being who she is. Self-acceptance and self-approval, becoming strong in her own identity, will start the healing process.

People born in 1905, 1917, 1929, 1941, 1953, 1965, 1977, and 1989 share the **Year of the Snake.**

Virgos have the **Snake** as the power animal for their sign.

Those born between **9 A.M. and 11 A.M.** incorporate this energy into their personality.

During the late 80s and for most of the 90s, **Aries** focused on Snake/Spleen issues and learned that, with their strong will, being right at any cost can have disastrous effects on their relationships. Other Arians expressed the other side and continually sought approval from others.

Where does this energy work in your life?

Everyone has Snake energy somewhere in his/her chart. Wherever this energy is concentrated, due to the time of your birth, you will seek perfection. This is where you will test to find out how much people will tolerate. This is where you will find the source of the lie or find where the bodies are buried . . . as in secrets. This is where you seek self acceptance, and the people who mirror this need approval.

Born 9 A.M.–11 A.M.: The Snake is the totem animal of the hour you were born, and you express this energy as a part of your everyday life. It's important for you to examine your relationships and the motives of others before you make decisions and take rash actions. Trust that you are acceptable in God's eyes, and that energy is expressed through your immediate environment, so that you don't test your relationships to the breaking point. Develop self acceptance so you aren't at the mercy of other people's approval.

Born 11 A.M.–1 P.M.: The Horse harbors feelings of rejection, but doesn't express them as does the Snake. They are always in the background, but don't come to the surface too frequently. The Horse tends to want to belong and will do what's necessary to achieve it.

Born 1 P.M.–3 P.M.: The Sheep has friends who have Snake energy. With the Sheep dealing with issues of victim/victor, being continually tested by his Snake friends can be a real trial. This is also where the Sheep receives love from his mate. When you have a spouse who is tentative about proffering affection, thinking the Sheep is going to reject it, and the Sheep sensing victimization, the two have a real trust issue.

Born 3 P.M.–5 P.M.: The Monkey has a Snake as father energy and employer. It's also the energy the Monkey displays to the world. In his work, the Monkey wants perfection and will accept nothing less.

Born 5 P.M.–7 P.M.: The Rooster has Snake people as coaches or ministers. It is hard for the Rooster to be heard by these people as they hold firm to their opinions. If the Rooster is a "whistle blower," it will be hard for the establishment to hear the truth.

Born 7 P.M.–9 P.M.: Part of the Dog's fear of intimacy comes from the Snake being energized in the area of sexuality. It's so hard to give yourself to someone totally when you fear rejection.

The Dog can feel the need to be perfect in its performance and thus create anxiety over not being good enough in bed.

Born 9 P.M.–11 P.M.: The Boar has a Snake for a mate. He's always trying to reassure her that she's the one for him, but the Snake is rarely secure. If the Boar finds himself alone, he will reflect these qualities as he faces his shadow issues and runs before he gets rejected. Self-acceptance is a big step in creating a hopeful attitude.

Born 11 P.M.–1 A.M.: The Rat draws in Snake people to learn from on the job. They fine-tune his need to do a good job and he finds that he can be embarrassed if everything doesn't come out perfectly. He hates to have the boss see his work as other than complete, and the boss expects perfection.

Born 1 A.M.–3 A.M.: The Ox finds that Snake energy is mirrored by the second sibling after him, and the first child. These people are anxious, worry about their popularity, and should not eat sugar. The Ox continually has to reassure them of her undying loyalty. The Ox may be fascinated by the Snake, but will marry a Sheep.

Born 3 A.M.–5 A.M.: The Tiger's roots are steeped in Snake energy. It was the mother's job by word or deed to instill in the Tiger a sense of significance. If that wasn't done, Mom's fear of rejection and trying to please her man no matter what left a lasting impression.

Born 5 A.M.–7 A.M.: If the Cat has a sibling born after him, this sib will reflect the Snake energy. It also shows that the Cat has Snakes as teachers . . . literally or figuratively. They will be strong taskmasters who demand the Cat be precise in his studies.

Born 7 A.M.–9 A.M.: The Dragon bases his financial empire on the Snake. The Dragon will consider his options carefully, so as not to make a mistake. The Dragon may have based his financial acumen on a lie that was established in childhood that he needs to define and change.

I Belong

Ms. Horse needs to belong—to love, to be in love . . . to belong to something or to someone, to cease to be the outsider looking in. Yes, to be the insider, to belong. She's felt like the odd horse out all her life, and her dearest wish is to be a part of the whole. She'll work hard and prove her worth. She's not afraid to get her hands dirty—although she doesn't like it—she'll carry her load and probably part of yours. She has a huge heart, which she wears on her proverbial sleeve, and she won't be ashamed to tell you she loves you.

To touch and be touched is Ms. Horse's desire. She's open, affectionate, and demonstrative when she trusts you, and she needs to be surrounded with people who will let her express this love. She loves beauty and needs to live in symmetrical surroundings. The ordinary or the sordid makes her cringe.

Don't rebuff this sensitive Horse offhand. Her heart will break and she'll walk away, head bowed and she won't risk again for quite awhile. She's vulnerable to the proffering of love and seeks to be one with her mate. She's loyal and trusting, but once you've proven that you aren't worthy of that loyalty, Ms. Horse can close down and not let herself be hurt again . . . or at least not for a long, long time. She'll "forgive and forget" a million times, but should there come a "million and one," it can be the straw that breaks the horse's back (rather than the camel's), and she can walk away and never look back.

"Have a heart," "cold heart," "hard-hearted"—all these "heart" phrases deal with the Horse who has been hurt one too many times. Then she can seem self-absorbed and may be remote, as she seeks to protect her heart from any more battering. If she's been touched inappropriately anywhere along the way, she can withdraw into her self and not allow anyone to touch her.

Born in the Year, Month, Hour, Minute of the

Horse

The Horse who has been "saddled" since birth may have been "broken" somewhere along the way. The Horse is always looking for that free-spirited animal that debuted on this Earth so many years ago.

The Heart is the meridian/organ for the Horse personality. The heart has to work all the time for us to live, and so, too, the Horse is in harness most of her life, doing what needs to be done, pushing herself too much sometimes in order to make her loved ones happy.

The affirmation for the Horse is, **"I belong."** The Horse needs to be one with another, to merge and belong. She is bereft when she walks a solitary road. When she's a maverick horse, cut out from the herd, she can become mangy, indeed, as her body reflects her separateness.

People born in 1906, 1918, 1930, 1942, 1954, 1966, 1978, and 1990 share the **Year of the Horse**.

Libras have the **Horse** as the power animal for their sign.

Those born between **11 A.M. and 1 P.M.** incorporate this energy into their personality.

During the late 80s and most of the 90s, **Pisceans** focused on Horse/Heart issues, reaching out to touch, to belong, and have learned in the process that forgiveness is the key to healing.

Where does this energy work in your life?

Everyone has Horse energy somewhere in his/her chart. Wherever this energy is concentrated, due to the time of your birth, you will give and receive love. This is the arena where you want to get in touch and have a tactile knowledge of everything that goes on within it. This is where you feel you truly belong.

Born 11 A.M.–1 P.M.: The Horse is your primary animal, and you long to belong, to be one with another. You'll strain like the mighty steed against the reins that keep you from seeking your true mate. You are vulnerable to others, and, once burned, you can feel that vulnerablity as being weak and shut down.

Born 1 P.M.–3 P.M.: The Sheep hides his heartfelt impulses. Perhaps forgiveness is the one thing that can bring the Sheep victory.

Born 3 P.M.–5 P.M.: The Monkey's mate shows love in a very heartfelt manner. She can be open and loving . . . or she can harden her heart for protection and pull away if she feels her love is not reciprocated. If the Monkey makes the decision to deny himself the relationship, the broken heart of the Tiger (mate) may not mend for some time. He has Horses for friends.

Born 5 P.M.–7 P.M.: The Rooster puts her heart into the career. The Rooster can be the beloved of her father or boss ("her" is used because it is yin/feminine energy). Or the Rooster can close down her heart to rise to the heights of business (after all, she's the first to rise in the morning) and can appear coldhearted. The Rooster is a workaholic, after all, and can love being at the office.

Born 7 P.M.–9 P.M.: The Dog can fall in love with far-away places and can be forever on the go, traveling the world. The Dog can have Horses for professors or traveling companions . . . or a second mate.

Born 9 P.M.–11 P.M.: The Boar gives his all in love. He is an ardent lover, who can lose his heart in romance. The Boar wants to feel the object of his affection close to his body. A lost love or a broken relationship can send him to his bog of despair.

Born 11 P.M.–1 A.M.: The Rat has a Horse for a mate. She can be quite a handful for the little Rat, but if she allows him to perch on her head and give directions, they get along quite well. If the Rat fears abandonment and the Horse becomes invulnerable—watch out!!

Born 1 A.M.–3 A.M.: The Ox has a big heart and he leans his shoulder into the plow and can go long distances without much appreciation. He longs to be free of the yoke and belong with others. He can have a Horse type for a boss, or find that he can really put his heart into his work.

Born 3 A.M.–5 A.M.: The Tiger finds the Horse energy reflected in his children and his lovers. They show the love the Tiger is capable of expressing. The Tiger is drawn to Horses, but marries Monkeys. His children are huggy, touchy little souls that need a sense of belonging.

Born 5 A.M.–7 A.M.: The Cat finds the Horse energy as the base of his personality. With the Cat's struggle with self-esteem, he needs a mother who creates a warm, loving home where he feels he belongs. If Mom is self-absorbed, the Cat can feel as if nothing he does is good enough.

Born 7 A.M.–9 A.M.: The Dragon speaks from the heart. He has siblings who are Horses or who display the Horse energy that needs to merge with another. He frequently has Horses for teachers.

Born 9 A.M.–11 A.M.: The Snake is open and generous with his resources when he feels appreciated. Push him too far, however, and he can flip his wallet shut, and moths will spawn inside.

I Am Victorious

Mr. Sheep seeks to be a person of refinement. He seeks a station in life where he can be respected and revered. He has a commodity in his wool, and he wants to get the highest price for it. Mr. Sheep seeks out friends and companions who are of a higher quality than most. No, he is not a bigot; he discerns who is healthy for him and who is not. For if Mr. Sheep does not discriminate, he can be pulled down into a quagmire of dissolute compadres who can lead him into less-than-honorable escapades.

If Mr. Sheep was raised in a family where he was allowed to say "no," and respected for his views and opinions, then he grew up knowing that he could expect to be victorious in confrontations with those in authority. He can then stand up and be reckoned with as an individual and not fall in with the herd. He knows that, by negotiating, both sides can win and there doesn't have to be an either/or in victory.

However, if he was not raised in this environment, he lives with a feeling that he won't be heard or understood no matter what he does. Family life was strict and authoritarian and one did not talk back to elders. In the extreme, this type of sheep can develop a "poor me" attitude in order to survive a very difficult childhood.

Mr. Sheep has tremendous talents—talents that can take him far and wide. That "wool" can be whatever he does best, and can literally be turned into gold if he proceeds cautiously. The problem is that he has a great zeal to be victorious, and, when the energy is imbalanced, he can ride over others in order to achieve it.

"Responsibility" is a key word for the Sheep. Sheep personalities need to accept responsibility when it is theirs to own, and yet also need to know when something is not their responsibility and be able to state it, and be able to delegate. Roles tend to blur with Sheep unless they are clearly defined in who they are.

Born in the Year, Month, Hour, Minute of the

Sheep

The meridian/organ for the Sheep is the Small Intestine. In order to be equal, in order to be victorious, the Sheep needs to be careful with whom he associates and choose people of the highest caliber who will be scrupulously fair with him and let him be victorious in situations where it is warranted. Then he can succeed in life.

There can be a codependent element in the Sheep's personality when his character isn't defined. It's too easy for the Sheep to "get along" at the expense of himself. When others run roughshod over him for too long he needs to say "enough!" The Sheep needs variety and to set clear boundaries about what he will accept and not accept in his life . . . just as the small intestine discerns what is healthy for the body and what needs to be removed through the intestines.

The affirmation for the Sheep is "**I am victorious.**" The Sheep needs to know who/what is good for him and who/what isn't. The Sheep needs to take "right action" and be responsible for his own behavior. The Sheep tends to bleat, and blame others for his sorry lot in life if he was victimized as a child.

People born in 1907, 1919, 1931, 1943, 1955, 1967, 1979, and 1991 share the **Year of the Sheep.**

Scorpios have the **Sheep** as the power animal for their sign.

Those born between **1 P.M. and 3 P.M.** incorporate this energy into their personality.

During the late 80s and for most of the 90s, **Aquarians** focused on Sheep/Small Intestine issues, finding themselves victimized in certain arenas of their lives, needing to find a win-win situation and not fall into a "poor me" attitude.

Where does this energy work in your life?

Everyone has Sheep energy somewhere in his/her chart. Wherever this energy is concentrated, due to the time of your birth, you will find that you have to act extra-scrupulously. This is the area where you can be victimized unless you, and they, act in the highest manner. This is also the area where you seek refinement—in the people it represents and the surroundings it reflects. This is where you find responsible—or irresponsible—people.

Born 1 P.M.–3 P.M.: The Sheep is your power animal. You can be a person of discrimination in the best sense, and have a nose for what is healthy for you and what isn't. You have experiences where you can choose to be a victor or a victim. The Sheep needs to let go of any victim tendencies and say, "I don't have time for this," whenever it comes up and refuse to devote any time to it. The Sheep must follow a spiritual path and not get involved in the daily machinations of life.

Born 3 P.M.–5 P.M.: The Monkey can be a "closet victim." Perhaps he controls his world, because he is determined that he won't be a victim . . . again. He needs to be aware of those "hidden enemies" who tend to work behind his back. These are most often self-destructive thoughts and behavior patterns.

Born 5 P.M.–7 P.M.: The Rooster needs to choose his friends wisely. Those he draws into his life can be of the highest caliber or be victims and the Rooster can be drawn into scenarios with them where it can be victimized through no fault of its own. Dad may be victimized in money dealings. A sibling who is the next oldest also reflects this energy.

Born 7 P.M.–9 P.M.: The Dog has a Sheep for a father. Dad could have been victimized in life, or sometimes, he could have been the perpetrator. In business dealings, the Dog can be victimized if he's not careful. He draws Sheep into his life through his career.

Born 9 P.M.–11 P.M.: The Boar needs to be sure he doesn't follow the herd in his religious experience. He must define himself and become an individual in his own right. The Boar tends to attract Sheep as ministers and travel agents . . . and second mates.

Born 11 P.M.–1 A.M.: The Rat can be victimized by a mate's money. The Rat might think there is money available in the joint account, only to find it isn't there. The Rat is better to keep his own money separate. The Rat may be eased out of an inheritance, or someone else's actions could cause tax problems.

Born 1 A.M.–3 A.M.: The Ox's natural mate is the Sheep (being on the opposite side of the wheel), as is its second child . . . and Mom's mom, i.e., Grandma. These people reflect the Ox's shadow self—needing to market herself wisely to bring the most for her "wool," and making sure that she raises her Sheep child to be victorious in life.

Born 3 A.M.–5 A.M.: The Tiger has fellow employees or an employer who is a Sheep. The Tiger, as an employer, needs to make sure his employees share in the profits and feel that they are part of the decision-making process, so they feel victorious.

Born 5 A.M.–7 A.M.: The Cat has Sheep for children, and the first child in particular. The Cat can also have a sibling two in line younger than him who has Sheep qualities. The Cat needs to ride herd on them a bit, and keep them motivated to achieve their highest goals. The Cat, too, needs to listen to his child and allow him/her to be victorious in dealing with its parents.

Born 7 A.M–9 A.M.: The Dragon has a Sheep for a mom. Mom needs to have a husband who respects and admires her and allows her to win, just as her parents needed to let her be victorious with them whenever possible. Otherwise, Mom can bleat and blame everyone else for her lot.

Born 9 A.M.–11 A.M.: The Snake has a Sheep for the brother or sister after her. She had Sheep types for teachers in grammar school. Some teachers have valuable "wool" to convey to kids; some don't. The Snake's parents need to make sure of the quality of her education and what is being instilled.

Born 11 A.M.–1 P.M.: The Horse has a Sheep for a banker or real estate agent. The Horse has to watch her money and make sure she deals with positive Sheep who will help her increase her assets.

I Am Faith

Thy Will Be Done—not "*My* Will be Done"—should be the hue and cry of Mr. Monkey. The Monkey needs to learn faith . . . faith in a world that is ultimately fair and will provide all that the Monkey needs. When Mr. Monkey experiences stress in childhood, he can opt to control his world instead—better to keep it under control than to trust that ol' universal energy, i.e. God, to do what's right!

In order to control his world, Mr. Monkey has to create a version that works for him . . . and often he will see, hear, speak nothing else. Even in visualization work, his world is "just fine, thank you," with a steely gaze that says don't tread any further into *that* subject!

Looking at the famous three monkeys of "Hear No Evil, Speak No Evil, See No Evil" fame, it actually speaks of denial—evil being anything that is other than the Monkey's conception of reality. Hence, you get:

1) **(Denial)**—everything is just fine. There is also self-denial, so that the Monkey . . .
2) **(Deny)**—. . . will deny himself something he wants very much in order that he . . .
3) **(Denied)**—. . . won't be denied something that subconsiously he wants more deeply, and may not even know what it is.

There is also a payback in this configuration somewhere. Mr. Monkey doesn't trust the universe to exact his revenge and often takes it in his power to do so himself. And the frustrating thing is that, in controlling one's world and paying someone back for a real or imagined slight, it tends to have a scorpionic effect. The Monkey turns the energy on himself in order to get the results he wants. For, in order to control his world and exact revenge, he denies himself something in order to achieve it, and, in the process, builds up this anger because, with all his efforts to control his life,

Born in the Year, Month, Hour, Minute of the

Monkey

still it is not going the way in which he wants. The Monkey who holds on too tightly to his world will sometimes find that Fate yanks it away from him periodically.

Sometimes the Monkey seems to have a dual personality. There is one person who is open and affectionate and demonstrative. Yet, there is another aspect of the personality that will override the natural inclinations and decree that, for whatever reason, he will control this aspect and not allow it to express very often. He places duty before his own needs.

The urinary Bladder is the meridian and the organ that takes the effect of this energy. Bladder-control problems, bladder infections and irritations occur when life tries to wrestle away control. Certain herbs are good for bringing the body back into balance, but the best cure is to let go and see just what the universe would do if it had a chance. In whatever area you are experiencing something you want to change very badly and it won't seem to budge, look to see where you might have a greater subconscious need to fulfill; so you will deny yourself that very thing. You need to reverse the energy and let go, so that you get what you need and allow the universe to mete justice in whatever way it deems appropriate . . . even if that is no justice at all.

The affirmation for the Monkey is **"I am faith."** The Monkey needs to let go and allow life to flow—to step back and be detached and watch it play out on a movie screen and realize there is a reason for everything.

People born in 1908, 1920, 1932, 1944, 1956, 1968, 1980, and 1992 share the **Year of the Monkey.**

Sagittarians have the **Monkey** as the power animal for their sign.

Those born between **3 p.m. and 5 p.m.** incorporate this energy into their personality.

During the late 80s and for most of the 90s, **Capricorns** focused on Monkey/Bladder issues and learned that life runs much smoother when they can pull back on their natural need to control and direct the course of their lives and watch the universe provide the perfect solution.

Where does this energy work in your life?

Everyone has Monkey energy somewhere in his/her chart. Wherever this energy is concentrated, due to the time of your birth, you will find the need to control, or have Monkey people mirror to you controlling elements. This is where you need to let go and trust the most. This is where you place an importance on duty.

Born: 3 P.M.–5 P.M.: You express the polarity of the Monkey most strongly, because you were born at the Monkey time of the day. You tend to take your experiences into the bladder and its corresponding acupuncture meridian. Depending on your childhood, you express the positive qualities of trust and faith and flow with the universe, or the negative, whereby you tend to be rigid and inflexible, stiff and unyielding, creating a world where you can survive. . . . or somewhere in-between. The better your childhood, the better opportunity you have to express more of the positive.

Born 5 P.M.–7 P.M.: The Rooster is a "closet controller" because the Monkey tendencies rule the subconscious. After all, the Rooster does decree that everyone wake up at the crack of dawn . . . whether they want to or not!

Born 7 P.M.–9 P.M.: The Dog is drawn to high-powered people who express the Monkey energy. If the Dog is too good-natured, she can come under their control. Sometimes, the Dog has to growl and establish her boundaries in order not to be absorbed into the lives of her Monkey-energy friends.

Born 9 P.M.–11 P.M.: The Boar finds the Monkey energy is expressed by his father and his boss. Authority figures tend to be demanding and exact payment when the Boar's work does not measure up. That is why he sometimes tends to be bogged down in his own morass of depression.

Born 11 P.M.–1 A.M.: The Rat experiences the Monkey energy in his world through contact with other cultures or on the competitive sports field. He can find coaches overbearing in exacting their control. Private schooling could provide this same Monkey influence, as teachers and religious figures can have a dogmatic approach to life.

Born 1 A.M.–3 A.M.: The Ox finds that a mate can turn into a Monkey when it comes to money and how it should or should not be spent. If you split up, you can rest assured your mate will do what is necessary to protect the assets.

Born 3 A.M.–5 A.M.: The Tiger has a Monkey as its mate and second child; also Mom's mom. These are highly formidable people whom the Tiger has to make sure recognize him and appreciate him for who he is. Monkey mates who try to take control can have a tussle.

Born 5 A.M.–7 A.M.: The Cat tends to be rather stubborn when it comes to his health. The Cat tends to wear rose-colored glasses and be in denial about what is going on in his body. On the job, the Cat seems to gravitate to those situations where there is Monkey energy from which to learn. The Cat can have Monkeys as bosses.

Born 7 A.M.–9 A.M.: The Dragon has Monkey children and Monkey lovers and it becomes the Dragon's quest to move these people out of their denial and open them up to the mythical, magical world of fantasy and allow them to color "outside the lines."

Born 9 A.M.–11 A.M.: It's amazing the Snake is as fluid and mobile as it is, because she viewed her mother as a Monkey. The Monkey's philosophy is the bedrock on which the Snake's concept of life is based, and she found her home life very structured. Mom had a concept of life that was not to be challenged.

Born 11 A.M.–1 P.M.: The Horse can find her education hampered by no-nonsense educators who tend to rein her in. She also finds that she lives in a neighborhood or community where the Monkey energy is strong. Her siblings are Monkey types, too.

Born 1 P.M.–3 P.M.: The Sheep becomes very Monkey-like if you try to take his money. The Sheep takes control whenever money is in the picture . . . and yet can be in Monkey denial on the status of his finances.

I Am Peace

The Rooster is anxious . . . always looking over her shoulder to see if danger is coming. (We use "her" for the Rooster, referring to the yin energy of the Kidneys. You may superimpose "chicken" if needed.) That is why Rooster people usually have tight necks.

The Rooster can't fly very far or very high. It is vulnerable on the ground, so it scurries about trying to stay out of harm's way . . . and harm is surely just around the corner, to it's way of mind.

That is why it procrastinates . . . always putting things off. "Well, what if this happened?" or "What if that happened?" The Rooster is always weighing the pros and cons and deciding the worst is probably going to happen, so let's not face it at all. And when it gets backed into a corner over some inaction, it "bawk . . . bawk . . . bawks," and flutters its wings and complains about its fate.

The Rooster, who is full of energy, gets up at the crack of dawn and "cock-a-doodle doos" the world awake. It has high energy and gets a lot accomplished. The Rooster seems to be drawn to the media and politics, exposing (and showing the world what's to be feared) the wrongs of the world. But, lots of times, the Rooster is low on chi (energy, life force), and kind of drags around. The energy invested in fear and fretting over what might happen next, can leave it exhausted and it lays around wishing that life were more peaceful.

Sexually, the Rooster can have problems. It wants to be in partnership, it wants a sexual relationship, but sometimes its experiences have been harsh, so it backs away. The Chicken can have fertility problems and not get pregnant easily.

The Rooster tends to be phobic, and can go through periods of time where it must face its basic fears.

The Kidney is the meridian/organ for the Rooster. It is involved in "chi," the life-force energy of the body. It relates to sexuality and reproductive functions. It filters

ROOSTER

Born in the Year, Month, Hour, Minute of the

metabolic wastes and secretes urine. The Kidney meridian is concerned with bones and teeth and the knees. In order for the Rooster to be upright and strong, it needs to stay away from the media, which motivates us with fear tactics.

The affirmation for the Rooster is **"I am peace."** The Rooster has to deal with all the media and larger forces of this world (government, religion, insurance, etc.) motivating the populace through fear. It has to turn off the TV news and be selective in what it reads in the newspaper in order to find the truth or its peace, which cannot be assailed by anything.

People born in 1909, 1921, 1933, 1945, 1957, 1969, 1981, and 1993 share the **Year of the Rooster.**

Capricorns have the **Rooster** as the power animal for their sign.

Those born between **5 P.M. and 7 P.M.** incorporate this energy into their personality.

During the late 80s and for most of the 90s, **Sagittarians** focused on Rooster/Kidney issues and learned that fear has kept them from living their lives to the fullest . . . something that infuriates a Sagittarian who loves to be the adventurer.

Where does this energy work in your life?

Everyone has Rooster energy somewhere in his/her chart. Wherever this energy is concentrated, due to the time of your birth, you will hold fear and procrastinate. This is where you particularly have to find your peace of mind.

Born 5 P.M.–7 P.M.: The Rooster is your primary totem animal. Your chi tends to be low, and you can be motivated by fear unless you are a person who has fought those demons and are at peace. You tend to be a workaholic and can have issues with your sexuality. The Rooster who has mastered these issues is a person who is truly at peace within and without.

Born 7 P.M.–9 P.M.: The Dog's sexuality is hidden. It's hard for her to tap into the deep recesses of her soul to tap her sensual nature, so she barks and gets territorial and tries to chase everyone away. Once she has opened up and has allowed herself to be intimate with another, she can be a warm, open, loving individual.

Born 9 P.M.–11 P.M.: The Boar has friends who can drain him. Or, his father's money could have been drained away. The Boar's mate feels that loving him means working long hours to provide rather than being together.

Born 11 P.M.–1 A.M.: The Rat has a Rooster as father energy and boss. The Rooster can be a pusher and a prodder, getting the Rat up before he wants to be, pecking at him to get something accomplished.

Born 1 A.M.–3 A.M.: The Ox has Roosters for coaches and spiritual advisers. They may be motivated by fear and be too cautious, causing him to stick to the row that he has tilled for so long, rather than chucking the yoke for something better.

Born 3 A.M.–5 A.M.: The Tiger has sexual issues and perhaps performance anxiety. The Tiger's mate may be fearful if the Tiger wants to invest their joint income in schemes that aren't conservative.

Born 5 A.M.–7 A.M.: The Cat is married to a Rooster and has a Rooster type as a second child. The Cat has self-worth issues to battle in this lifetime, and the Rooster is there to get the Cat going at the crack of dawn and not dillydally.

Born 7 A.M.–9 A.M.: The Dragon frets over his health, and can drive himself too hard. The Dragon needs to attend to his job and not procrastinate, letting things slide.

Born 9 A.M.–11 A.M.: The Snake has affairs with the Rooster, but marries the more sedentary Boar. The Snake tends to have Rooster types for children, especially the first one. They can be more fearful than most children and need to be reassured all the time. The Snake needs to create a life for his children that gives them courage to go out and experience life. The Snake may have trouble conceiving.

Born 11 A.M.–1 P.M.: The Horse has a Rooster for a mother. The Horse's foundation may have been built upon fear, and the Horse has issues around courage. The Rooster may have provided the Horse with food and a home, but may be too preoccupied with her own fears and sexual issues to make the Horse feel a sense of belonging.

Born 1 P.M.–3 P.M.: The Sheep has Roosters for teachers and siblings. The Sheep may have been taught a conservative course that keeps him from venturing forth from the herd.

Born 3 P.M.–5 P.M.: The Monkey is cautious about money. He puts funds away for a rainy day. He's rather rigid about his sexual encounters and it takes awhile for him to feel safe enough to experience his partner totally.

4743

CUSTOMER'S ORDER NO.		DEPT.			DATE: 5/10/03		
NAME:							
ADDRESS:							
CITY, STATE, ZIP							

SOLD BY:	CASH	C.O.D.	CHARGE	ON ACCT.	MDSE RTD.	PAID OUT

QUANTITY		DESCRIPTION	PRICE	AMOUNT	
1	1	Chinese Power Animal		16	95
	2			1	25
	3				
	4			18	25
	5				
	6				
	7				
	8				
	9				
	10				
	11				
	12				
	13				
	14				
	15				

RECEIVED BY:

I Am Intimate

Ms. Dog has two sides to her personality. She'll be open and friendly like a puppy dog, and look at you so adoringly that it will melt your heart. She'll follow you around, and be content just to be at your side. Her loyalty will never be suspect. However . . .

At other times, the Dog will get ferociously territorial, and bark loudly to scare you away. *No Trespassing!* she's saying. It's she who's scared, of course. Scared of sexual intimacy. Scared of connecting with another human being. So she'll find a reason to get huffy and scare you off and then return to the sanctuary of her doghouse. No one enters her doghouse (i.e. "her space") without permission. But you can easily get in her "doghouse" if you don't live by society's standards. Ms. Dog can get morally uptight and be highly judgmental about other lifestyles that are not circumspect and conservative.

Ms. Dog can be so scared of intimacy that she'll withdraw behind a facade of moralistic righteousness, finding anything erotic and sexual "dirty." She will often stay celibate for long periods of time until the right person comes along.

The Dog tends to marry infrequently and will go for extended periods of time between relationships. It does seem strange to the Dog at times, because she is so loyal and lovable, that her love does not seem to be reciprocated. It's harder for her to find a new relationship than the other animals. She doesn't realize, however, that at times her energy field pushes people away rather than attracts them.

The myth of Psyche and Eros is a very appropriate metaphor for the Dog. Psyche is a beautiful maiden who has much more to offer than her sisters, but they marry well and she is left behind. Many suitors admire her, but go off and marry someone else. The god Eros (Cupid) is smitten with Psyche and refuses to obey his mother, Aphrodite,

Born in the Year, Month, Hour, Minute of the

Dog

who wants to dispose of her. In the end, Psyche and Eros unite, and she becomes the heavenly bride of Eros as she is made immortal. So, too, does the mind (Psyche) have to merge with the emotions (Eros) and become one to be truly open and intimate . . . which is the Dog's quest. When the Dog achieves this alchemical union, she is truly a complete person. At some point, the Dog has to truly step into the fire and realize that alchemy.

The Circulation-Sex meridian (also known as the Pericardium) is a process, rather than an organ, that governs the Dog. As its name states, it has to do with sex, but more with the psychology of sexuality than with procreation. It also deals with circulation—of the blood as well as how we "circulate" in society.

The pericardium is the membrane sac that protects the heart. It takes the frequent blows that would normally wear down the heart and protects us in an emotional clinch. It not only has to do with intimate encounters, but with how comfortable we are in groups and other social interactions. People who have this meridian prominent frequently have cold extremities. They complain about having cold hands and feet. They are the ones that are always bundled up when everyone else thinks it's simply cold. Their body tends to be cold and restrictive. They tend to shy away from intimacy, and frequently find themselves filled with regret and remorse as they get older for not taking a chance on love when it was offered. Men can have the proclivity for prostate problems because of this.

The affirmation for the Dog is **"I am intimate."** The Dog needs to become that open, trusting, loyal Dog, in order for the barriers to come down and allow people in, and to become fully, totally intimate, with a mate as well as interacting with others. The Dog needs to learn to come forward when meeting someone, not retreat.

People born in 1910, 1922, 1934, 1946, 1958, 1970, 1982, and 1994 share the **Year of the Dog.**

Aquarians have the **Dog** as the power animal for their sign.

Those born between **7 P.M. and 9 P.M.** incorporate this energy into their personality.

During the late 80s and for most of the 90s, **Scorpios** focused on Dog/Circ-Sex issues and dealt with intimacy and impotence, mental and physical. The normal sexuality of Scorpio was challenged. They may have changed and used sex in a power play, by withholding it rather than exercising it.

Where does this energy work in your life?

Everyone has Dog energy somewhere in his/her chart. Wherever this energy is concentrated, due to the time of your birth, you will find yourself being more modest and withdrawn. This is where you have to forge that intimacy . . . whether it be in a personal relationship or speaking before a coliseum full of people.

Born 7 P.M.–9 P.M.: Your motivation is based on these emotions. You have a reserve and shyness about you that can keep others at bay. You are highly sexual if well-balanced, and know the connection between sex and love; but your reserve needs to be penetrated by a persistent (and ardent!) individual, who will get past your territorial boundaries and dwell with you in your inner sanctum.

Born 9 P.M.–11 P.M.: The Boar hides his sexual fears and rarely confronts them. He tends to be lusty and earthy, rooting around in the earth, but there is a loneliness that is hard to reach.

Born 11 P.M.-1 A.M.: The Rat has friends who are Dogs. The Rat can feel abandoned sometimes, because of the Dog's natural reticence. The Rat is looking for unconditional love, and the Dog doesn't proffer that lightly.

Born 1 A.M.–3 A.M.: The Dog represents the Ox's father. The Ox can feel stifled because of the Dog's high moral judgment that didn't allow the Ox to express himself as a child. Any attempt on the Ox's part to be his earthy, sensual self could have been met with a down-the-nose stare.

Born 3 A.M.–5 A.M.: The Tiger has problems with competition. religion, sports, travel. It may be difficult for the Tiger to let loose and allow the sport to take over. He can have difficulties getting beyond the mechanics.

Born 5 A.M.–7 A.M.: The Cat can be very reserved and inhibited in bed. It takes some time for her to warm up to the situation. She can look on sex as dirty and feel the need to clean herself frequently.

Born 7 A.M.–9 A.M.: Born in the Hour of the Dragon, its natural mate is the Dog. Sometimes the Dragon can overpower the Dog and the smaller animal can feel that nothing she does can make her an equal. If the Dragon regales her with his magic, however, the Dog can open up and be full of fun and intimacy.

Born 9 A.M.–11 A.M.: The Snake has to work with Dogs. The Snake needs to transform and move beyond the traditional, and he often finds coworkers that are strict moralists.

Born 11 A.M.–1 P.M.: The Horse draws in lovers who are Dogs, and yet their natural mate is the Rat. The Horse will generally have children who reflect the Dog energy. These children tend to be very conservative and look askance when the Horse tries to kick up her heels. Unless her lover is a great big puppy dog, the Horse will opt for the more altruistic Rat.

Born 1 P.M.–3 P.M.: The Sheep had a childhood that was dominated by Dog energy. Mom may have been her best friend, all warm and cuddly, or have been the type of mother the Sheep could never reach, a mother who was not demonstrative and established a foundation that this was not done, leaving the Sheep confused, which caused problems in adulthood.

Born 3 P.M.–5 P.M.: The Monkey can't monkey around very much at school, because of its Dog teachers. They tend to be those tight-collared types who look down their noses at any thought of play. The Monkey got strokes for being a straight arrow, and, later in life, finds it hard to let loose.

Born 5 P.M.–7 P.M.: The Rooster values the energy of the Dog, and can be quite good at using the Dog energy to dig a hole and deposit her money, push the ground over it, and leave it there for a rainy day.

I Am Hope

Mr. Boar has the potential to transform into a swan . . . a lovely white, graceful swan. But somehow, he doesn't know it. Mr. Boar has doubts . . . big doubts. He questions everything and wants to be shown. When his questions are answered and his doubts quelled, he moves into a state of certainty, a place of hope, that can never be assailed.

Mr. Boar is large and lugubrious. He moves slowly and with determination. He tends to root in the soil for legumes, and at times, can get mired in the bog. Mr. Boar's metabolism isn't very good, so he tends to be sluggish. The Boar tends to feel that he is ugly, and can suffer tremendous humiliation and ridicule. The Boar needs to awaken to the beauty that is in his soul.

Boars in the wild have a natural bent toward suicide, and as an archetype, Mr. Boar shows us where our self-destructive tendencies reside. He can either be bogged down in depression, or the depression can make him foolhardy, taking risks, seeing how close he can come to the brink without going over, and contemplating if going over isn't the better of the two options.

Often Boars need a shock to their system in order to get them moving. Then they can move from the negative into the positive and transform their lives.

Mr. Boar seeks to be included, and yet, to him, always seems to be on the outside looking in. He fears ridicule and will often take the safe way.

There is an old proverb from the medieval times about two knights who were being sent into battle. One feared death more than ridicule and so refused to go. The other feared ridicule more than death, and so went out to meet his fate, not being able to face the townspeople if he didn't. So, too, the Boar fears ridicule and will go to great lengths to avoid it . . . yet, at other times, when all seems lost, he will take risks and be foolhardy, almost inviting the inevitable.

Born in the Year, Month, Hour, Minute of the

Boar

The Triple Warmer process is the focus of the energy for the Boar. It has an overall governing effect on the system. It deals with breathing, assimilation, and elimination. It rules our self-destructive tendencies or self-constructive* ones. It is where, in the extreme of depression, our system can break down.

The affirmation for the Boar/Triple Warmer is **"I am hope."** The Boar needs to know there is always a light at the end of the tunnel or that the glass is half full. The Boar is too prone to dive into pessimism and not be able to get out of it.

People born in 1911, 1923, 1935, 1947, 1959, 1971, 1983, and 1995 share the **Year of the Boar.**

Pisces have the **Boar** as the power animal for their sign.

Those born between **9 P.M. and 11 P.M.** incorporate this energy into their personality.

During the late 80s and for most of the 90s, **Librans** focused on Boar/Triple Warmer issues and learned that self-destructive tendencies can lead to crisis . . . crises they subconsciously sought to take them out of their pain, but didn't actually want to manifest when the time came to pass.

Where does this energy work in your life?

Everyone has Boar energy somewhere in his/her chart. Wherever this energy is concentrated, due to the time of your birth, you can find yourself bogged down. This is where you tend to be pessimistic and where you need to move into a solid resolve of certainty.

Born 9 P.M.–11 P.M.: The Boar is the animal that reflects your personality. You need to concentrate on the positive all the time and purposefully put yourself with positive people, so that you don't get bogged down in depression. If you are at all "in the dumps," another Boar is the last person you want to be with. They could pull you down even further. You tend to be serious, and it's hard for you to see the light side of life, unless you have dealt with these issues and have found your hope and cling to it like a life raft.

---

*Phrase coined by author to turn the energy of self-destructive tendencies into positive energy.

Born 11 P.M.–1 A.M.: The Rat questions life and its spiritual aspects. He has a dour side that few see. The Rat shouldn't be too solitary or introspective, as this can draw him into his dark side.

Born 1 A.M.–3 A.M.: The Ox has to watch that he doesn't bring pessimistic people into his life to bring him down. He needs to see ways of throwing off the yoke and getting out of his rut. He doesn't need to be pulled down into the Boar's morass.

Born 3 A.M.–5 A.M.: The Tiger has a Boar for a father or employer . . . or both. The Boar is a heavy influence and can be part of the reason for the Tiger's own depression. These two shouldn't spend a lot of time together unless they are committed to being full of light. One of them usually has to be the positive one for the twosome.

Born 5 A.M.–7 A.M.: The Cat tends to have a Boar as second mate, or as ministers and professors. The Cat really has to settle down when he marries a Boar, who isn't going to like the Cat coming and going as he sees fit.

Born 7 A.M.–9 A.M.: The Dragon finds that his mate can become quite boorish when it comes to money. The mythical Dragon isn't going to be able to spend much joint income on frivolous things to lighten the heart. The Dragon has a big job to loosen the purse strings.

Born 9 A.M.–11 A.M.: The Snake has a Boar for a mate. If the Boar is full of hope, he'll help the Snake to transform. If not, she will find it hard to move beyond the heaviness of the relationship.

Born 11 A.M.–1 P.M.: The Horse can get pessimistic when she gets sick. She needs to hear positive feedback in order not to sink into a bog of pessimism. She does wonders with positive affirmations.

Born 1 P.M.–3 P.M.: The Sheep is attracted to Boars. Together they can reach the heights of positive living . . . or they can feed each other's negative tendencies. The Sheep will have Boar-type children, who need to be constantly reminded the glass is half full.

Born 3 P.M.–5 P.M.: The Monkey has a Boar for a mother. A religious faith is frequently important to her to have something to hold on to. She may have been self-destructive and provided an unsettling foundation for the Monkey. If the Boar mother wasn't living from the positive, she set self-defeating programs as part of his lineage that he must strive to overcome.

Born 5 P.M.–7 P.M.: The Rooster experiences the Boar as a teacher or mentor. These are the ministers and teachers who can preach "hellfire and damnation" and see history from a doom-and-gloom perspective.

Born 7 P.M.–9 P.M.: The Dog can be sober about her finances and hide her money in a tin can buried in the yard. She'll know exactly where every dime is, however, and you can count on her as the one person who will have money when others don't.

Chinese Power Animals and the Meridians

Power animals reflect our base nature on an instinctual level. They are archetypes, much like Roman and Greek gods and goddesses, of our psychological behavior patterns. The fairy tale on page xiii was based on the life and Chinese power animals of Prince Charles of Great Britain. With just a little imagination, it was easy to create a story based on these primitive archetypes. As you can see, the animals and their archetypal energy accurately depicted the Prince's life, and allowed us to see it in a more picturesque way.

In ancient Chinese practice, each year is assigned to an animal, whose archetypal, primal instincts reflect generally on those persons born during that year. The Year of the Rat was 1996, 1995 was the Year of the Boar, 1994 was the Year of the Dog, 1993 was the Year of the Monkey, etc. There is a cyclical group of twelve animals that represent our basic emotional drives. The animals that the Chinese have used for thousands of years are:

Rat	Ox	Tiger	Cat/Rabbit*
Dragon/Buffalo*	Snake	Horse	Sheep/Goat*
Monkey	Rooster	Dog	Boar/Pig*

Personality profiles have been delineated by Eastern and Western astrologers, showing the psychological makeup of each animal type. Since this becomes very general for everyone born in any given year, in recent times, Western astrologers have broken the profile down even further—i.e., how a Pisces Rat is different from a Sagittarius Rat, etc.

These Chinese animals are full of symbolism and lore. How they act on a primal, instinctive, animal level shows us basic characteristics that we act out in what we think is our more "civilized

---

*In some Chinese cultures, the second animal is used in place of the twelve I refer to in this book.

way." How can that be, you ask? Haven't we evolved beyond that? What do these ancient Chinese animals mean to us? How can an animal that represents thousands and thousands of people born in any particular year be of any significance on an individual basis?

The animal of the year we are born in gives us a general makeup. O.J. Simpson was born in 1947 and his ex-wife Nicole was born twelve years later, in 1959; each in the sign of the Boar. You will read later that this gives them a tendency toward self-destructive behavior.

What makes us different from the thousands of others born in the same year is that the Chinese refine the cycle in two ways. Their lunar calendar relates generally to the astrological Sun signs, so that we have an animal to correlate with our Sun sign:

Rat	Aries	Horse	Libra
Ox	Taurus	Sheep	Scorpio
Tiger	Gemini	Monkey	Sagittarius
Cat	Cancer	Rooster	Capricorn
Dragon	Leo	Dog	Aquarius
Snake	Virgo	Boar	Pisces

In other publications, you may have seen a different list attributed to the astrological signs. After much research, however, I find that these animals have the closest connection to the signs from a meridian perspective, which you will learn about on subsequent pages.

Time of Day Wheel
The Chinese also have a "Time of Day" wheel, that ascribes these same animals to specific hours as well—one animal for each two-hour period of the day, starting at odd-numbered intervals. Hence, we become a composite of the time and the year we were born under, as well as the month—or astrological sign. As in Western astrology, we aren't just our Sun sign, but a composite of the planetary positions for that moment, accented by the time we were born.

For instance, a friend was born at 6:53 P.M. PT, on August 30, 1942, which is the Year of the Horse. The period from 5 P.M.–7 P.M. is the Hour of the Rooster. The Snake is the animal for Virgo. Hence, she is a Horse born in the Hour of the Rooster and the Month of the Snake. A number of books have been written delineating the demeanor and habits attributed to

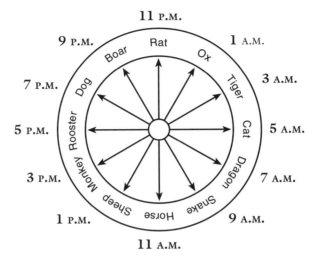

Figure 1. Time of Day Wheel.

these animals. What has been missing from previous books, however, is that these animals are power animals and they become potent archetypes in describing our personalities and the emotions that motivate us when we relate them to the meridian system of the body.

Chinese Meridians
The ancient practices of acupuncture and acupressure are based on the five-element system. The elements are much as we attribute them in the West: fire, earth, air (metal), water . . . and the Chinese add a fifth, wood. Everything in life can be attributed to one of these elements, just as in the practice of Western astrology. However, within these elements lie the meridians. "Meridians" are invisible pathways of energy that go up and down the body. They are named after ten organs and two processes of the body. Acupuncturists are able to release blockages by knowing which points along the meridians to stimulate with their needles. The fascinating aspect of these meridians is that they resonate to a polarity of core emotions. Hence, when we join the power animals to the meridians, we have a way of accessing the deep resources of core emotions, and can facilitate change on fundamental levels.

Meridians and the Time of Day Wheel
In the Chinese meridian system of acupuncture, the Time of Day Wheel, which designates each two-hour period during the day to

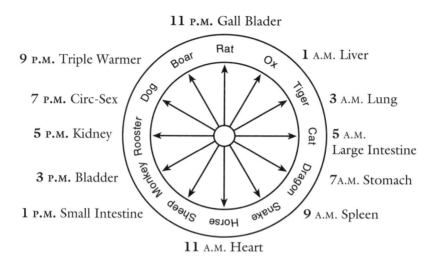

Figure 2. Time of Day Wheel
with Meridians and Power Animals.

a power animal, also designates these same two-hour increments to a meridian of the body. At any given time of day, the meridian that "rules" that period of time is at its peak—or strongest—and twelve hours later, it is said to be at its weakest. The meridians are named, for the most part, after organs of the body: Lung, Large Intestine, Stomach, Spleen, Heart, Small Intestine, Bladder, Kidney, Gallbladder, and Liver—plus two processes, Circulation-Sex, or the Pericardium, and Triple Warmer (also Triple Burner, Triple Heater). The Time of Day clock separates the wheel into twelve sections, in odd-hour increments. These meridians are assigned to the five elements, and, in this work, the animals will be correlated to them.

The Minute of the Power Animal
As I developed this process, it occurred to me that, even though we were defining the animals more closely to each individual as we moved from the year to the month to the hour, there are still thousands of people born within any two-hour period. With some experimentation, I found that, quite accurately, the minute we are born is quite specific to our own particular journey in life. Working in ten-minute increments, it is quite easy to see your specific journey to heal in this lifetime (see page 310).

The Power Animal
for the Year You Were Born

Indicate Your Power Animal Here:

Year: Animal:

You may wonder how the animal for the year you were born could be influential, when thousands upon thousands of people are born during any given year. From observation, I've deduced that the power animal for the year we are born is the foundation, much like the base of a pyramid.

If you were born in the Year of the Monkey, how do you express that energy? By the month, hour, and minute you are born, you define that Monkey more individually. So, the animal for the year you are born becomes a base upon which all the others are balanced.

The power animal of the year you were born becomes a powerful metaphor that you can use in visualization to see the state of your inner self in general. Reading up on the ways of your animal will show you a great deal about how you feel about yourself and how others see you.

Are you a small animal or a large one? Are you a predator or prey? Are you lithe and quick or are you slow and cumbersome? Do you work for others or are you free and liberated? An animal such as the horse can be wild or she can be domesticated; she can be a thoroughbred racehorse or she can be a dray horse. If you were born in the years

1906 • 1918 • 1930 • 1942 • 1954 •1966 •1978 • 1990

you might want to go into a light meditative state and see what your Horse looks like, because that is truly what makes you different from the other hundreds of thousands of people born in those years. We place our own perception on how our Horse or Tiger or Dragon or other power animal is going to manifest in our life.

In fact, let's try this now. Look on page 307 and ascertain which animal represents the year you were born.

Now, turn off the telephone and handle any extraneous noises that might disturb you (kids, TV, etc.). You might want to tape-record the next part and play it to aid you.

Take some deep breaths, settle down, and get comfortable.

Today we are going to go to your secret place where the power animal of the year you were born resides. You know exactly where to go; trust yourself. See a path ahead of you . . . leading down to your secret place . . . moving down the path one step at a time . . . each step taking you ten times deeper than before . . . moving down the path now . . . 10 . . . 9 . . . 8 . . . 7 . . . 6 . . . 5 . . . 4 . . . 3 . . . 2 . . . 1 . . . opening up into your scene . . . taking note of where you are . . . a meadow? . . . oceanside? . . . mountains? . . . desert? . . . jungle? etc. (The locale will also reveal a lot about the environment in which your animal currently resides.) Is it a nice day? A cloudy day? A blizzard? Just take note of where you are and how you feel about the surroundings of your power animal. . . .

Now ask your power animal to enter the scene . . . what does s/he look like? Healthy? Strong? . . . or not? Is s/he confident? Timid? If your animal is small, how does s/he feel about that? Is s/he intimidated? Scared? Confident? If your animal is large, is it aggressive, arrogant, intimidating? Or secure in its personality?

Dialog with your power animal at this point, asking it such things as how s/he is? . . . What does s/he want (if anything) . . . What would s/he like . . . etc.

If s/he is wounded in any way, or scared, or feels threatened . . . you can create a fortress of some type that you can put your animal in and allow it to rest and heal, untouched by predators. Then check in with it from time to time as you go about your day to see how s/he's doing and making any adjustments, visually, which you feel you need to.

Your power animal is imbued with wisdom that is for you alone. S/he is always ready to share this knowledge with you, in fact, s/he's just been waiting for you to come and dialog so s/he can reveal it to you.

Ask your power animal now . . . what wisdom s/he has for you today? And listen . . . it might come easily . . . it might come with time . . . it might be audible . . . it might just be a feeling . . . trust that whatever comes up right now is perfect. (Sometimes you might not get a direct answer, but ask and let it incubate and then watch your daily life for clues and signs; in some form it will be revealed to you if you pay attention.)

Spend as much time as you like with your power animal and when you are complete for this time period, let it know that, now you have come in touch with it, you'll be back to check on it, nurture and care for it . . . and in turn s/he'll reveal the wisdom it has for you.

Coming back up now. 1 . . . 2 . . . 3 . . . 4 . . . 5 . . . fully back in your body . . . 6 . . . 7 . . . 8 . . . 9 . . . 10, fully awake, fully alert, fully back in the present time.

The Power Animal
for the Sign You Were Born Under

Indicate Your Power Animal Here:

Sign: **Animal:**

To get in touch with the energy of the power animal which is assigned to the month you were born, refer to page 301 to find the animal for that period of time.

If you did the visualization with the power animal for your year, you found out some deep, profound truths. The sign of the power animal becomes more significant to your makeup, because it represents only 1/12th of the year. Now, let's do another visualization with the power animal for the sign you were born under (if this animal is the same as the power animal for the year, see how the animal acts differently in the sign compared to how s/he does in the year).

Take some deep breaths, settle down, and get into a comfortable position. . . .

Today we are going to go to your secret place where the power animal of the sign you were born under resides. You know exactly where to go; trust yourself. See a path ahead of you . . . leading down to your secret place . . . moving down the path one step at a time . . . each step taking you ten times deeper than before . . . moving down the path now . . . 10 . . . 9 . . . 8 . . . 7 . . . 6 . . . 5 . . . 4 . . . 3 . . . 2 . . . 1 . . . opening up into your scene . . . taking note of where you are . . . meadow? . . . oceanside? . . . mountains? . . . . desert? . . . jungle? etc. (The locale will also reveal a lot about the environment in which your animal currently resides.) Is it a nice day? A cloudy day? A blizzard? Just take note of where you are and how you feel about the surroundings of your power animal. . . .

Now ask your power animal to enter the scene . . . what does s/he look like? Healthy? Strong? . . . or not? Is s/he confident? Timid? If your animal is small, how does s/he feel about that? Is s/he intimidated? Scared? Confident? If your animal is large, is it aggressive, arrogant, intimidating? Or secure in its personality?

Dialog with your power animal at this point, asking it such things as how s/he is? . . . What does s/he need (if anything) . . . What would s/he like . . . etc.

If s/he is wounded in any way, or scared, or feels threatened . . . you can create a fortress of some type that you can put your animal in and allow it to rest and heal, untouched by predators. Then check in with it from time to time as you go about your day to see how s/he's doing and making any adjustments, visually, which you feel you need to.

Your power animal is imbued with wisdom that is for you alone. S/he is always ready to share this knowledge with you, in fact, s/he's just been waiting for you to come and dialog so s/he can reveal it to you.

Ask your power animal now . . . what wisdom s/he has for you today? And listen . . . it might come easily . . . it might come with time . . . it might be audible . . . it might just be a feeling . . . trust that whatever comes up right now is perfect. (Sometimes you might not get a direct answer, but ask and let it incubate and then watch your daily life for clues and signs; in some form it will be revealed to you if you pay attention.)

As you contemplate this wisdom, the animal for the year you were born in enters the scene. How do they react to each other? Are they friends? . . . or enemies? . . . or something in between? Do they strengthen each other as a team? . . . or not?

Spend as much time as you like with your power animals and, when you are complete for this time period, let them know that, now you have come in touch with them, you'll be back to check on them, nurture and care for them . . . and in turn they'll reveal the wisdom they have for you.

Coming back up now. 1 . . . 2 . . . 3 . . . 4 . . . 5 . . . fully back in your body . . . 6 . . . 7 . . . 8 . . . 9 . . . 10, fully awake, fully alert, fully back in the present time.

The Power Animal
for the Hour You Were Born

Indicate Your Power Animal Here:	
Hour:	Animal:

The hour you were born defines your power animals more precisely. An Ox born in the Month of the Horse and the Hour of the Monkey is going to be different than the Ox born in the sign of the Horse and the Hour of the Boar.

Refer to page 310 to ascertain the animal for the time you were born; always correcting war/daylight time to standard time.

The power animal for the time you were born is the cornerstone of your totem. It reflects who you are on an individual basis. It's habits, traits, and idiosyncrasies will manifest more specifically in how you react, and what organs and muscles are affected in your body.

Your time of birth is a crucial element in delineating your power animals and how they work in your life. People born in the Hour of the Tiger (3 A.M.–5 A.M.) are going to take their traumatic experiences into their lungs, while people born in the Hour of the Rooster (5 P.M.–7 P.M.) tend to be fearful and hypervigilant, with backaches caused by the kidney's reaction to this fear. People born in the Hour of the Rooster can have reproductive problems, and those born in the Hour of the Cat (5 A.M.–7 A.M.) can have colon issues. More about this in the section on health.

By knowing the hour you were born and the animal associated with it, you have direct access to your body and you can see what areas you need to work with to relieve the symptoms associated with it.

If you did the visualizations with the power animal for your year and your sign, you found out some deep, profound truths. Now let's do the same with the power animal for the time you were born. This will reveal even more, and this time the actions will be most specific to who you are as a human being. Even if this happens to be a duplicate power animal in your triple totem, I urge you to do this visualization, if no other, because it defines you as a person more specifically.

Take some deep breaths, settle down, and get into a comfortable position. . . .

Today we are going to go to your secret place where the power animal of the time you were born resides. You know exactly where to go; trust yourself. See a path ahead of you . . . leading down to your secret place . . . moving down the path one step at a time . . . each step taking you ten times deeper than before . . . moving down the path now . . . 10 . . . 9 . . . 8 . . . 7 . . . 6 . . . 5 . . . 4 . . . 3 . . . 2 . . . 1 . . . opening up into your scene . . . taking note of where you are . . . and how you feel about the surroundings. . . .

Now ask your power animal to enter the scene . . . what does s/he look like? Healthy? Strong? . . . or not? Is s/he confident? Timid? If your animal is small, how does s/he feel about that? Is s/he intimidated? Scared? Confident? If your animal is large, is it aggressive, arrogant, intimidating? . . . or secure in its personality? . . . Note that the accuracy to who you are as a person is more precise with this animal. . . .

Dialog with your power animal at this point, asking it such things as how s/he is? . . . What does s/he need (if anything) . . . What would s/he like . . . etc. If s/he is wounded in any way, or scared, or feels threatened . . . you can create a fortress of some type that you can put your animal in and allow it to rest and heal, untouched by predators. Then check in with it from time to time as you go about your day to see how s/he's doing and making any adjustments, visually, which you feel you need to.

Your power animal is imbued with wisdom that is for you alone. S/he is always ready to share this knowledge with you, in fact, s/he's just been waiting for you to come and dialog so s/he can reveal it to you. Ask your power animal now . . . what wisdom s/he has for you today? And listen . . . it might come easily . . . it might come with time . . . it might be audible . . . it might just be a feeling . . . trust that whatever comes up right now is perfect. As you contemplate this wisdom, the animals for the year and month you were born in enter the scene. How do they react to the animal of the hour? Are they friends? . . . or enemies? . . . or something in between? Do they strengthen each other? . . . or not?

Spend as much time as you like with your power animals and when you are complete for this time period, let them know that, now you have come in touch with them, you'll be back to check on them, nurture and care for them . . . and in turn they'll reveal the wisdom they have for you.

Coming back up now. 1 . . . 2 . . . 3 . . . 4 . . . 5 . . . fully back in your body . . . 6 . . . 7 . . . 8 . . . 9 . . . 10, fully awake, fully alert, fully back in the present time.

Reconciling Your Power Animals:
Introducing Your Power Animal for the Minute Your Were Born

Indicate Your Power Animal Here:	
Minute:	**Animal:**

As you can see by now, just because we are born in the year of a certain animal, it is not just a generic depiction. By the time we delineate the month, hour, and minute that is specific to an individual, the combinations of power animals that we humans pull from to create the unique individuals that we are are countless. Of course, this applies not only to people, but to animals, countries, and corporations as well—in fact, to anything that is "born" at any given time. The United States is a Monkey, born in the month of the Cat (Cancer), the Hour of the Ox, and the Minute of the Monkey—July 4, 1776 at 2:17 A.M. Interestingly, the transformed, higher-octave energy of the Ox is the Eagle, and the Eagle is our national bird (see chapter on the United States).

Let's look at the combination under which you were born. Do you like it or not? Do you have animals of equal strength and power, or do they seem unbalanced? Are they traditional protagonists or not (i.e., the Cat and the Dog, the Rat and the Snake)? Are their energies similar or drastically different? This can show you how your personality changes from one situation to another.

Reconciling these animals and getting them to cooperate in visualization will help you to integrate them into your life. Depending on your circumstances, you may have 4, 3, 2, or maybe only 1 power animal, if, say, you were born in Leo, in 1952 at 7 A.M., which would make you a quadruple Dragon. In that case, use your visualization to see how your animal acts differently in each aspect of year, sign, hour, and minute.

We've spent some time with our animals, but let's stop and do another visualization now, and see how your personal power animals relate to each other in more detail.

Take some deep breaths, settle down, and get into a comfortable position. . . .
You are going to go to your secret place now, where your three power animals reside. Once again, you know exactly

*where to go. . . . See your path loom ahead of you . . . lead-
ing to your secret place . . . moving down the path one step
at a time . . . each step taking you ten times deeper than before . . . moving down the path now . . . 10 . . . 9 . . . 8 . . .
7 . . . 6 . . . 5 . . . 4 . . . 3 . . . 2 . . . 1 . . . opening up into your
scene . . . taking note of where you are . . . a meadow? . . .
oceanside? . . . mountains? . . . desert? . . . etc. (Again, the
locale will also reveal a lot about the environment in which
your animals currently reside.) Is it a nice day? A cloudy
day? A blizzard? Just take note of where you are and how
you feel about the surroundings of your power animals. . . .*

*Now ask your power animals to enter the scene, one at a
time. First, ask the power animal of the year in which you
were born to enter. Is s/he any different from the last time
you met? How does s/he feel there alone? Does s/he want com-
panionship or not?*

*Ask the power animal of the sign you were born under to
enter. What does the first animal think about that? What is
their body language toward one another? How do they relate?
Do they like each other? Do they not like each other? How are
they positioned to one another? Close? Far away? Take in the
whole scene and watch them interact for a spell. . . .*

*Dialog with your power animals at this point, asking
them such things as how each feels about the other? . . . Are
they happy to be together in this relationship with you? Do
they respect each other? Do they interact well or not? What
would it take for them to support each other totally, and thus
be a supportive element in your life?*

*Now, ask the power animal of the hour you were born to
enter. As before, note how they interact . . . do they get along?
Do two gang up against one? or not? Are they willing to
band together and be a united form for your health and
well-being?*

*Dialog and observe how the three interact. . . . At this
point, ask the power animal of the minute you were born to
join them. . . . This is the animal of your personal Achilles'
heel. How do they react to it? Do they welcome it? . . . or are
they afraid? Do they nurture it or are they repelled by it? . . .
or somewhere in between?*

*If they are wounded in any way, or scared, or feel
threatened . . . once again you can create a fortress of some*

type that you can put your animals in and allow them to rest and heal, untouched by predators. Maybe one is threatened by the other. If they fear each other, or one fears another, dialog to find out what the problem is and see how it can be resolved . . . maybe the other animal isn't aware of how s/he comes across.

Offer a safe haven to the weaker one, and allow it to strengthen so it becomes equal to the stronger one and can stand with it on equal footing. Check in with them from time to time to see how they're doing and make any adjustments, visually, you need to, to effect harmony and balance.

Together, your power animals have some special wisdom that is for you alone. Ask your power animals now, one at a time . . . what is the wisdom they have for you today? And listen . . . again, it might come easily . . . it might come with time . . . it might be audible . . . it might just be a feeling . . . trust that whatever comes up right now is perfect. Watch your daily life for clues and signs; in some form these will be reinforced for you if you pay attention.

Spend as much time as you like with your power animals and, when you are complete for this time period, let them know that you'll be back to check on them, nurture and care for them . . . and in turn they'll reveal the wisdom they have for you as the days unfold.

Coming back up now. 1 . . . 2 . . . 3 . . . 4 . . . 5 . . . fully back in your body . . . 6 . . . 7 . . . 8 . . . 9 . . . 10, fully awake, fully alert, fully back in the present time.

By visiting your four power animals, you have gotten in touch with key elements of your psyche. When these animals are working in harmony and balance with each other, you have valuable allies to support you in your everyday life. When they are at odds, elements of your body are at odds with each other. How they work as powerful archetypal energies with the meridian system of the body enable you to bring your spirit, mind, body, and affairs back into harmony by knowing their emotions and motivations and working with them to facilitate change.

Fundamentals of the Meridians

Life is the movement of energy, and the basis of this energy is the four elements: fire, earth, air, and water. There must be a balance of these four elements in nature in order for us to function. We need air to breathe, the Sun for light and warmth, water to conduct the electricity of our living, breathing bodies, and the earth as the form and structure of our being to be individualized from other forms. Without one, the others could not exist. Even in an automobile, the form (earth) of the car cannot move without the ignition (fire), carburetor (air), and the gasoline and oil and water (liquids = water) to keep it cool and moving freely.

Every strata of being needs to strive continually to keep these elements in balance for our survival. In the five-element system, the Chinese relate these power flows to the four elements and add a fifth, wood. In some systems, wood is equated with earth, and the earth element is regarded as the center of the system, just as our earth is the center of our "world," from which all else flows. Within these elements are meridians: flows of energy that move up and down the body.

Table 1. *The Meridians Divided between the Five Elements.*

ELEMENT	MERIDIAN
Fire	Heart, Small Intestine, Triple Warmer, and Circulation-Sex
Earth	Stomach and Spleen
Air (**Metal** in the Chinese system)	Large Intestine and Lung
Water	Kidney and Bladder (Urinary)
Wood	Liver and Gallbladder

The Meridians

Meridians are flows of energy that must move unblocked through the body to maintain health and vitality. Six go up and down the body and six go up and down the arms. They are the pathways that acupuncturists use to release blockages and facilitate health. They correlate to organs in the body and react to core emotions as well as to the acupuncturist's needles. In the stress and strain of daily experience, we block this energy in the way we experience life. Our emotions are at the core. The way we react emotionally affects our bodies. Positive and negative emotions are running through our body/mind all the time and, if we have a larger percentage of negative than positive, we will feel blockages to the extent that the positive doesn't neutralize and heal the negative.

Acupuncturists use their needles to release the blockage and facilitate the energy flow. Acupressurists do the same thing with touch. When the body is able to gain strength and equilibrium and get closer to balance, we restore our health.

Each meridian not only responds to the needles of the acupuncturist on a physical basis, they also react to a polarity of emotions—positive and negative—such as sad/happy, deprived/fulfilled, victim/victor, etc. Acupuncturists can tell by our emotions which organs are being affected in the body. If you become angry, or "livid," your liver is being affected. If you have lost your job or have just gone through a divorce, if you feel you have the lost the identity you have so carefully carved for yourself, the Stomach meridian can become unbalanced. If you feel tired and fatigued, there can be a Kidney imbalance, etc. We take our emotions into specific areas of the body. The way the organs function gives us a clue to the emotions that affect them: i.e., the large intestine eliminates feces and, when it is imbalanced, we have problems of self-worth, or feeling "dirty" and neuroses can ensue.

E-motions are "Energy in Motion"

E-motions are "Energy in Motion"; they are encoded in the musculature of our bodies. Every muscle has been documented to a corresponding meridian. In the 20s, research discovered that, as each muscle was put through its range of motion and viewed through a fluoroscopy, there was a reaction in a particular meridian/organ. Every experience, then, good or bad, becomes a hologram. It goes to the muscle, then to the associated meridian, and then to the organ to be processed or held.

There are twelve meridians that relate to ten organs and two processes in the body. The twelve meridians respond to a duality of core emotions. Do you know that we can restore the positive by knowing the emotions that correlate to each meridian and, by using those emotions, tap into the inner being and effect change? We can. When we experience dis-ease, it becomes apparent that, to be in good health, we must vibrate from the positive emotions of each meridian, and the power animals can help us to do that, by showing us in metaphoric form how they relate to and interact in our bodies.

As an astrologer who has studied the principles of acupuncture, when I saw that the hours of the animals were in odd-hour increments just as the meridians, it seemed reasonable to assume that these animals were archetypes of the meridians. It has proven to be a very insightful, profound way of working with the meridians for health and healing. (Although you've seen that there are five types for each animal in Chinese lore—a Water Rat, a Wood Rat, a Metal Rat, a Fire Rat, an Earth Rat, etc.—in this work, we are applying the elements as they refer to the meridians.)

The Time of Day Wheel

Every emotion in the universe can be attributed to one of these meridians. When we experience an emotion, it goes to its host meridian, and hence the organ behind it. If we have been conditioned in childhood to expect the positive, most often we experience the positive in our interactions. But life seems to be a stage for overcoming challenges and, quite often, the negative is established in childhood. It is the quest, then, to awaken to the positive polarity and change our life for the better.

In Applied Kinesiology and Touch for Health, which is the core for my Body-Mind Synergetics™—a system that uses both hypnotherapy and body work to effect change—we use muscle testing to find the truth of our being. We bypass the conscious mind and access these emotions in our musculature by testing its integrity. It is more or less a lie-detector test. When we are stating something that the body believes to be true, the muscle will stay strong when we test it. If it is not the truth—no matter how logical our conscious mind may deem it to be—the muscle will not be able to hold. It becomes weak. You might say, "I want to lose weight" and your conscious mind can deem that the best thing for you to do, but if your subconscious has a vested interest in protecting you and feels the added weight accomplishes that, all your conscious protestations aren't going to get you very far. If you muscle tested "I want to lose weight," you'd most likely find that your muscle will become weak; your body likes it just the way it is, thank you very much. When you access the body's truth, you're halfway to finding out the reasons behind it. When you release the subconscious motiviations, then your body will cooperate and drop the excess pounds.

When we find blocks in the meridians, through muscle testing, we clear them through lymphatic points and allow the body to experience the emotion with the body's energies flowing. When the body realizes it doesn't have to defend itself, it can allow itself to return to balance.

What we reveal through these tests is that the meridians and their corresponding emotions and animals are there as archetypes to show us what is really going on at the base of our being.

For instance, one day Amy got a big surge of energy and went out to weed the backyard. She had bought a new electric weeding tool to clear the weeds, and had to put it together. She started to use it and was making terrific progress when the handle turned in her hand a bit; she realized later she obviously hadn't tightened it enough when she put it together. But, as she released the trigger for the power, she naturally expected it to stop. But the weed-whacker started bumping along the ground toward her. Figuring it was a different brand than she had before, she thought she just didn't know its idiosyncrasies and it would stop in a second. Well, it bumped it's way toward her and took a couple of little whap-whaps at her ankle; still she thought, "This will stop in a second." When it took a whole bunch of whap-whaps out on her leg, she jumped back, disengaging her finger from the trigger completely, which she found she hadn't done before. As the shaft had turned in her hand she thought she had let go of it, but she found she was holding down the trigger a little bit. Fortunately, it wasn't on at full power.

After Amy got over the shock, she nursed the area, and started to look at what this was telling her. . . . "Be sure to always disengage one's hand completely from a weedwhacker"? Yes, but there was much more to the metaphor.

The offended part of her body was the outside of her right ankle. The meridian that goes down the outside of the body is the Gallbladder. The Gallbladder's animal is the Rat. The Gallbladder's emotions deal with abandonment and betrayal vs. being adored, loved, and supported unconditionally and not being judged.

As we looked at the incident, I shared with her the research I had done to correlate the meridians to the astrology chart. I explained that, in her life, the Gallbladder archetype reflects her emotions about her parents and the 4th house of home. She never had a good relationship with her mother, but thought she was the apple of her father's eye. As she looked at the wound, she realized that she was still letting those feelings from childhood cut her up, and she was still giving them some power (because she hadn't released her finger fully from the trigger).

On her next visit we did some visualization with her Rat to get in touch with these emotions. Her Rat was angry, but more in a wounded way. He felt alone and isolated. She asked him what was the basis of his anger. When pressed a bit, he told her that he knew things weren't as they seemed. He had a gnawing feeling that produced this rage, that he was being betrayed in some way.

Amy didn't understand it at the time, but as her life unfolded from that point, she came to realize that she was being betrayed by her father. He was using this facade of adoration to manipulate and control her. At one point, she came to the realization that she was now acting similarly to her mother to survive this relationship.

The Energy Polarity

Within the elements, there is a masculine (yang) meridian and a feminine (yin) meridian for each element. In the fire element, there are two of each: two organs and two processes.

Table 2. *The Energy Polarity*

ELEMENT	YANG MERIDIAN	YIN MERIDIAN
Fire	Small Intestine Triple Warmer	Heart Circulation-Sex
Earth	Stomach	Spleen
Air	Large Intestine	Lung
Water	Bladder	Kidney
Wood	Gallbladder	Liver

Throughout this book we will refer to the yang animals as "he" and to the yin animals as "she" to help you to relate the animals to their meridian gender. The Rooster happens to turn up under the yin energy. We will still use "she" here at times, in quotes, to remind you that it is yin energy. If that is disconcerting, you can replace the image of a chicken with the Rooster. Similarly, the Ox is an emasculated bull, and is also yin energy and will be considered as such.

The Organs
The meridians are named after ten organs of the body:

Lung	Large Intestine
Stomach	Spleen
Heart	Small Intestine
Bladder	Kidney
Gallbladder	Liver

There remain two meridians named after processes: Circulation-Sex and Triple Warmer. As the name implies, Circulation-Sex rules circulation and sexual intimacy. An alternate name is the Pericardium, the membrane sac that protects the heart from emotional bombardments. Triple Warmer—or Triple Heater or Triple Burner, as it is alternately called—refers to the three processes of life: breathing, assimilation, and elimination.

Because the Time of Day Wheel not only designates the meridians, but the power animals as well, there is a power animal for each organ. Haven't you felt at one time or another as if a dragon resides in your Stomach? The Dragon rules the Stomach meridian. When you're sexually secure, haven't you felt like crowing like a rooster? The Rooster rules the Kidney and their reproductive and sexual function. Or when you're proud of something you've accomplished, don't you want to pump up your chest and roar like a tiger? The Tiger rules the Lung. These animals are archetypes of the organs they rule.

When we relate the power animals to the elements we get the results seen in table 3 on page 74.

Table 3: *Elements, Corresponding Power Animals, Meridians*

ELEMENT	MERIDIAN	POWER ANIMAL
Fire	Heart	Horse
	Small Intestine	Sheep (Goat)
	Triple Warmer	Boar
	Circulation-Sex	Dog
Earth	Stomach	Dragon
	Spleen	Snake
Metal (Air)	Lung	Tiger
	Large Intestine	Cat (Rabbit)
Water	Bladder	Monkey
	Kidney	Rooster
Wood	Gallbladder	Rat
	Liver	Ox

The Muscles

In the 1920s, a noted chiropractor x-rayed his assistants while putting each large muscle through its range of motion. He found that each muscle is connected to a specific organ. For instance, the deltoid in the upper arm is connected to the Lung meridian. If your deltoid is aching, there is an imbalance of some sort in the Lung meridian, and, on some level, you are feeling the emotions of being neglected or unrecognized . . . or maybe you've been shot down recently, and your ego has been crushed. You wouldn't feel much like puffing out your chest and feeling good about yourself at that point.

In the early 90s, Rickey Henderson and Dave Henderson of the Oakland A's baseball team, both had hamstring problems that didn't go away with normal medical treatment. No one asked me, but if they had, I would have looked at the situation and, knowing that the hamstrings are connected to the Large Intestine meridian, I would have said that they were having subconscious problems about self-esteem and self-worth. Had their upbringing prepared them for the adulation they were now receiving? Were they able to acknowledge and accept that they are exceptionally talented? Or was there some sort of sacrifice involved, for the Large Intestine deals with sacrifice as well as self-worth issues. What were they sacrificing (home and family perhaps?) to attain their goals? Something was "hanging them up," as a hamstring will. Coming to terms with those emotions would have brought the hamstrings around much more quickly.

The muscles which are related to the meridians are:

Lung
Anterior serratus (under arms)
Coracobrachialis (front of shoulders)
Deltoids (in the arm)
Diaphragm (in the chest)

Large Intestine
Fascia Lata (down the outside of legs)
Hamstrings (lower back of legs)
Quadratus Lumborum (inside thighs)

Stomach
Pectoralis Major Clavicular (chest)
Brachioradialis (lower arms)
Levator Scapulae (up into neck)
Neck Muscles (front and back of neck)
Biceps (upper arms)

Spleen
Latissimus Dorsi (side of torso)
Trapezius (upper back)
Opponens Pollicus Longus (fingers)
Triceps (back of upper arms)

Heart
Subscapularis (deep in shoulder)

Small Intestine
Quadriceps (front of thighs)

Bladder
Peroneus (outside lower legs)
Sacrospinalis (back by spine)
Anterior Tibial (front legs)
Posterior Tibial (back of legs)

Kidney
Psoas (waist in back)
Upper Trapezius (sides of neck)
Iliacus (waist into leg bone)

Circulation-Sex
Gluteus Medius (derrière)
Adductors (inside thighs)
Piriformis (middle of derrière)
Gluteus Maximus (derrière)

Triple Warmer	Teres Minor (shoulder) Sartorius (waist to knee) Gracilis (groin area) Soleus (back of lower legs) Gastrocnemius (back of lower legs)
Gallbladder	Anterior Deltoid (upper arms) Popliteus (back of knee)
Liver	Pectoralis Major Sternal (chest) Rhomboids (upper back)

By knowing the muscles of the body and to which meridians they correspond, you can look at any muscle that is crying out to you and find what emotions are behind it, thus zeroing in on what is imbalanced and finding what you need to return to healthy stasis.

Part II

More About Your Personal Chinese Power Animals

Wood Element
Rat and Ox

Rat

Time of Day: 11 P.M. to 1 A.M.

Element: Wood

Color: Green

Energy: Yang

Meridian: Gallbladder. The Gallbladder meridian begins at the eye, goes around the ear, into the scalp, over the shoulder, picks up under the arm, and moves down the side of the torso and the leg into the fourth toe.

Organ: Gallbladder. The gallbladder is a small sac attached to the liver. It is a storage site for bile, which it receives from the liver. It concentrates bile by reabsorbing water from it. The gallbladder processes fats.

Motivation: Betrayal vs. Unconditional Love. The need to choose autonomously and not feel we are without choices. Taking things too personally and not being objective. To trust, to judge, to make wise choices. When stressed, we see too subjectively and can't see "the forest for the trees." Anger and its acting out, rage, are seated in the gallbladder. This is where we can't be objective, but act out our inner turmoil. And yet a Rat can be the most altruistic of the signs, doing for others without thought for themselves.

Those Who Share the Year of the Rat: Lauren Bacall, Pat Nixon, Alan Alda, Prince Andrew, Marlon Brando, Prince Philip, Robert Redford, Burt Reynolds, George H. Bush, Spencer Tracy, John Madden, Ruth Buzzi, Dennis Hopper, Ben Hogan.

Those Who Share the Month of the Rat . . . are generally **Aries.**

Those Who Share the Hour of the Rat: Gloria Swanson, Susan Atkins (Manson follower), Dianne Feinstein, Amelia Earhart, Indira Gandhi, Sissy Spacek, Beverly Sills, Brooke Shields, Pearl Buck, Lizzie Borden (ax murderer), John F. Kennedy, Jr., Dolly Parton, Jessie James (outlaw), Sephen King (macabre author).

Muscles: Anterior Deltoid, Popliteus. The anterior deltoid flexes the shoulder when the elbow is bent. The popliteus turns the foot and the knee in, and flexes the leg. If you were born between 11 P.M. AND 1 A.M., you tend to have more problems with these muscles than others. Look to where you have built up anger and resentment.

Emotions: Abandoned vs. Adoration. Also, betrayed, unconditional love, judgment, choices, trust, pleasure, blame, devastated, fair/unfair, fault finding, justify, possessive, risk, used, and hidden agendas.

Born in the Year, Month, Hour, Minute of the Rat
Positive: You feel unconditionally loved, and you make a good impression, which draws people to you. You are a natural magnet for positive energy. You can be counted on to make wise choices.

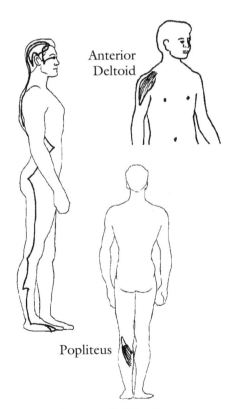

Anterior Deltoid

Popliteus

Figure 3. The Rat:
The Gallbladder Meridian.

You plan and strategize well. You feel blessed by God and feel supported by an abundant universe. You are altruistic and do for others simply because it's the right thing to do. You play fair and expect others to do the same. You have trust in your fellow man and they live up to that trust.

Negative: Born in the Year or Month of the Rat or between 11 P.M. and 1 A.M., you have issues with being betrayed and abandoned. Where anger resides in the liver, rage is born in the gallbladder. Rage is the acting out of anger. If you were born during this time, or in the Year of the Rat, you carry your rage internally and can lash out at others. If you consistently wake up between 11 P.M. and 1 A.M., your anger is being triggered when the gallbladder is activated in its time spot. Your temper can be legendary and, when challenged, you do a perfect "Incredible Hulk" impersonation. Remember the old Bill Bixby series, when he turned into this hideous green monster? . . . with buttons popping and his suit ripping as his anger turned him into the Hulk?

People sense you can be manipulated through threats of abandonment. To clear your "worst case scenario," visualize everyone close to you being removed, one by one, and realizing you will survive; then they don't have any emotional power over you. The liver houses the soul, and, being closely aligned with the gallbladder, we eat fats that the gallbladder has to process in order to stuff our bodies because of the anger at having our soul trampled upon. You may place your focus on the one you perceive as betraying you, but, on some level, you feel betrayed by whichever god you pray to. The opposite is being adored, and the word "adoration" originally comes from being adored by God, by His face shining upon you and being gracious unto you, as the phrase goes. When you feel betrayed, it's as if the higher forces are not in your corner.

When you crave fats, you know you are feeling betrayed and abandoned.

Antidote: Being loved unconditionally, being clear to make wise choices and draw people into your life who will be trustworthy and who will not pull the rug out from under you when you least expect it. Removing the charge of emotional blackmail. Acting out of true altruism and not expecting anything in return.

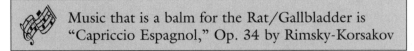 Music that is a balm for the Rat/Gallbladder is "Capriccio Espagnol," Op. 34 by Rimsky-Korsakov

Rate Yourself and Others in Your Life

On a scale of 0–100, where 0 is most negative, 50 is neutral, and 100 is most positive, where do you think you fall with these traits? We usually fluctuate between 40 and 60, but when we've experienced trauma in our lives, we sometimes dip into the lower end of the spectrum.

0	50	100

Ox

Time of Day: 1 A.M. to 3 A.M.

Element: Wood

Color: Green

Energy: Yin

Meridian: Liver. The Liver meridian starts at the big toe, goes up the inside of the legs, extends to the side of the torso, and then darts to a point just below the nipples.

Organ: Liver. The liver is a large, glandular vertebrate organ located in the upper right portion of the abdominal cavity that secretes bile. It's color is reddish brown. The liver is active in the formation of certain blood proteins and in the metabolism of carbohydrates, fats, and proteins. The liver has approximately 360 known functions. It breaks down protein and fats, and creates enzymes. It detoxifies the body.

Motivation: Stifled vs. Growth. Being free and independent (autonomous) or feeling frustrated. Anger over being held back and not being able to grow into one's full creative potential. Having one's vision cropped, as having blinders on.

Those Who Share the Year of the Ox: Mary Tyler Moore, Warren Beatty, Johnny Carson, Merv Griffin, Dustin Hoffman, Paul Newman, Jack Nicholson, Dennis Weaver, Bing Crosby, Clark Gable, Jack Lemmon, Jeff Bridges, Phil Carey.

Those Who Share the Month of the Ox . . . are generally **Taurus.**

Those Who Share the Hour of the Ox: Queen Elizabeth, Margot Fonteyn, Lily Tomlin, Lauren Bacall, Ginger Rogers, Phyllis Diller, Robert Wagner, Frank Gifford, Winston Churchill, Yogi Berra.

Except for Ginger Rogers, there is a certain sedentary presence about these Ox types. You really wouldn't expect them to dash about, willy-nilly. They are deliberate, moving toward a goal one step at a time.

Muscles: Pectoralis Major Sternal, Rhomboids. The pectoralis major sternal muscles move the arm in, turning and drawing it forward. They are behind the breasts.

The rhomboids are muscles in the back of the shoulders. They pull in and turn the shoulder blades. It's where you feel "stabbed in the back."

Emotions: Happy vs. Unhappy. Stifled, stunted, repressed vs. validation, being independent, autonomous, and free. Feelings of being frustrated, blinders on, yoke around the neck, not being able to express life freely.

Born in the Year, Month, Hour, Minute of the Ox
Positive: Born in wee hours of the morning, as well as the year, month, or minute, you are creative. You can project into the future and follow through and complete projects. You have vision and can see what few of us can. You are autonomous and independent and

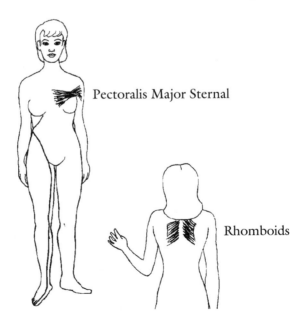

Pectoralis Major Sternal

Rhomboids

Figure 4. The Ox:
The Liver Meridian.

move forward with confidence. You are like a redwood tree, irrevocably moving higher and higher to fulfill your majesty. You see the world in glorious color and have a vision for the world as well as yourself. You can "see" beyond the common man to visualize what humanity can be.

Negative: Born in the Year or Month of the Ox, or between 1 A.M. and 3 A.M., you tend to be "liverish"—irritable, impatient, or, conversely, you implode your anger and insist you aren't an angry person at all. This can express itself in "eruptions" on the body: i.e., rashes, psoriasis, etc.

The liver houses the ethereal soul and affects the eyes, which is why it is said the eyes are the windows to the soul. Your eyes can appear drawn and tired. Your experiences as a child tend to stifle and repress you; you may not have been validated and honored for who you were as an individual. You may have been kept from growing by those in authority. There is an element of immaturity about you, even if you are a responsible adult, simply because you weren't allowed to experience life and grow as a child. You may have had adult caretakers who were fearful for your safety and did everything for you.

The liver rules the ability to execute and follow through. You can become impatient with little things and not be adept at working with machinery or tools. You tend to jump around from project to project and not complete things. If you wake up between 1 A.M. and 3 A.M. consistently, you can be pretty sure there is some anger rearing its head, begging to be acknowledged.

Antidote: You need to seek avenues where you can grow into your full potential. Go out and experience more of life. Push yourself beyond the barriers that were set up for you as a child. You need to be validated by those in authority and given full rein to be who you are inherently. Your happiness is derived from being creative and expressive and transforming yourself into a fully functioning human being. You need to move your life from black and white into color.

Music that is a balm for the Ox/Liver is Sonata in B Minor for Flute and harpsichord by Bach. Also, Sonata in A Major and Sonata in E Major for Flute and other instruments, by Bach.

In modern music, we find Uzca's CD, "Slice of Light," healing for the liver.

Rate Yourself and Others in Your Life

On a scale of 0–100, where 0 is most negative, 50 is neutral, and 100 is most positive, where do you think you fall with these traits? We usually fluctuate between 40 and 60, but when we've experienced trauma in our lives, we sometimes dip into the lower end of the spectrum.

0	50	100

Metal Element
Tiger and Cat

CAROLINE
PATRICK

Tiger

Years: 1902 · 1914 · 1926 · 1938 · 1950 · 1962 · 1974 · 1986 · 1998

Time of Day: 3 A.M. to 5 A.M.

Element: Metal (Air)

Color: White

Energy: Yin

Meridian: Lung. The Lung meridian starts on the torso near the crease of the arm, parallel with the top of the breast, and goes down the arm on the inside and out the thumb.

Organ: Lung. Taking a breath is the first thing we do in life, and the last thing we do. The lungs have to do with removing the foreign bodies that enter through the breath. The lung removes carbon dioxide from the blood and provides it with oxygen.

Motivation: The need to be recognized and stand out. Conversely, the need to hide behind a mask when that recognition is glaring and harsh. The need for the ego to be acknowledged. The need to feel alive. Depression results when we mask our true feelings, or numb them with alcohol or cigarettes—when we can't express who we are.

Those Who Share the Year of the Tiger: Markie Post, Gary Larson, Jay Leno, David Canary, Elliot Gould, Janet Reno, Ruta Lee, Marilyn Monroe, Julie Kavner, Jerry Brown, John Dean, Evil Knievel, Dwight David Eisenhower, Tracy Austin, Hugh Hefner.

Those Who Share the Month of the Tiger . . . are generally **Geminis.**

Those Who Share the Hour of the Tiger: Diane McBain, Ethel Kennedy, Carol Burnett, Ann-Margaret, Helen Hayes, Sally Field, Pat Nixon, Chris Evert, Tatum O'Neal, Elvis Presley, Ludwig von Beethoven, Ted Kennedy, Ingrid Bergman.

There is a certain majesty about these Tigers; a regal bearing. Helen Hayes was the "Queen of the American Theater," Pat Nixon was first lady, and Chris Evert the queen of tennis. Diane McBain always displayed a refined sophistication on the screen during her stardom at Warner Bros. People like Carol Burnett, Ann-Margaret, and Elvis Presley are first in their fields and have the lung capacity of the Tiger to belt out a song with the best of them.

There is an aloofness, which is attributable to the air quality of the element, and within that is the desirability to wear a mask when facing the world to protect them. Pat Nixon is a prime example, masking her feelings from the world. She wasn't really "Plastic Pat"; she was wearing a mask to hide her pain.

Muscles: Anterior Serratus, Coracobrachialis, Deltoids, Diaphragm. The anterior serratus draws the shoulder blade forward.

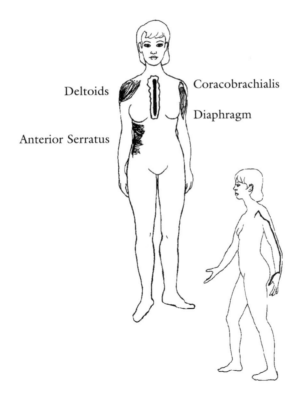

Deltoids

Coracobrachialis

Diaphragm

Anterior Serratus

Figure 5. The Tiger:
The Lung Meridian.

A weakness in this meridian will make it difficult to push things forward when the arms are straight. This causes the shoulder blades to wing out in the back. It also raises the ribs. The anterior serratus, then, is important when we breathe in and out.

The coracobrachialis helps to straighten the arm when it is held over the head. It also aids the shoulder when the elbow is bent—for instance, when you comb your hair. You would use this muscle in school when you raise your hand to get attention.

The deltoids cap the shoulders. They draw the arm away from the body and lift the elbow. The diaphragm is the main muscle used in breathing. The diaphragm separates the chest from the abdominal cavity.

If one of your animals is the Tiger, some of your emotions go to your lungs, and the foregoing muscles are involved; you might find you have frequent imbalance with them. If you find yourself waking up between 3 A.M. and 5 A.M., consider about what you might be grieving.

Emotions: Recognized vs. Ignored, neglected. Also, the feeling of being dead vs. alive, ego vs. egolessness; wearing a mask, depression, inspiration, enthusiasm. Sadness and grieving also come under the auspices of the Lung meridian.

Born in the Year, Month, Hour, Minute of the Tiger
Positive: Born in the Year or Month of the Tiger or in the early morning hours, from 3 A.M. to 5 A.M., you can be truly inspired. Operating from the positive aspects of the Lung meridian, you are enthusiastic and inspire others. You wake up in the morning, glad to be alive and look forward to each new day. You enjoy being recognized and have a need to be reckoned with. You seek positions of importance where you can stand out in the crowd. People may say to you, "You are so full of life!"

Negative: You tend to be depressed and feel as if you have a black cloud continually over your head. There can be a sense of being numb inside, having shut down your emotions early, for it was too painful to feel. People who smoke are numbing their lungs, dulling the nerve endings in regard to being neglected or having their ego crushed. The anger results in depression; the sadness can become pervasive. You don't feel totally alive. At some point, the ego has taken a bashing and you can either feel egoless or force people to recognize you. Issues of pride are expressed in Lung-meridian imbalances. When the senses are assaulted for too long, some of you resort to wearing a mask to the outside world, to protect youself. When negative, there can be a lack of pride of ownership, and yet you can be too proud to accept help. Wolfgang Amadeus Mozart's music causes the Lung meridian to respond. It is a healing balm. Country and western music, and most specifically the Sons of the Pioneers, also resonates to the lung. Country and western music itself, with its "she done me wrong" themes, is well-suited to lung issues. However comforting at the time, one needs to use it only temporarily, for it is feeding the grief, not healing it. Then move on to Mozart.

Antidote: You need to be recognized and appreciated for who you are. The heaviness on your chest needs to be lifted, so that you feel the air filling your lungs to their full capacity, "drinking in the wellspring of life" and feeling alive again. You need to cease enduring things and being long-suffering. You need to recapture that dream that eluded you. You need to know that it's okay to be proud of who you are and your accomplishments.

 Music that is a balm for the Tiger/Lung meridian is music by Mozart.

Rate Yourself and Others in Your Life

On a scale of 0–100, where 0 is most negative, 50 is neutral, and 100 is most positive, where do you think you fall with these traits? We usually fluctuate between 40 and 60, but when we've experienced trauma in our lives, we sometimes dip into the lower end of the spectrum.

| 0 | 50 | 100 |

Cat

Years: 1903 · 1915· 1927 · 1939 · 1951 · 1963 · 1975 · 1987 · 1999

Time of Day: 5 A.M. to 7 A.M.

Element: Metal (Air)

Color: White

Energy: Yang

Meridian: Large Intestine. The Large Intestine meridian starts on the index finger and goes up the inside of the arm on the anterior side, over the shoulder and up to the nose.

Organ: Large Intestine. The large intestine and the colon are the elimination organs of the body. It is the portion of the intestine that extends from the ileum to the anus, and forms an arch around the small intestine that includes the cecum, colon, rectum, and anal canal. Since it relates to feces, this organ/meridian concerns itself with what we are conditioned as children to regard as "yukky," hence its emotions deal with the spectrum of feeling clean or dirty.

Motivation: The Cat is motivated from a need for self-esteem. To respect themselves and feel their value, so that they do not sacrifice and become a martyr when their self-worth is questioned.

Those Who Share the Year of the Cat: Joan Crawford, Claire Booth Luce, Ingrid Bergman, Lily Tomlin, Sidney Poitier, Bob Hope, George C. Scott, Richard Thomas, Elizabeth Ashley, Erma Bombeck, Tatum O'Neal, Richard Crenna, Kurt Russell.

Those Who Share the Month of the Cat . . . are generally **Cancerians.**

Those Who Share the Hour of the Cat: Barbara Streisand, Lucille Ball, Rosalyn Carter, Joan Kennedy, Barbara Walters, Julie Andrews, Grace Kelly, Kathryn Crosby, Judy Garland, Imelda Marcos, Richard Strauss, Ty Cobb, Linda Evans, Pete Rose,

Leonard Bernstein, Aristotle Onassis, Jack Nicklaus, Abraham Lincoln.

Along with Tigers (because they are part of the air [metal] element with the Cat), there is a certain aloofness about most of these Cats. You'll not see them rushing out and trying to get publicity; it comes to them simply because of their presence. You wouldn't think any of them would have self-esteem issues to deal with, but I bet if you asked them, they would all say they do, to varying degrees. Sometimes it is this very thing that pushes people to great heights. Most are certainly overachievers.

Most of these people seem "light on their feet," always able to "land on their feet" as well when challenged. The exception might be George C. Scott, which may indicate he was born in a different year or one of his other animals is stronger.

Muscles: Fascia Lata, Hamstrings, Quadratus Lumborum. The fascia lata muscle aids in bending the thigh, drawing it out from the body sideways, as well as keeping it turned in.

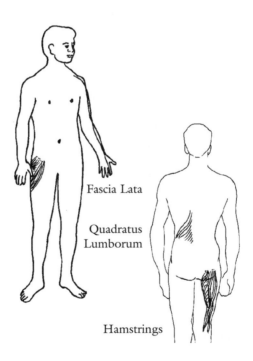

Fascia Lata

Quadratus
Lumborum

Hamstrings

Figure 6. The Cat:
The Large Intestine Meridian.

The hamstrings are the muscles in the back of the thigh that flex the leg and turn it sideways when you bend your knee.

The quadratus lumborum is in the lower back around the waist and flexes the vertebral column sideways, toward the hip.

If you were born between 5 A.M. and 7 A.M., when you react to life, you tend to take it to your large intestine, and these muscles are involved. You may have more problems with them than others. If you tend to "sleep in" past these hours or find it difficult to wake up between 5 A.M. and 7 A.M., look at what emotions you might be trying to avoid in relation to sacrifice, martyrdom, and self-esteem issues.

Emotions: Self-Esteem vs. Defective. Sacrifice, martyrdom, feeling clean or dirty about oneself.

Born in the Year, Month, Hour, Minute of the Cat
Positive: Born at daybreak, or the year or the month of the Cat, you can have a true sense of self. If the positive emotions of the Large Intestine meridian were established in your youth, you can be secure in your self-worth and self-esteem. You know you are valuable and don't have to sacrifice yourself for the sake of others. You have a positive sense of self-love, and feel clean and good.

Negative: If you were raised with the negative emotions of the Large Intestine meridian, your early environment could have caused you to feel unclean about yourself, that there's something shameful about you from which you just can't escape.

Once I was in the grocery store and a little girl was in my path. Her mother said scornfully, "Get out of the lady's way, you little shit." I cringed. How many times must that be repeated in that little girl's life for her to take it on subconsciously?

Born at daybreak, your childhood environment held different levels of unworthiness. Some Cat people's experiences were mild. Others were severe. At worst, you feel unworthy to take up the space your body requires in this world. You had parents and teachers who always talked down to you. One mother told her son not to even think about the girl next door—"She's too good for you." This is what you have to deal with to varying degrees. There is the intrinsic shame that John Bradshaw talks about: feeling defective—that no matter what you do you can't get clean enough, you are defective merchandise, you came that way, that's the way it is, and there's nothing you can do about it. The large intestine processes the waste—the feces—which is why, born at this time, you can have issues with not feeling clean enough. Because of this, neuroses can develop.

Antidote: You need to realize you are to God what a drop of water is to the ocean. God could not express totally if you were not alive. You are sacred space with divine talents to express during your time on this earth.

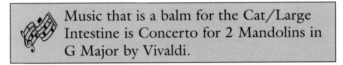

Music that is a balm for the Cat/Large Intestine is Concerto for 2 Mandolins in G Major by Vivaldi.

Rate Yourself and Others in Your Life

On a scale of 0–100, where 0 is most negative, 50 is neutral, and 100 is most positive, where do you think you fall with these traits? We usually fluctuate between 40 and 60, but when we've experienced trauma in our lives, we sometimes dip into the lower end of the spectrum.

0	50	100

Earth Element
Dragon and Snake

Dragon

Time of Day: 7 A.M. to 9 A.M.

Element: Earth

Color: Yellow

Energy: Yang

Meridian: Stomach. The Stomach meridian starts under the eye, makes a "U" around the cheek, and then goes down the neck and the torso to each leg to the second toe.

Organ: Stomach. The stomach receives the food and starts the process to transform the nutrients into energy for the body; it is the principal organ of digestion.

Muscles: Pectoralis Major Clavicular, Levator Scapulae, Neck Muscles, Brachioradialis. The pectoralis major clavicular is a chest muscle that aids the arm to bend and turn at the shoulder.

The levator scapulae are muscles in the shoulder that go up into the neck and are connected to the head's stability.

The neck muscles, the ones that go up the back and front of the neck are related to the Stomach meridian, and when you eat something your body doesn't like, they will often get tight.

The brachioradialis is found in the forearm and flexes the elbow as well as turns the wrist.

The biceps flex the forearm.

Many of the finger muscles are related to the stomach meridian, and can show us our "graspingness" in getting what we need.

If you were born between 7 A.M. and 9 A.M. you can be prone to any of these muscles being "out" more often than others. If you persistently sleep beyond 9 A.M., you might want to look at what feelings of disappointment you are dealing with. A good affirmation might be: "I wake up with high expectations that are met."

Those Who Share the Year of the Dragon: Ethel Kennedy, Shirley Temple, Raquel Welch, Patti (Reagan) Davis, Bruce Lee,

John Lennon, Jack Nicklaus, Christopher Reeve, Martin Sheen, Rosemary Clooney.

Those Who Share the Month of the Dragon . . . are generally **Leos.**

Those Who Share the Hour of the Dragon: Pearl Bailey, Cher, Anne Frank, Barbara Stanwyck, Lucie Arnaz, Penny Marshall, Twiggy, Deborah Kerr, Goldie Hawn, Caroline Kennedy, Leigh Taylor Young, Liza Minelli, Jimmy Carter, Eddie Fisher, Ferdinand Marcos, Billy Joel, Johnny Cash, Paul Newman, Tom Selleck, Johnny Carson, Meryl Streep, Bob Mackie, Lawrence Welk, J. Paul Getty, Joseph Kennedy, Sr., Desi Arnaz, Jr., Jamie Lee Curtis, President Bill Clinton.

These are people who "touch the magic." They are artists, visionaries and people with imagination who can dream big. They have large appetites for power and fame. They want to accumulate the best and live the high life. They enjoy the material pleasures

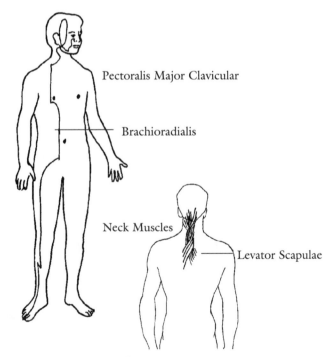

Figure 7. The Dragon:
The Stomach Meridian.

and position life has to offer. Some of them can be dominant and "breathe fire" when displeased.

Emotions: Content vs. Deprived. Disappointed, dispossessed, hunger, and greed vs. fulfilled, content. Also, feeling attached to something—person, place, or thing. Having identity issues. Knowing something's value, its "cash" value as opposed to the esteem and worthiness as with the Cat. Addictions, compulsions, and obsessions fall in the realm of the Dragon. Being larger than life and having appetites that reflect this demeanor.

Born in the Year, Month, Hour, Minute of the Dragon
Positive: At best, you are a person who is truly contented, who has reasonable expectations and the ability to see them through to a proper conclusion. You don't hunger after anything or feel deprived. There is a sense of being fulfilled; your tummy is full and you appreciate the good things in life. You realize that you aren't what you do. You know you will wear many hats in your lifetime and can segue from one to another easily.

Negative: Born between 7 A.M. and 9 A.M., you were born at the time of day we usually have breakfast—when we break our fast from the previous night. We're hungry, we've gone the longest spell of the cycle without eating. We seek to nurture ourselves for the coming day. Born during these hours, you take your experiences into your stomach to "digest" them. The Dragon and the Stomach meridian deal with disappointment, feeling deprived and what the Chinese call "dispossessed." When we lose a job, get a divorce, change residence, or the kids move out, etc., we have lost the identity that we have created for ourselves over an extended period of time; an identity that nurtures us. At that time, the stomach churns, turns upside down, and doesn't deal well with things. You tend to excess—whether it be food, gambling, or simply going off on a shopping spree to help you forget. It helps fill an emptiness that can seemingly never be filled for you.

Antidote: It is particularly important for babies born during these periods to be fed when they are hungry, to have all their needs met as an infant and small child. Not that it doesn't apply to us all, but Dragon people need to have a feeling of contentment as babies. You need to know that, when you cry with an empty belly, someone will come and fill you up. When babies are fed on a schedule they get the idea that they may never be fed again, so they must gobble up everything in sight when they are fed. They are also told subliminally that their needs aren't going to be met, and they live a life of continued disappointment. There are issues with security and this is where the excesses reside; compensating for the lack that you feel consistently.

 Music that is a balm for the Dragon/Stomach is Concerto for 2 Violins in D Minor by Vivaldi. Also, Concerto in D Major by Mercadante, particularly the version played by James Galway.

Rate Yourself and Others in Your Life

On a scale of 0–100, where 0 is most negative, 50 is neutral, and 100 is most positive, where do you think you fall with these traits? We usually fluctuate between 40 and 60, but when we've experienced trauma in our lives, we sometimes dip into the lower end of the spectrum.

0	50	100

Snake

Years: 1905 · 1917 · 1929 · 1941 · 1953 · 1965 · 1977 · 1989

Time of Day: 9 A.M. to 11 A.M.

Element: Earth

Color: Yellow

Energy: Yin

Meridian: Spleen (Pancreas). The Spleen meridian starts on the big toe, moves up the inside of the leg, and goes up the torso to the armpit, then ends about 4" below it.

Organ: The spleen transforms the food into energy. It stores blood, disintegrates old blood cells, filters foreign substances from the blood, and produces lymphocytes.

Motivation: Rejection vs. Approval. Significance vs. insignificance. The Snake can perceive rejection when it isn't even there, anticipating rejection and needing approval just for being who it is. It wants to be perfect and can be overly critical. There can be issues around bonding with parents, and secrets to be found out about. In the extreme, the Snake can be self-rejecting.

Muscles: Latissimus Dorsi, Trapezius, Opponens Pollicis Longus, Triceps. The latissimus dorsi starts in the middle of the back near the spine and ends under the armpit. It contributes to keeping the back straight and the shoulders down. It is used in many sports activities.

The trapezius is in the upper back and extends from the spine to the upper shoulder. Its job is to keep the shoulder blade in and it also turns it.

The opponens pollicis longus is in the palm of the hand.

The triceps, located in the back of the arm, aid in straightening the elbow.

Those born between 9 A.M. and 11 A.M. generally have more muscle problems because the Spleen/Pancreas meridian works directly on the muscles. It was thought in the past that the liver related to muscles, but now the theory is that the spleen has a direct correlation. When you have problems with these muscles, look to see where you are dealing with rejection and insignificance in your life. Also, there may be someone lying to you on some level.

Those Who Share the Year of the Snake: Diane McBain, Jackie Zeman, Ann-Margaret, Brooke Shields, Gloria Allred, Phyllis Diller, Marcia Clark, Jackie Kennedy Onassis, Grace Kelly, Ryan O'Neal, Robert Duvall, Stacy Keach, Beau Bridges, Zsa Zsa Gabor, Muhammad Ali.

Those Who Share the Month of the Snake . . . are generally **Virgos.**

Those Who Share the Hour of the Snake: Veleka Gray, Marilyn Monroe, Wallis Simpson (Duchess of Windsor), Della Reese, Sally Struthers, Princess Anne, Billie Jean King, Mia Farrow, Kurt Russell, Mickey Mantle, Harrison Ford, Michael Caine, Jimmy Connors, Steve Wozniak, Michael Douglas, Mark Harmon, Madalyn Murray O'Hare.

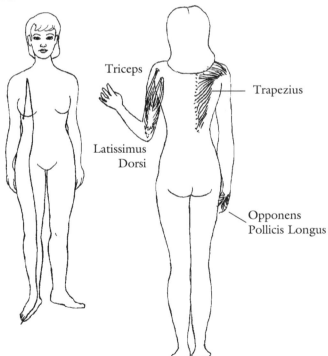

Figure 8. The Snake:
The Spleen/Pancreas Meridian.

This seems to be a group of people who have had battles to fight, and rejection with which to contend. Wallis Simpson received the highest accolade of approval by having a future king throw over his throne for her, and yet they lived, for all intents and purposes, in exile. Billie Jean King was forced to wear a tennis skirt and wasn't allowed to wear shorts in a childhood match and it became the catalyst for her becoming a champion . . . and dictating her own rules. Madalyn Murray O'Hare seemed to defy it all by taking on the country and the world when she blocked prayer in the schools.

Emotions: Appreciated vs. Rejected. Significance vs. Insignificance. Adequate vs. Inadequate. "The Lie" vs. Truth. Being able to be wrong, or admitting one isn't perfect, is part of the Spleen meridian. When one can't be wrong, they can create lies and secrets in order to maintain the image.

Born in the Year, Month, Hour, Minute of the Snake
Positive: Just like the Snake, its related organ, the spleen, is an agent of transformation in the body. When you radiate the positive emotions of the Snake, you have a sense of yourself that is unshakable. You know that not everyone is going to like you in this world, and that is okay. You realize some energies just don't jibe and it is no fault of either party. You are secure in yourself, don't have any need to succumb to peer pressure, and radiate a sunny personality. You have a sharp mind and can remember details. The ability for memorization and concentration occurs in the Spleen meridian. It is important in taking tests and one can see that it shouldn't be imbalanced by the consumption of sugar when students want to stay up and cram and drink sodas for the caffeine and sugar. You are very sensitive to the energy of others and can find yourself seeing right through to the core of who they are or saying, "That person makes my skin crawl" when someone is not acting with integrity. You are a loyal friend and rush in to help and support friends and family when they need you.

Negative: As a Snake person, you fear rejection. If things aren't going the way you want, you can feel you might be rejected and need to reject before you get rejected. Sometimes you misperceive and you can jump the gun and hurt a relationship in the process. You aren't going to wait around very long for someone to make up their mind. If they don't find you the most fascinating person in the world, you'll be off to replace them pronto . . . even if it isn't a personal rejection. Sometimes children who are put up for adoption are born at this time period, and have an inborn sense of being rejected, regardless of the altruistic motivation of the parents.

Another aspect of the Snake personality, is "The Lie." The meridian here is the Spleen and the spleen secretes insulin. Note the play on words with "secrets." The spleen deals with lies that are necessarily kept "secret." People born at this time sometimes find they are operating from some lie that was established in their childhood that they have believed, and upon which they have built their lives. They find they have perpetuated the lie out of innocence, or it is perpetuated around them.

Antidote: The Spleen person needs to acknowledge that not everyone is going to like them and learn not to take it personally. Some people just "click"—the chemistry is perfect. Some people grow on each other. And some people just don't click—the tumblers just don't fall into line, and it's got to be okay. Both people can be equally fantastic; the chemistry just isn't there. It's harder on someone born at Snake (Spleen) time to understand. It's not a personal rejection when the world isn't in their corner 100 percent of the time. You need to find appreciation and approval within yourself and in your security be able to distinguish rejection from other emotions that people are experiencing. The Snake needs self-approval and self-love.

 Music that is a balm for the Snake/Spleen is Music by Telemann, particularly the Suite in A Minor for Flute, and Trumpet Concerto in D.

Rate Yourself and Others in Your Life

On a scale of 0–100, where 0 is most negative, 50 is neutral, and 100 is most positive, where do you think you fall with these traits? We usually fluctuate between 40 and 60, but when we've experienced trauma in our lives, we sometimes dip into the lower end of the spectrum.

0	50	100

Fire Element
Horse and Sheep

Horse

Years: 1906 · 1918 · 1930 · 1942 · 1954 · 1966 · 1978 · 1990

Time of Day: 11 A.M. to 1 P.M.

Element: Fire

Color: Red

Energy: Yin

Meridian: Heart. The energy of the Heart meridian starts in the armpit and goes down the inside of the arm and out the little finger. This meridian affects not only the heart, but the brain as well. It is where long-term memory resides.

Organ: The heart is the central organ of the body. It is the chambered, muscular organ that pumps blood received from the veins into the arteries, maintaining the flow of blood through the entire circulatory system.

Motivation: Love vs. Indifference, Hate. To belong, to be touched, to dwell in reality; to be passionate about life; to believe.

Muscles: Subscapularis. The subscapularis is behind the shoulder blade. It aids in drawing the arm in when it is raised above the shoulder. It is used for many things, most prominently in music conductors, which is one reason it has been noted that conductors live to such a ripe old age, because the subscapularis is connected to the Heart meridian. The combination of the music, the motion of the arms above the shoulders using the subscapularis, and the eyes darting around to key members of the orchestra, aid the body in keeping the heart strong. Most people don't use the subscapularis that much. We don't do many things in our daily activity to raise the arms. Sports activities such as tennis use this muscle, and tennis players, too, seem to be fit and live longer as a general rule.

If you were born between 11 A.M. and 1 P.M., you take your emotions personally into your heart. People can reach you by appealing to your heart impulses. All the heart metaphors pertain to the Horse and the Heart meridian: warmhearted, coldhearted, heartened, disheartened, don't have the heart for it, hard-hearted, tenderhearted, stouthearted, heavyhearted.

Those Who Share the Year of the Horse: Pearl Bailey, Betty Ford, Barbra Streisand, Chris Evert, Patty Hearst, Leonard Bernstein, Sean Connery, Clint Eastwood, John Travolta, Wayne Newton, Sandra Dee, Frank Gifford, Michelle Lee, Robert Wagner, Annette Funicello.

Those Who Share the Month of the Horse . . . are generally **Libras.**

Those Who Share the Hour of the Horse: Mary Tyler Moore, Anne Morrow-Lindbergh, Rose Kennedy, George H. Bush, Napoleon Bonaparte, Eleanor Roosevelt, Willie Nelson, Kenny Rogers, Roy Rogers, George Gershwin, Burt Reynolds, Dan Rather, Phil Donahue, Jack Nicholson, Arthur Ashe, Albert Einstein, Carrie Fisher, Michael Landon.

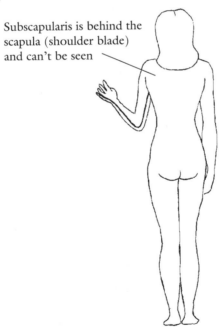

Subscapularis is behind the scapula (shoulder blade) and can't be seen

Figure 9. The Horse:
The Heart Meridian.

Many of these celebrities have had long, illustrious careers; there's a lot of staying power and stamina in Horses. Arthur Ashe was felled by a heart attack before he succumbed to AIDS. On screen, Roy Rogers frequently put his horse before his romantic interest, and, in reality, had quadruple bypass surgery at one point. He eventually died of heart complications. Being born in the Hour of the Horse doesn't mean you will have heart problems, but it certainly shows that you should take care of your heart, eat well, and exercise. The rose is another symbol for the Heart meridian, and the Kennedy matriarch was named Rose.

Emotions: Love vs. Hate. Caring vs. Self-Absorbed. Being in and/or out of touch, feeling vs. numbness, understanding the meaning of life. Belief vs. non-belief, passion vs. indifference, being in or out of touch with reality, being grateful or ungrateful.

Born in the Year, Month, Hour, Minute of the Horse
Positive: You tend to be strong, lighthearted, and have the ability to appreciate your circumstances and have a grateful heart. You have a sense of belonging, and are welcome wherever you go. You have a tender heart and can be counted upon to help those in need. You are a tactile person and enjoy being in touch with people, either by physical touching or communication. You have a solid sense of reality and can see things as they are.

Negative: Born at midday, or in the year or month of the Horse, you can laugh a little too loudly or at the wrong time. You may have the tendency to talk incessantly when the energy is out of balance. You can give too much and reach a point where you can't extend yourself anymore, and can seem to be self-absorbed to others. It's really a defense to protect your sensitive heart. You have a long memory and can recall things that others have forgotten. You have a need to be touched, but if you were inappropriately touched as a child, you can withdraw and not allow anyone to come too close. Emotional issues touch you deeply: "heartbroken," "heartache," "broken promises," etc. all touch the Horse. Jealousy resides in the Heart meridian, and forgiveness is the best antidote for jealousy and hate. It has been said that envy takes two, but jealousy takes three. Imbalances in the Heart meridian generally concern relationship issues.

Antidote: The Horse person needs to be vulnerable and open up to be loved and touched. They need to set health limits and boundaries about how much they give and insist that people in their life reciprocate in kind. This is where we receive the ability to form meaningful relationships and relate to others in general. The Horse and the Heart meridian is where we learn to develop the ability to respond to others.

 Music that is a balm for the Horse/Heart is Appalachian Spring by Aaron Copeland; also waltzes, because of the quarter-time beat, and Baroque styles.

Rate Yourself and Others in Your Life

On a scale of 0–100, where 0 is most negative, 50 is neutral, and 100 is most positive, where do you think you fall with these traits? We usually fluctuate between 40 and 60, but when we've experienced trauma in our lives, we sometimes dip into the lower end of the spectrum.

| 0 | 50 | 100 |

Sheep

Time of Day: 1 P.M. to 3 P.M.

Element: Fire

Color: Red

Energy: Yang

Meridian: Small Intestine. The Small Intestine meridian starts at the outside of the little finger, works its way up the posterior side of the arm, takes a dip into the shoulder blade and then comes back up, goes to the eye, and stops at the ear.

Organ: Small Intestine. The small intestine decides which nutrients are good and should circulate throughout the body, and what is waste and should be released. It is the narrow, upper part of the intestine where digestion is completed and nutrients are absorbed by the blood. The small intestine extends from the pylorus to the cecum and is made up of the duodenum, the jejunum, and the ileum.

Motivation: Victimization vs. Victor. Being discriminating or not being able to separate the wheat from the chaff in relationships or any other aspect of life. Being responsible for your own actions and being clear on what is not your responsibility; taking the blame if need be, but not taking the blame for others.

Those Who Share the Year of the Sheep: Tuesday Weld, Valerie Perrine, Barbara Walters, Penny Marshall, Amy Carter, Billie Jean King, Ram Dass, James Dean, Robert DeNiro, John Denver, Willie Mays, Fabian, Leonard Nimoy, Dan Rather, Madalyn Murray O'Hare, William Colby (CIA), Howard Cosell, Bonnie Franklin, Shelley Fabares.

Those Who Share the Month of the Sheep . . . are generally **Scorpios.**

Those Who Share the Hour of the Sheep: Lillian Carter (Jimmy's mother), Jacqueline Kennedy Onassis, Patti (Reagan) Davis,

Bette Midler, Madame Marie Curie, Tonya Harding, Fidel Castro (Cuba's leader), Sen. Gary Hart, Sen. Orrin Hatch, Desi Arnaz, Stephanie Powers, Barbara Mandrell, John Travolta, Babe Ruth, Rich Little.

Penny Marshall's voice can bleat like a sheep. Patti Davis is certainly a maverick sheep, not going along with the herd, and Bette Midler, too, seems to be a lady who does her own thing. Jackie O, although seemingly not a victim on the surface, was a participant in one of the most tragic moments in history.

Muscles: Quadriceps, Abdominals. The quads are in the thigh and straighten the knee and flex the thigh. They are one of the biggest muscle groups in the body. They aid in getting up and down from chairs and climbing stairs. They relate to the statement, "I won't stand for this," or "I can't stand this anymore."

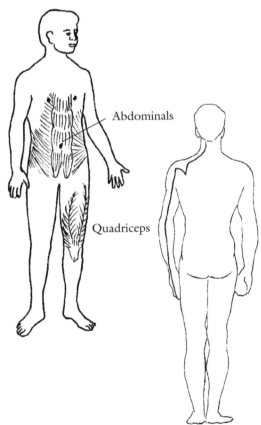

Figure 10. The Sheep:
The Small Intestine Meridian.

The abs are in the front and at the sides of the front of the body.

When the quads and abs are weak, one is feeling victimized in some way. Look to see how you are running with the herd and not being true to yourself. This is also one of the reasons why, when we get in shape, we feel better about ourselves. As we strengthen the body, we strengthen the corresponding concept in our brain and feel more victorious.

Emotions: Victim vs. Victor. Discrimination vs. Codependency. Responsibility vs. blaming others, empowerment vs. powerlessness.

Born in the Year, Month, Hour, Minute of the Sheep
Positive: You have a strong work ethic and dutifully carry out your duties. You can be counted on to be at work every day, and to have all your tasks completed by day's end. If not, you don't mind working overtime or putting in some hours on the weekend. You are a boss's best employee. You are careful in your diet and with whom you choose to associate. You read health articles, read labels, and are disciplined in your ability to stay away from foods and products that are not good for you. In the same way, you are meticulous in whom you associate with, and do not idly take on new friends without putting them through intense questioning to see if they pass muster. You know what your responsibilities are, and you carry them out on time. You take the path that leads to empowerment.

Negative: Born in the early afternoon, you can have persecution problems. If your parents didn't raise you to feel you were the greatest and that you could succeed at anything you wanted to, you can perceive yourself as a victim of your experiences, and thus victimize others in the process. In the extreme negative, sometimes your environment is your enemy and you can have environmental allergies and never leave the house because of them.

This is the time of day when most football and baseball games commence, which is quite appropriate when we recognize it is the time when we engage in an activity that produces a victor.

You can also use your victimization to play upon others' emotions.

It has been reported, one or two time in print, that Tonya Harding was born at 2:30 P.M. and this one seems to work best. Regardless of the merits of her personal involvement, with the energy of the Sheep operating negatively in her life, the media reported that she had a challenging childhood that could have planted the seeds of "poor me" and the perks that we can unwittingly perceive as positive by being the victim of the subconscious. Even if the time isn't accurate, there is the element of Sheep in her life somewhere, which acted out here.

I have reached a point in my practice where I will seriously consider not taking a client born between 1 P.M. and 3 P.M., if their victim role is highly developed, and they aren't living out the positive side of responsibility, simply because they project the sessions will not be beneficial, hence they aren't, hence it is my fault . . . it couldn't possibly have anything to do with their mindset!

Antidote: The small intestine discriminates. It takes the food and decides just what is healthy and should continue on through the system and what should be eliminated through the large intestine. So we, too, need to be discriminating. We've been taught in this generation not to discriminate, but bigotry and discrimination are two different things. To discriminate is to discern, to be refined and to separate the wheat from the chaff in life. If, as a culture, we aren't allowed to discriminate, then our bodies will mirror that energy, and we will keep cheesecake and eliminate tofu because we/it can't differentiate between what's good for us and what isn't. If the small intestine receives the same food over and over again, it will get tired of sending the same thing in the same direction. It wants variety, in life as well as in the food it distributes. To become empowered by life is your quest.

 Music that is a balm for the Sheep/Small Intestine is Pathétique, Symphony No. 6 in B Minor, Op. 74 by Tchaikovsky. Also, Peer Gynt Suite No. 1, by Edvard Grieg.

Rate Yourself and Others in Your Life

On a scale of 0–100, where 0 is most negative, 50 is neutral, and 100 is most positive, where do you think you fall with these traits? We usually fluctuate between 40 and 60, but when we've experienced trauma in our lives, we sometimes dip into the lower end of the spectrum.

0	50	100

Water Element
Monkey and Rooster

Monkey

Time of Day: 3 P.M. to 5 P.M.

Element: Water

Color: Blue/Black

Energy: Yang

Meridian: Bladder. The Bladder meridian is the longest one of all. It travels from the eyes, up over the head, down the neck, and down the back of the torso and the legs into the fifth toe. Interestingly, with a meridian where the emotions deal with control, this one is practically the only one we cannot reach and control ourselves; we have to ask for help.

Organ: The urinary bladder is an elastic, muscular sac in the anterior part of the pelvic cavity where urine collects before excretion.

Motivation: Being Controlled or Taking Control vs. Having Faith and Going with the Flow of the Universe. Being dutiful or following your heart. Being in denial vs. accepting truth.

Those Who Share the Year of the Monkey: Debbie Reynolds, Elizabeth Taylor, Bette Davis, Angela Davis, Lisa Marie Presley, Dorothy Hamill, Michael Tilson Thomas, Chris Darden, Shari Lewis, Leigh Taylor-Young, Jimmy Stewart.

Those Who Share the Month of the Monkey . . . are generally **Sagittarians.**

Those Who Share the Hour of the Monkey: Jackie Zeman, Anita Bryant, Doris Day, Betty Ford, Elizabeth Montgomery, Shirley MacLaine, Brenda Vacarro, Christina Onassis, Helen Keller, Farrah Fawcett, John Kennedy, Robert Kennedy, Jesse Jackson.

These are strong men and women who have the courage of their convictions. They enjoy taking control, and yet faith, as symbolized by Helen Keller, is the epitome to which they can aspire. These people create a reality and will not budge from its perimeters.

Muscles: Peroneus, Sacrospinalis, Tibials. The peroneus muscles are in the lower leg and flex the side of the foot upward and out. Pronounced, "pair-o-knee-us," some will mispronounce it and say "pear-*roan*-e-us," echoing "erroneous." Plays on words often help us to zero in on key issues about a power animal or meridian. When I hear that, I start to look at how "erroneous" is part of this meridian . . . some erroneous perception that has led the Monkey person to seek control in his/her environment.

The sacrospinalis goes up and down the back from the neck to the waist, on either side of the spine, and is a group of muscles that are an integral part of much of the back's activity. They help to keep the body upright, "in control."

The tibials are in the lower leg at the back of the calf, and flex the foot out and upward.

If you were born between 1 P.M. and 3 P.M., your emotional holograms are generally going to go to these muscles. If anyone finds them weak, look to where you are feeling controlled by others, or where you feel the need to control to keep your world safe.

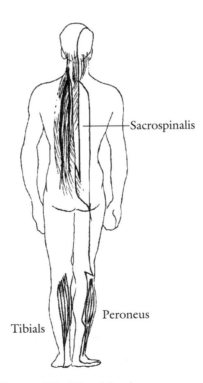

Figure 11. The Monkey:
The Bladder Meridian.

Emotions: Control vs. Faith. Denial vs. truth. Controlling one's destiny, creating a world one can live within safely.

Born in the Year, Month, Hour, Minute of the Monkey

Positive: At best, the Monkey allows life to unfold. You recognize that the universal force (God, what have you) knows far better than you do. You are willing to surrender and trust the universe to exact retribution, no matter what it is—or to exact none. You are up front with yourself and others, and you have no ulterior motives. You are an open expression of life, and you allow it to flow to and through you in an ever-expanding circle. You are willing to throw the monkey wrench away and stop altering your experience, so a loving universe can give you All.

Negative: As a Monkey, you can bolt when something gets too close to cracking open the cosmic egg. You created a world you can control, a world you have structured so that you can live and function. When a person or event comes along that has the potential of cracking it wide open, making you look at the pain, face the music, move through the darkness to find healing, you'll often leave precipitously. "It's not you," you say, "this is the best thing that's ever happened to me, but I'm outta here." Well, of course, it's you. Not because you're the wrong person. It's because you're probably the right person to lead the Monkey through its "stuff" and maybe it's "better the devil you know than the devil you don't know." As a Monkey, you just have a devil of a time letting the universe give to you. What if you let go? What would you do if you weren't holding your world together day after day? Let go and receive? Hard for the Monkey to do.

The Monkey holds on so tightly that, sometimes, events happen suddenly that take things completely out of his/her control. The more you can let go, the less tendency the universe has to pull the rug out from under you periodically to force you to let go and experience what it's like to have to trust the universe.

The Monkey person has issues with control because its corresponding organ is the bladder, and the bladder deals with control vs. faith. It may be overt, or it may be covert, but control is a mitigating factor in your life. Because of being controlled as a child, you make a decision somewhere along the way to take control in your adult life in order to make sure you aren't buffeted around by fate anymore. Stiff, rigid, and erect, you won't even allow your visualizations to take their own course; everything is fine, just fine, thank you.

Denial is another aspect of the bladder, also self-denial and denying yourself something on a conscious level so you won't be denied something psychologically deeper: i.e., wanting to lose weight consciously, but subconsciously you need it for protection.

The Monkey can be hard to muscle test and will be able to block or supersede the truth of your being, simply because you are so used to overriding life when it doesn't suit. You hate change, and try to maintain your life the way you've constructed it. The bladder is said to be the seat of the emotions, and thus, many emotional disorders can be reached through this meridian.

A favorite expression about the Monkey is, a "monkey on our back." Certainly when we have the need to control everything around us, it is the monkey on our backs that needs to come off. A positive expression is to visualize the monkey as a free spirit up high in a tree, seeing far and wide, providing vision for the path ahead.

Another expression is "throwing in a monkey wrench." In order to stay in control, the Monkey person often employs a "monkey wrench"—something to cause a problem—to control the situation, in order to keep the other person off balance.

Antidote: A Monkey needs to let go, to surrender to the universe and trust it to give you everything you want, to recognize when you get into denial and decide not to express that anymore. You need to realize that it wasn't God who mistreated you as a child, but other mere mortals who were trying to control their world. You need to be tough enough to allow someone or something (therapy) to crack open that cosmic egg and face what's inside in order to get that monkey off your back; to know that only you can deprive yourself of anything.

 Music that is a balm for the Monkey/Bladder is Scheherazade by Rimsky-Korsakov. Also, Sonata in E Major for Lute and Basso by Bach.

Rate Yourself and Others in Your Life

On a scale of 0–100, where 0 is most negative, 50 is neutral, and 100 is most positive, where do you think you fall with these traits? We usually fluctuate between 40 and 60, but when we've experienced trauma in our lives, we sometimes dip into the lower end of the spectrum.

0	50	100

Rooster

Time of Day: 5 P.M. to 7 P.M.

Element: Water

Color: Blue/Black

Energy: Yin

Meridian: Kidney. The Kidney meridian starts in the ball of the foot and moves all the way up the inside of the leg, up the torso, and ends in the chest. This meridian regulates procreative areas of the body and is responsible for short-term memory.

Organ: Kidney. The kidneys are the blood filtration system. They are a pair of organs in the dorsal region of the vertebrate abdominal cavity. They function to maintain proper water and electrolyte balance. The kidneys regulate acid/base concentration, and filter the blood of metabolic wastes, which are then excreted as urine.

Motivation: Fear vs. Peace. Sexual security or insecurity. Fear creates procrastination, hypervigilance.

Those Who Share the Year of the Rooster: Simone Signoret, Elizabeth Montgomery, Jayne Mansfield, Carol Burnett, Jane Russell, Dianne Feinstein, Goldie Hawn, Caroline Kennedy, Bette Midler, Mia Farrow, Kim Novak, Hugh Downs, Henry Winkler, F. Lee Bailey, Brian Keith.

Those Who Share the Month of the Rooster . . . are generally **Capricorns.**

Those Who Share the Hour of the Rooster: Debbie Reynolds, Denise Pence, Katherine Hepburn, Raquel Welch, Julie Kavner, Mary Frances Crosby, Linda Ronstadt, Mary Baker Eddy, Lisa Marie Presley, Patty Hearst, Frederic Chopin, Warren Beatty, Sean Connery, Robert Duvall, Bob Hope, Adolf Hitler, Suzanne Somers.

"I gotta crow" seems to be both the hue and cry and the thing to shrink from. There are singers who like to belt a song, there are actors who like to be in front of the crowd; and yet there are the reclusive ones who prefer the quiet side of life. Roosters are hypervigilant and some Roosters can be politicians and "whistle blowers," bringing injustices to our attention. Some are sex symbols and some have sexual issues.

Muscles: Psoas, Upper Trapezius, Iliacus. The psoas aids the lumbar curve of the spine. It is part of the hip-flexing muscle group.

The upper trapezius are muscles that go up the sides of the neck. They tilt the chin, and pull in the shoulder blade. Tension in the trapezius is often the result of fear.

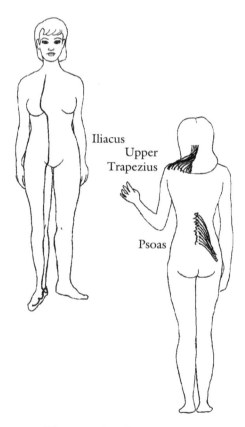

Figure 12. The Rooster:
The Kidney Meridian.

The iliacus is in the front of the body, extending down toward the leg.

If you are born between 5 P.M. and 7 P.M., you can take your emotions and feelings into these muscles and have more problem with them than most. When your upper traps in the neck are tight on the sides of your neck, you are probably in an environment that is fearful, or you actually feel "trapped" in some way.

Emotions: Fear vs. Peace. Stuck, trapped, sexual insecurity vs. sexual security. Willpower, courage, ability to take action, hyper-vigilance, paranoia.

Born in the Year, Month, Hour, Minute of the Rooster

Positive: Raised in an atmosphere of peace, you ignore the hubbub going on around you and stay centered. You are secure in your sexuality and hold it as a positive experience. You are fertile and experience the joy of procreation. You are heard by others, and are open to hear the opinions of others. You wake up each morning full of energy and call to others to follow your lead.

Negative: As a Kidney person, you are motivated by fear (being called "chicken" is not out of context here). You are hypervigilant; you read the newspaper, watch the news. You are up on the latest news, so that if there is a strangler in the area, you can get out of town. Tell you California is going to fall into the sea and you believe it and make plans to move to another state. If someone wants to motivate you, fear is their most potent weapon. It takes the realization of this and the desire to move into a place of peace, of well-being, to rise above the constant fear propaganda that is spoon-fed to us every day on TV and the media. Fear is always in the background somewhere.

A Kidney person needs to eat nutritiously and keep the chi, the life-force energy, up. You tend to be tired and procrastinate. You fear confrontation and will try to appease people. Those who are living other people's lives will tend toward chronic fatigue and Epstein-Barr. It's just too much effort to fight, so you give in and it's easier to sleep than to think about getting out of the situation. It takes a lot to take action, stand up for one's self, and do something.

Sex is also an issue. You can be sexually insecure and not want to be the one who asserts themselves in a relationship. You tend to be more passive and let people come to you. Then, backed into a wall, you can be forced to deal with your sexuality.

Beethoven had sexual problems in his life, he also had a kidney stone and was deaf—all kidney issues. His music will either be a balm or an irritant to an imbalanced Rooster person.

Antidote: Examine what makes you fearful, ascertain how much validity there is to it, and discard the rest. Confront your "worst-case scenario" and take the charge out of it. Bring yourself into a state of peace, where you can take action to effect positive change in your life. Be aware that you are being motivated by fear all the time—by the media, by insurance companies, by the government. You are being bombarded with fear-generating propaganda all the time, and you take it on more than anyone else. Moving into a state of peace will allow you to draw into your life only those people who will support this peace—and maybe you'll just turn off the TV and the radio.

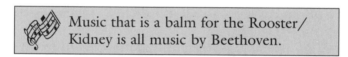

Music that is a balm for the Rooster/
Kidney is all music by Beethoven.

Rate Yourself and Others in Your Life

On a scale of 0–100, where 0 is most negative, 50 is neutral, and 100 is most positive, where do you think you fall with these traits? We usually fluctuate between 40 and 60, but when we've experienced trauma in our lives, we sometimes dip into the lower end of the spectrum.

0	50	100

Fire Element
Dog and Boar

CAROLINE PATRICK

Dog

Years: 1910 · 1922 · 1934 · 1946 · 1958 · 1970 · 1982 · 1994

Time of Day: 7 P.M. to 9 P.M.

Element: Fire

Color: Red

Energy: Yin

Meridian: Circulation-Sex (Pericardium). The Circ-Sex meridian starts at the nipple, comes up and enters the arm at the armpit, and travels down the inside of the arm through the elbow crease into the palm, ending at the middle finger.

Organ: The pericardium is the membranous sac filled with serous fluid that encloses the heart and the roots of the aorta and other of the large blood vessels.

Motivation: Inhibition vs. Connectedness. The ability to connect with another, whether it be in a sexual, one-to-one relationship, or a hall full of people when giving a speech.

Those Who Share the Year of the Dog: Gloria Steinem, Doris Day, Shirley MacLaine, Cher, Judy Garland, Susan St. James, Sophia Loren, Suzanne Somers, Sally Field, Helen Gurley Brown, Sandy Duncan, Liza Minelli, Richard Chamberlain, Pat Boone, Candice Bergen, President Bill Clinton.

Those Who Share the Month of the Dog . . . are generally **Aquarians.**

Those Who Share the Hour of the Dog: Princess Margaret, Jane Fonda, Betty White, Elizabeth Taylor, Geraldine Ferraro, George Deukmejian, Richard Burton, Princess Diana, Franklin D. Roosevelt, Mozart, Tony Conigliaro, Robert Redford, Rick Springfield, Dorothy Hamill, Charles Chaplin, Zsa Zsa Gabor, Morgan Fairchild, Hillary Rodham Clinton.

There is a sense of refinement, of being apart from the crowd. These people draw back and do not readily jump in and get their feet muddy . . . nor their nails. There is an element of intimacy that is never really bridged. Pressed by more forceful individuals, these people get quiet and pull back, feeling uncomfortable when people get too intimate and move into their space too fast. These are people, like Betty White, who love animals, particularly dogs.

Muscles: Gluteus Medius, Adductors, Piriformis, Gluteus Maximus. The gluteus medius pulls the thigh out and rotates the leg. The adductors bring the thigh in, flexing it and rotating it inward. The piriformis is a hip muscle that is important in a person's posture. It rotates the hip. The gluteus maximus is actually the "derrière." It stabilizes the lower back, it extends the thigh and aids in pulling the leg in.

These muscles relate to the psychology surrounding sexual issues and inhibition. Women tend to take their excess weight to their derrière and stomach to regain lost power.

Emotions: Uninhibited vs. Inhibited. Fear of sexual intimacy vs. connecting love with sex; stingy vs. generous; spontaneous and authentic vs. rehearsed and held back.

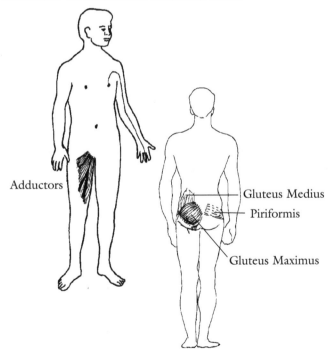

Figure 13. The Dog:
The Circulation-Sex Meridian.

Born in the Year, Month, Hour, Minute of the Dog

Positive: You are a satisfied individual, safe in your sexuality. You are generous and giving—of yourself, your time, and your talents. You are open and devoted like a puppy dog. You reach out to people and feel the connectedness of the universe. You are comfortable speaking before a crowd, or tapping into the depths of a one-to-one relationship. You are open, spontaneous, loyal and authentic, not afraid to be who you are.

Negative: Born in the evening, or the year or month of the Dog, you are often reserved. You tend to be inhibited in your sexuality, perhaps because of early experiences. You don't have a lot of partners. On the other side of the coin, some people born at this time can overcompensate in sexual encounters. Because of this inherent "block," you feel you must liberate.

There are elements of stinginess vs. generosity. It's hard for you to share unless you are very well-balanced. You can sense sexual tension more acutely than most. Regret and remorse over the past tend to "dog" your efforts to make progress. It is very difficult for you to let go of a relationship once it has proven to be over. Television and movies are full of sexual tension, particularly in their advertising, and the Circ-Sex meridian can be unbalanced a good deal of the time as it reacts to this stimuli.

When the Dog is imbalanced, you can become overtly self-righteous and be morally outraged over the sexual media, which others don't see as being nearly as salacious as you do. What is erotic to others can seem pornographic to you.

The Dog has a clear definition of what is sex and what is a relationship. There is a clear distinction between the two. The Dog needs to alchemize the two and come to a union in order to see the two as one.

Antidote: Within this meridian is the ability to connect love with sex. To be sexually intimate is the quest here. To love and be loved openly and honestly. To link love with the sexual act and bring it to a higher level. To feel satisfied and secure in a relationship. To be able to bring others into your "space" and feel comfortable. To open up to your sexuality and allow the beauty of it to permeate your being. To stand in the fire and allow the alchemy to take place. To be fully authentic and spontaneous in your interactions with others.

The music of Johannes Sebastian Bach is a balm for the Circ-Sex/Pericardium meridian.

Rate Yourself and Others in Your Life

On a scale of 0–100, where 0 is most negative, 50 is neutral, and 100 is most positive, where do you think you fall with these traits? We usually fluctuate between 40 and 60, but when we've experienced trauma in our lives, we sometimes dip into the lower end of the spectrum.

0	50	100

Boar

Years: 1911 · 1923 · 1935 · 1947 · 1959 · 1971 · 1983 · 1995

Time of Day: 9 P.M. to 11 P.M.

Element: Fire

Color: Red

Energy: Yang

Meridian: Triple Warmer. The Triple Warmer meridian starts on the fourth (ring) finger, zigs over to the opposite side of the wrist, and then goes up the arm and behind the elbow, continuing up over the shoulder, around the ear, stopping just above the outside of the eye.

Organ: The triple warmer is not an organ. The terminology is for the three "burning areas" of the body—the lungs and the ability to breathe and take in oxygen; the assimilation function of processing foods; and the elimination process to remove that which is no longer necessary.

Motivation: Hope vs. Hopeless. To fear ridicule and humiliation and to try to do anything to prevent it. To be self-constructive or self-destructive. To be foolhardy and risk-prone because of losing the meaning for life and wanting to opt out . . . or, not having the energy to do anything because of the futility. Needing to dwell in hope instead of hopelessness.

Muscles: Teres Minor, Sartorius, Gracilis, Soleus, Gastrocnemius. The teres minor is a shoulder muscle that rotates the arm and the forearm.

The sartorius is a thigh muscle that flexes the leg and thigh and turns it sideways. It is the longest muscle in the body.

The gracilis is another thigh muscle. If you are lying facedown, it is the first muscle that bends the knees. The soleus is a calf muscle that flexes the foot and the lower part of the leg. It steadies the foot.

The gastrocs are calf muscles that work in tandem with the soleus to flex the foot and the lower part of the leg.

If you are born between 9 P.M. and 11 P.M., you take your emotions into these muscles. If any person is having problems in this area, look to where you are feeling depressed, where life seems futile.

Those Who Share the Year of the Boar: Magic Johnson, Diahann Carroll, Eileen Brennan, Albert Brooks, Henry Kissinger, Richard Karn, Jack Kemp, Robert Dole, Jane Curtin, Hume Cronyn, Arsenio Hall, Hillary Clinton, Geraldine Ferraro, Estelle Getty, John Ritter, Pete Sampras, Sondra Locke, Kevin Spacey.

Those Who Share the Month of the Boar . . . are generally **Pisces.**

Those Who Share the Hour of the Boar: Joan Crawford, Gloria Steinem, Bette Davis, Clare Booth Luce, Shirley Temple, Greta Garbo, Shari Lewis, Gloria Allred (attorney), Elisabeth

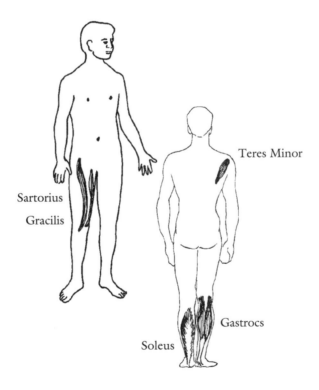

Figure 14. The Boar:
The Triple Warmer Meridian.

Kübler-Ross, Prince Charles, Prince Philip, Christa McAuliffe, John McEnroe, Richard Nixon, Willie Mays, Candice Bergen, Howard Hughes.

Some in this group exhibit the classic qualities of the Boar. John McEnroe with his "over the edge" behavior exhibits the self-destructiveness of youths who taunt authority, while Gloria Allred is more balanced in her defense of people against the system. Elisabeth Kübler-Ross has written on death and dying, and the Boar can have a deep understanding of death that few others perceive.

Emotions: Hope vs. Hopeless. Ugly vs. Beautiful. Optimism vs. pessimism, humiliation vs. respect; depression, self-destruction vs. self-construction. In its extreme, suicidal.

Born in the Year, Month, Hour, Minute of the Boar
Positive: You are full of hope and see the glass always half full, never half empty. There is a sense of elegance and grace about your demeanor. You move easily and people admire you for your grace and beauty. You are optimistic and expect the good things in life to happen for you, so they usually do. You are cautious, yet willing to take risks when they are appropriate.

Negative: The seeds of self-destruction are inherent in the Triple Warmer meridian. At the core are the emotions of hope vs. hopelessness. When you feel hopeless, there is a need to "get off the planet, and one can engage in a variety of self-destructive behaviors in order to achieve that dubious goal. You can be depressed and feel the weight of the world is on your shoulders. In the other extreme, you can be foolhardy and take risks, tempting fate, not really caring if you survive or not to various levels, according to the balance between positive and negative. When we talk about people being survivors or not, the emotions of the Triple Warmer come up, because the power animal is the Boar, who feels big, awkward, and ugly and who, in the wild, has an irrational bent for suicide.

The Triple Warmer meridian also deals with humiliation and ridicule, and is the prime meridian for depression. When we are angry at the way we've been treated and yet have to hold it in, we become depressed.

A narcissistic quality belongs to the Boar. Boars can be self-centered and feel that the world revolves around them alone, that their needs and desires are the only ones that count.

Antidote: In order to neutralize this energy, you need to see yourself as light and buoyant and full of light. Know there is always a light at the end of the tunnel; know that, with the new day, comes hope and the prospect for life to change. Know that the answer is inherent in the problem and keep working toward it until you get the change you want. Parents who instill hope in their little boars will neutralize this tendency.

 Music that is a balm for the Boar/Triple Warmer is Pines of Rome by Respighi. Also, Mahler's Symphony No. 2, Resurrection, and Wagner's The Ring.

Rate Yourself and Others in Your Life

On a scale of 0–100, where 0 is most negative, 50 is neutral, and 100 is most positive, where do you think you fall with these traits? We usually fluctuate between 40 and 60, but when we've experienced trauma in our lives, we sometimes dip into the lower end of the spectrum.

| 0 | 50 | 100 |

Part III
Relationships with Power Animals

Primal Relationships

In astrology, the time you were born is a key component of your personality. It is the rising sign, your mask to the world.

It is how we protect the vulnerability of our Sun sign. It defines us as individuals over the other thousands of people who are born on the same day.

In *Chinese Power Animals,* we've just demonstrated that the animal on the ascendant (the rising sign), at its strongest during that time frame, becomes the animal we will most often look to as the animal that embodies the individual over the animal that signifies the year we are born or the animal of the sign we were born within.

In my practice, I use the astrology wheel to work with the power animals. From it, I know which animal represents mom, dad, spouse, kids, aunts, uncles, in-laws, etc. But to incorporate that into this book would take us off course (it will be covered in a future book based on this work). To get around that, I have devised figure 15 on page 142. Generally speaking, the animals that represent parents and spouses will be these animals.

In each circle, there is the name of the meridian and its time of day in the center. To the left is the power animal for that time period; i.e., the animal for Gallbladder is Rat. At the bottom of that circle is a Cat. On the right, opposite the Rat, is a Horse, and on top is a Rooster. In this chapter, you will want to use the animal at the time of your birth, and the behavioral characteristics of the animals that fall in order around the wheel for those of mom, dad, and mate. While you can pick up some basic information from the animal's relationships to your year and month, that is more general, while the animal of your rising time is most specific to you and your relationships.

In this wheel, the animal on the left represents you—or, more specifically, the person born during that time frame, in this example, the Rat. The Cat on the bottom represents mother and the

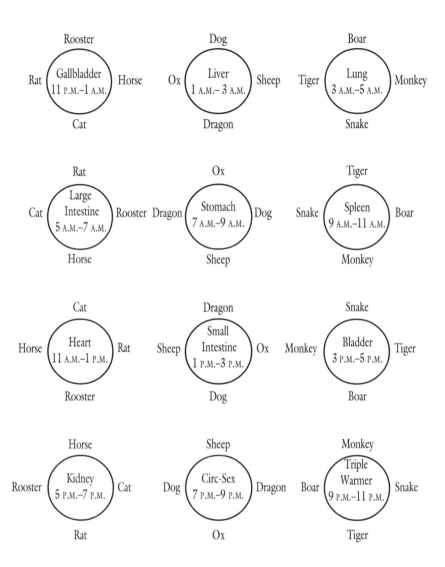

Figure 15. Relationships of the Power Animals.

Rooster on top represents father. The Horse directly across is spouse and, more specifically, first spouse.

Each animal depicts key people in your life, and represents your interaction with them. This may or may not mean they are born in the year or time or sign the animal symbolizes (quite frequently they are, but we're looking at energy interaction here, not a sign-to-sign correspondence). This is why children can have varied reactions to parents and vice versa, because the animal of their rising sign will create a different pattern with their parents than with their siblings.

This is how people mirror back to you the issues you are resolving in this lifetime. The father of a friend was born in 1915, the Year of the Cat, at 10:58 P.M., the Hour of the Boar. In her own chart, with Rooster in residence at the hour of birth, the Sheep symbolizes father for Her. She experiences the Sheep qualities in dealing with her father, because that is what her dad mirrors to her; she's felt victimized and had to take the blame for things her father did. Her mother, on the other hand, born in the Hour of the Dragon, has the Dog symbolizing her mate, and she experienced those qualities in their marriage. He was inhibited and remote, and disdained sex.

For people born in the United States (and the depth of the band around Earth that the United States spans, just above the equator), this will stand up pretty well. If you get too far north or get below the equator, then other factors are involved. But, as a general rule, this will work for you. If you are born north or south of this band, then look to the sign above or below yours to see where you fit in to this scheme.

The other consideration would be when you have a birth time that is in the second hour of the two-hour span, approaching the next sign/meridian. If you want to get clear on issues with Mom, and you were born around 4:00 A.M., say, in Tiger time, but approaching Cat time, ask yourself, "What type of energy represents Mom—Snake or a Horse?" (because Snake is the power animal for Mom for the Tiger, and Horse is the power animal for Mom for the Cat). You know; your instincts will tell you specifically. This would also pertain if you live considerably above the equator.

In the following examples, we are going to be talking about the contention and/or stress. Obviously, if all is going well in your closest relationships, you aren't going to be drawn to a self-help book to try and figure them out. That taken into consideration, how can you use these animals for transformation?

Mom

Mom is represented by the power animal at the base of your relationship circle. This is your foundation, your Rock of Gibraltar. It is where you get your bedrock philosophy, from which you motivate.

It is a mother's responsibility, by word or deed, as you are growing up, to instill in you the positive emotions of the animal/meridian. To the degree that she does, you will have a solid foundation from which to define yourself as an individual. To the degree she doesn't (and again, because this is a plane of learning, most don't to varying degrees), you will have these issues to sort out. It is also a key issue with her.

This placement shows the primary emotions and meridian/organ your mother deals with in her life, and she may have illness in this area. It also shows where you can keep the emotions of dealing with your mother-child relationship, and exhibit similar illness. Again, if you are born on or after the even hour (2-4-6-8-10), look to the next power animal and synthesize the two readings.

Mother's energy shows a daughter what to expect as a woman and mother, and shows a son what to expect from his wife and other women. She is his role model for the feminine energy.

The Rat

The Rat has a Cat for a mother. By word or deed, it was her responsibility to create a home where his self-esteem and self-worth were developed; a place where he felt valuable and had a reason for being on this Earth. But the Cat may have played "cat and mouse" with the child, never really feeling confident. If the Cat continually criticized the Rat, then he grew up not feeling good about himself. The Cat mother had self-esteem issues, and passed them down to the Rat. The roots of the Rat's feelings of abandonment lie in his feelings of self-esteem.

Because Mother is a Cat, she deals with colitis, and other large intestine problems. She may have sacrificed for her family and can feel as if she is a martyr. Some Cat mothers have neuroses. When the Rat has to deal with Mom, he can feel his self-esteem being attacked, and his hamstrings could give out.

The Ox

The Ox has a Dragon for a mother. This is a formidable combination. By word or deed, it was Mom's responsibility to create a home life that was full of fun, fancy, and mirth, where the Ox felt content and had his tummy filled. But, to whatever degree Mom felt hungry, that her needs were never met, she conveyed this to her child. So, the Ox is always plowing ahead, trying to take care of everyday needs, rather than reaching for the stars . . . because his stomach hunger is more important than his dreams. The roots of the Ox's feelings of resentment lie in his inability to be independent and free, not tied to duty and responsibility.

Because Mother is a Dragon, she can have stomach problems. She could have obsessions, compulsions, or addictions, always hungering after something. When the Ox deals with the Dragon, "she" feels frustrated and angry, and her pectoralis major clavicular can act up.

The Tiger

Mom is a Snake. By word or deed during childhood, her role was to provide a safe haven, where the Tiger felt significant. Mom needed to provide a base where the Tiger could learn to handle relationships and develop a solid ego that could never be assailed by the moods of other people. Mom is a transformative agent, and at her best can make the Tiger feel the full might of her ego and accomplish much in her lifetime.

But because Mom's a Snake, she's elusive, easily slighted, and must always be right. It's hard for the Tiger to develop her ego when she can have no opinions that differ from Mom's, fearing that she will cause rejection. The Tiger's depression can ensue from trying always to be perfect to make Mom happy. In the extreme, perhaps bonding never took place between mother and child. The roots of the Tiger's depression lie in this need to match this perfect template.

Because Mom is the Snake, she has issues with sugar, and possibly has diabetes or hypoglycemia or other spleen problems. She needed self-acceptance. If the Tiger is having issues with her, she can head for the sugar or maybe her "lat" muscles start giving her problems.

The Cat

Mom is the Horse; full of instinctive, dynamic energy. By word or deed throughout childhood, it was her responsibility to develop the Cat's self-worth by making him feel loved, that he belonged. Mom needed to be the touchy, huggy type of Mom that always drew the Cat close.

But the Cat being a cat, picked up on any energy that sparked of self-absorption and often took off, being the independent type it is. The Cat obviously had to tread lightly and be sure of where he was in relation to the Horse. Not that the Horse was particularly negative, just so-ooo much bigger. The Cat could have gotten trampled by default; Mom just may not have seen him underfoot in time. Mom could have been a giver, or could have sealed herself off from emotion if her love wasn't reciprocated, causing the Cat self-esteem issues. The roots of the Cat's self-worth lie in whether Mom's heart was open or closed.

Because Mom is a Horse, she "leads with her heart" and can have heart issues during her lifetime. The heart meridian also includes the brain, and there is susceptibility to strokes if planets stress this area. When the Cat deals with Mother, he can feel "hard-hearted" at times, or the subscapularis muscle can cause fits.

The Dragon

The Dragon has a Sheep for a mother. By word or deed as he was growing up, she was responsible for developing in him a sense of priorities, and knowing how to discriminate . . . not the bad, bigotted type of discrimination, but to sort the wheat from the chaff and know what is good for him and what is not. She needed to develop a sense of responsibility in the Dragon that was neither over nor under, but which clearly defined his role in any endeavor.

The Sheep has issues with victim/victor, and Mom needed to set the foundation for the Dragon that he is a victor, and allow him to "win" whenever possible in their interactions. But, being a Sheep, she may have felt victimized by life and left the impression with the Dragon that life victimizes. The roots of the Dragon's issues with hunger lie in his feelings of victimization.

Because Mom is a Sheep, she can have illnesses related to the small intestine. When the Dragon deals with her, he can get a pain in his gut or his quads (those big muscles on the upper thighs) can cause problems.

The Snake

The Snake has a Monkey for a mother, who can take on a variety of shapes as a primate: a lightweight monkey up in the trees, chattering about, or an ape or gorilla or other large monkey, controlling the home and the family. By word or deed, Mom needed to establish roots for the Snake that created a feeling of trust . . . observing the universe and allowing it to play out in its way, not Mom's way. But, Mom probably brooked no interference. She could have been in denial and wanted no one to scratch the surface and reveal any truths about her existence that did not match what she had established. The Snake may have had to slither around to keep out of her way. Certainly, she has realized that confronting Mom head-on did not work, so she tended to go around her to Dad (the Tiger). The roots of the Snake's rejection complex, as well as the source of the "secrets" of childhood, lie in Mother's need to control to whatever degree.

Because Mom is a Monkey, she has issues with control that could lead to bladder control problems later in life. When the Snake deals with Mom, she constantly has to try and get beyond the denial and control. She can feel she needs to establish her own boundaries, or her peroneous muscles in the back of the legs could give her problems when she's frustrated.

The Horse

The Horse has a Rooster for a mother. By word or deed, it was her responsibility to create a base where the Horse felt at peace and had nothing to fear. But the Rooster is up at daybreak, heralding the dawn and looking around for whatever might cause fear, creating an unstable place for the Horse to grow up. The Rooster Mom may actually peck (criticize) the Horse. The Horse has fear as her foundation and must battle it all the time. Sexuality is an issue, too. Mom has problems with her sexuality and can cause the Horse to back off from relationships because of her experiences. The roots of the Horse's need to belong lie in the "henpecking" of her upbringing.

Because Mom is the Rooster, she battles fear, fatigue, and perhaps fertility problems . . . so the Horse may be adopted. The kidneys are the affected organ, and Mom can have issues with kidneys or hearing. When the Horse deals with Mom, she can have her own fears come up around her, and the "upper traps" alongside the neck can get tight.

The Sheep

The Sheep has a Dog for a mom. It was her role, by word or deed to convey to the Sheep that sex is natural and normal, and to see the beauty in it. But, Mom, as a dog, was always scurrying around, "herding" the Sheep, keeping it from getting into trouble. Mom was probably reserved and withdrawn and may have been sexually inhibited, conveying that message to her child that that's the way women should comport themselves. She may have even gone to the extreme and been uptight and morally indignant at what she saw on the movies or TV. The Sheep's feeling of victimization has its roots in Mom's inhibiting behavior.

Because Mom is a dog, she has issues with circulation, which can be the bloodstream, or also "circulating" with others on a social basis. And, of course, sex. She can look upon it as a duty and not get the full joy from it. When the Sheep has to deal with Mom, he can feel inhibited about addressing the situation, and can develop problems in the glutes or the adductors.

The Monkey

The Monkey has a Boar for a mother, who, if not self-constructive, was quite possibly self-destructive, indulging in drugs, alcohol, or other addictions. It was Mom's responsibility, by word or deed, to provide a home life where there was joy and hope, where the Monkey was optimistic and looked forward to the future. The seeds of his control are rooted in the degree to which futility was the cornerstone of his youth. If Mom ridiculed him in any way, the Monkey sought to control his reality so that he would never have to experience that again. The roots of the Monkey's control issues lie in the pessimism and depression of his youth.

Because Mom is a Boar, she has issues with depression and seeing the dour side of life. She can get bogged down and always be rooting around, staring at the ground rather than looking up to the stars. When the Monkey deals with Mom, he can get depressed at the prospect, or his gastrocs (in the calves) can cause problems.

The Rooster

The Rooster has a Rat for a mother. By word or deed, it was her responsibility to establish a childhood for the Rooster that showered the Rooster with unconditional love, and always provided choices so that the Rooster could develop its sense of self and not fear what was all around. But, to the degree Mom didn't do this, the Rooster feels some level of abandonment and/or betrayal by the Rat, maybe something tangible, or Mom simply "wasn't there" for "her," when she thought she should be. The roots of the Rooster's fear lie in the fear of abandonment.

Because Mom is a Rat, she has problems with the gallbladder, and can develop gallstones, or have problems digesting fats. When the Rooster deals with Mom, "she" can have digestion problems and head for the fatty foods, or the anterior deltoid or popliteus can act up. The Rooster is never passive about Mom. "She" either adores her or can't stand her; it's hardly ever neutral.

The Dog

The Dog has an Ox for a Mother. By word or deed, it was her responsibility to encourage the Dog to reach for the stars, to provide all that she needed to grow to her full potential, and release all her creative juices. But, the Ox can repress the Dog, and the Dog can't understand it. All it wants is love and affection and to be taken care of, and Mother Ox can stifle the Dog at every turn because of her own limited view. She may be overprotective and keep the Dog from experiencing love/life. The roots of the Dog's inhibition lie in the repression of the mother, not being able to experience life until later.

Because Mom is an Ox, she's conceivably had a yoke around her neck all her life and can only see what's in front of her. Mom is angry, certainly in subterranean depths, but perhaps on the surface as well, and she has liver ailments that can cause problems with the eyes. When the Dog deals with Mom, she can feel repressed at the thought, or her pectoralis major sternal muscles in her chest or the rhomboids in her back may act up.

The Boar

The Boar has a Tiger for a mother. The Tiger, by word or deed, was handed the responsibility to teach the Boar to feel alive and full of life and enthusiasm. The Tiger needed to encourage the Boar to develop a healthy ego and be proud of his accomplishments. But Mother Tiger could have been depressed, which only fed the Boar's depressive state. The Tiger may have grieved over past wrongs and never encouraged the Boar to be light and buoyant. The roots of the Boar's pessimism lie in how "alive" his mother felt. As one Boar person put it, "She just wanted me to breathe, and I wanted to feel alive."

Because the mother is a Tiger, she can have lung problems, or be saddled with grief. When the Boar has to deal with her, he can develop a cold or bronchitis, or his body can ache from the intercostal muscles that hold the ribs.

Dad

Dad is represented by the power animal at the top of your relationship circle. This is the pinnacle you reach toward in your life. Dad represents masculinity, power and authority, and your career. How successful your father was in his career can dictate how successful (or not) you will be in yours.

Dad is the perfect metaphor for your ambition. Look at what he did well and emulate that. Look at what he didn't do well, and do the opposite.

It's Dad's responsibility, by word or deed, to instill in you the drive to excel, to reach the maximum of your life's potential. His is conditional love, setting standards for you to achieve your place and feel you truly deserve it. As a role model, he needed to balance Mother's unconditional love by creating a positive mindset for you to attain your goals. To the degree that he didn't fulfill this mission, you will have these issues to overcome. They are also his issues.

The power animal at the top of your wheel shows the primary emotions and meridian/organ your father deals with in his life, and the illnesses to which he is prone. It also shows where you can keep the emotions of dealing with your father-child relationship, and exhibit similar illness in your interaction. Once again, if you were born on or after the even hour (2-4-6-8-10), look to the next animal and synthesize the two readings.

Father's energy shows a son how to be a man and compete in a man's world, and shows a daughter how to function "in a man's world" and how she should be treated by the males in her life. If you treated your father as if he were a god as a child, it can also reflect on how you expect your god-universe-power to treat you.

The Rat

The Rat has a Rooster for a father. He can be a military type, up at dawn's light, expecting everyone to be up and at 'em, too. He can pick, pick, pick until the Rat runs away. By word or deed, it was Dad's responsibility to instill in the Rat a sense of peace . . . with himself, with his sexuality, and with his god. "Instilling the fear of God in a child" probably came from a Rooster father. Instead, the Rooster needed to model for his child a sense that sex is a rich part of life and not denigrate it in any way. If the father were filled with fear, he could pass it along to his children. He may be a workaholic, or alcoholic, in order to run from his inner passions. The inability of the Rat to attain his goals lies in his fear.

Because Dad is a Rooster, he can have kidney problems, or fertility issues. He can be hard of hearing or have problems with bones and teeth. When the Rat has to deal with his Rooster father, he can be filled with fear and have problems with the psoas or upper trap muscles.

The Ox

The Ox has a Dog for a father. By word or deed, it was Dad's assignment to show his children, through his comportment with his wife, the connection between love and sex—that one is not truly fulfilled without the other. It was his role to go out and seize life and interact with others in order that the Ox could feel her independence and be able to create to her full potential. Dad, may, however, been sexually inhibited and withdrawn. He may have been a Bible-thumper who railed against anything that suggested sexuality, making the Ox feel that her libido was wrong. The Ox can have a lot of anger at the repression instilled by a father. The inability of the Ox to see beyond the row she tills is because of his inhibition.

Because Dad is a Dog, he can have problems with intimacy, and may have prostate problems as he gets older. When the Ox has to deal with her father, she can feel inhibited and withdrawn, and can feel it in her glutes (derrière) or adductors (inner thighs).

The Tiger

The Tiger has a Boar for a father. By word or deed, it was the Boar's responsibility to give the Tiger hope and faith in the future. He was to instill optimism and create a being who is self-constructive. The Boar, however, has levels of despair and self-destruction. He can get literally bogged down, and not be able to tap into the light and buoyancy that is part of him. The inability of the Tiger to feel enthusiastic and alive can stem from the Boar's depression.

Because Dad is a Boar, he can have thyroid problems, or deal with his own depression and destructive tendencies. When the Tiger has to deal with her father, she can feel hopeless that she can penetrate and make a difference, and she can have her hamstrings act up.

The Cat

The Cat has a Rat for a father. By word or deed, the Rat needed to instill in his child a sense of unconditional love—a man can be conditional with an unconditional base. The Rat needed to love his child and show his adoration, so that the Cat felt he was worthy of accomplishing and receiving all the good things of life. The Rat may have abandoned the Cat instead, or the Cat may feel the Rat betrayed him. No matter how the relationship goes, the Cat will always be subjective about the Rat. The adoration will be the highest, or the rage the most intense. The Cat will never be objective about his father. The inability of the Cat to sense his own worth lies in his quest for unconditional love.

Because Dad is a Rat, he can have a terrible temper and explode for no conceivable reason. He can have migraines, or gallstones, or sciatica. When the Cat has to deal with Dad, he gets very subjective and the anterior deltoids (on the upper arms) could act up, or he may get a migraine.

The Dragon

The Dragon has an Ox for a father. The Dragon has the potential for mirth and fun and fancy, and the father Ox has the option of encouraging it or squelching it. By word or deed, it is Dad's responsibility to encourage his son (or daughter) to be autonomous and independent, to allow them to be creative and to reach their goals unfettered. The Ox has that potential in himself. But if he was held back, if he was squelched or smothered himself, Father Ox may do the same to his offspring. The Dragon's hunger can lie in his inability to create.

Because Dad is an Ox, he can have liver problems and issues with his eyes. When the Dragon has to deal with the Ox, he can get "liverish" or feel "stabbed in the back" (where the rhomboid muscles are that relate to the Liver meridian).

The Snake

The Snake has a Tiger for a father. It was his responsibility as the little Snake was growing up, to instill in her by word or deed that she should be proud of who she is and acknowledge her accomplishments and skills—to be proud of her, as she should be proud of herself. But, it really isn't in our culture to allow our children to do that, and, to whatever degree the Tiger neglected or ignored her, her feelings of rejection are based in the Tiger's teachings.

Because Dad is a Tiger, he may smoke and have lung problems. To whatever degree he didn't live out his purpose, he can feel dead inside, and does not want to feel because the pain is too deep. The Tiger has a lot of grief to process over the past, and may be depressed or feel the weight of the world on his shoulders. When the Snake deals with the Tiger, she can feel that she is not acknowledged, so "why bother?" She can feel it physically in the latissimus dorsi muscles on the sides of the torso.

The Horse

The Horse has a Cat for a father. The Cat's responsibility, by word or deed, in the Horse's upbringing is to instill in the Horse a sense of self-worth and self-esteem . . . to define the Horse as an individual and show her how valuable she is in this world. To the degree he didn't, she has self-doubt over succeeding in her career, and may even sabotage herself because of it. The inability of the Horse to succeed in her life's work or be successful in her interaction with men (male or female people born in the Year of the Horse) lies in her father's acknowledgment of her skills and abilities.

Because Dad is a Cat, he can have physical issues with colitis and the large intestine, and with his own self-worth. If he doesn't value himself, it would be hard to allow a child to be better than he is. When the Horse has to deal with Dad, all the feelings of unworthiness can come up, and she can have problems with her hamstring muscles or with colitis.

The Sheep

The Sheep has a Dragon for a father. The Dragon father is undoubtedly larger than life, and may be intimidating to the Sheep. It is Father's responsibility, by word or deed, to teach the Sheep how to fulfill his own internal needs, so that he doesn't hunger in the outside world. To the degree the Dragon didn't, the Sheep has issues with a deep hunger that goes unanswered no matter what he eats . . . undoubtedly, a hunger for father's love and approval.

Because Dad is a Dragon, he can have problems with his stomach, and ulcers can be the result. When the Sheep has to deal with Dad, he can feel a knot in the pit of his stomach, and find the pectoralis major clavicular muscles in his chest acting up.

The Monkey

The Monkey has a Snake for a father. Dad was probably a sensitive man who could not tolerate being criticized. He needed to be right, and brooked no confrontation. It was Dad's responsibility, by word or deed, to approve of the Monkey and show him his significance in the world. To the degree he didn't succeed, the Monkey has issues with rejection, and pretends he doesn't need approval . . . from Dad or any other authority figure. In the extreme, there may even be issues with never bonding with Father.

Because Dad is a Snake, he may have problems with diabetes or hypoglycemia. When the Monkey has to deal with Dad, or other authority figures, he can do whatever is necessary to get his approval, or move into his self-denial if it isn't forthcoming. He may override his own emotions and believe "it doesn't matter."

The Rooster

The Rooster has a Horse for a father. Dad was probably a hard worker and wore his heart of his sleeve. If he had emotional traumas early on, he may have closed down and become unapproachable when his child was born. It is Dad's responsibility, by word or deed, to instill in the Rooster an open heart and give "her" a sense of belonging. To the degree that didn't happen, the Rooster can always be looking to be part of something greater.

Because Dad is a Horse, he can have heart problems or even deal with effects on the brain, because the Heart meridian governs the brain as well. When the Rooster has to Deal with Dad, "she" can have heart pangs or have the subscapularis muscle act up.

The Dog

The Dog has a Sheep for a father. If the Dog envisions herself as a Sheepdog, then the tables can turn and the Dog can always be shepherding her Dad. The Sheep can have a victim consciousness and convey that to the Dog. It is the Sheep's responsibility, by word or deed, to instill in the Dog the sense that she can be victorious in life, and in her relationships with men. The Sheep needs to let the Dog win as often as possible, to allow the Dog to feel what winning is all about. To the degree that didn't happen, the Dog has issues with being a victim, and blaming others for her lot in life.

Because Dad is a Sheep, he can have digestive problems, and issues with assimilating his food correctly. When the Dog has to deal with the Sheep, the iliacus muscle can act up, or the quads in the front of the legs can cause problems when the Dog has to "stand up" to her father.

The Boar

The Boar has a Monkey for a father. The Monkey can be an imperial parent who will brook no nonsense and lives in a world of his own. The Monkey can be dogmatic and hear nothing that doesn't agree with his own view of life. The Monkey father can place duty above love or authenticity. It is the Monkey's responsibility, by word or deed, to instill in the Boar a faith in God, the universe, Buddha, whomever, and teach him to flow with life. To the degree that he doesn't, the Boar can feel he has to override his own instincts and control his world just like Dad does. The Boar's depression can stem from a subconscious realization that, in controlling his world, he blocks the good from entering as well as the bad.

Because Father is a Monkey, he has problems with the bladder and bladder control later in life. He might also have multiple sclerosis. When the Boar has to deal with the Monkey, he can find his own dogma knocking heads with his father's, or find his teres minor acting up.

You and Your Shadow— Your Mate

In the traditional comparisons of compatibility and incompatibility among the Chinese animal signs, it has been suggested that there is incompatibility with the signs directly opposite one another. Thus, a Rat shouldn't marry a Horse, an Ox shouldn't marry a Sheep, a Tiger shouldn't marry a Monkey, a Cat shouldn't marry a Rooster, a Dragon shouldn't marry a Dog, and a Boar shouldn't marry a Snake. Yet, how many times do we do this and feel we are going against fate?

On the Time of Day Wheel in the five-element system, however, the meridian/organ is strongest during its designated time of the day, and conversely, it is weakest twelve hours later. Hence, we draw the energy of that other person into our lives to learn about it and draw on its strength. Together, we become whole as we merge.

In Western astrology, the opposite sign mirrors to us some of our least-desirable traits, our "shadow issues," and that is why we draw them into our lives. In my research, I have found, contrary to the traditional information, that we do "marry" the animal opposite our own. So, if you wonder why you were born in the Hour of the Boar and are married to a Snake-hour person, for example, or any of the other combinations that don't seem to work—according to older texts—this is why.

In Western astrology, the 1st house of the astrological chart is the House of Self, who you are, and the 7th house, directly opposite, is the House of Mate, or the Shadow Self. Even here, it is generally agreed that whatever signs are in the 1st and 7th houses are opposites, and yet opposites attract to compliment and compensate for qualities that are missing in the other.

So, too, with the power animals. You will be attracted to the animal who is opposite the one of your hour, and find that s/he reflects the patterns, traits, and illnesses of that animal. You might have wondered why you were attracted to someone the books say you shouldn't marry, but, because that person reflects your shadow issues, that's exactly what you do.

I was born at the time of the Rooster and the animal in my 7th house is a Cat, and I did marry someone who was born in the Year of the Cat, if not the Hour. In this work, it's the essence of the energy we're looking for, not specifically whether we will precisely draw in the mate who has the animal as his/her rising power animal.

For another example, I know a couple where the wife was born at the Hour of the Boar, while her husband is a Snake. After working with her in hypnotherapy and with the power animals, the Boar transformed into a Swan and no longer wanted to live with the Snake, but needed to go out into the world and establish her own life. The Snake used forms of rejection to get the Swan to stay, even developing diabetes in order to control the Swan (sugar imbalances are a Snake/Spleen tendency). This Snake could never be wrong and would never admit to a fault. To be divorced meant having to admit there was a problem in his marriage, and he couldn't deal with it.

Your mate, then, is the one directly across on the wheel . . . and most frequently, the one opposite the hour your were born.

Rat marries the Horse
Ox marries the Sheep
Tiger marries the Monkey
Cat marries the Rooster
Dragon marries the Dog
Snake marries the Boar

Now, because the location where most of us live is not precisely on the equator where the lineup would be directly opposite, the power animal for your mate could be the one before or after it on the wheel. The width of any animal's rulership, much like the houses in Western astrology, can be smaller in one section and larger in another. This can move the wheel, so that the animal above or below the one directly opposite can become the archetypal animal for any given person. For instance, Prince Charles, born in the Hour of the Boar, should have the Snake for his shadow. But, because he was born north of the equator there is a distortion, and the Horse becomes the archetype of his mate, with the Snake having some secondary energy to add dimension to the soup. The Horse more aptly describes Princess Diana than the Snake . . . although she was admiringly canny in the way she handled her divorce.

This pairing can also be used in any kind of partnership—personal or professional. It should be noted that politician Al Gore's wife, Tipper, was born on the same day, if not year, as Bill Clinton. When Gore was Vice President, he had the same partnership energy in both arenas of his life.

The Rat

The Rat needs to be adored. The Rat needs to feel he is loved without any conditions. The Rat can be very altruistic, so he needs to feel that concern is being reciprocated. He fears abandonment and betrayal. He is very subjective and doesn't need anyone who is going to make him jealous or angry.

The Rat's opposite mate is the Horse, but he can also have a Snake or a Sheep for a partner.

The Rat and the Horse

The Horse needs to proffer all the love she has to give, so the Rat will never feel he'll be abandoned. Then the Rat will do all at his disposal to make her feel loved in return. The Horse who has turned hard-hearted will only bring anxiety to the Rat's already anxious life.

The Rat and the Snake

The Rat and the Snake are natural foes in the animal kingdom. The Snake fears rejection, the Rat fears abandonment. This can be a dance to see who gets the upper hand and remains with the ego intact. The Snake needs to accept that what the Rat does for her is from a pure heart, and not be suspicious. The Snake needs to let go of the need for perfection and the need to be right. The Rat needs to stop reading abandonment into the actions of the Snake when she feels he's rejecting her . . . or simply not letting her have the last word! The Rat needs to express his altruism to the Snake, which will give her a sense of security.

The Rat and the Sheep

The Sheep needs to show the Rat he can be victorious in any situation, that the Rat has a right to be admired and that, with the victory-oriented Sheep at his side, betrayal is not an issue. The Sheep who feels victimized will only enhance the Rat's feelings of betrayal. When the Sheep is responsible and doesn't lay blame at the feet of the Rat, he will learn to trust.

The Ox

The Ox needs a partner who is her biggest fan, someone who will champion her in whatever she needs to do, a partner who will gently lead her away from the plow and take the yoke off her neck. The Ox needs to avoid the critic and the ones who dwell in fear, who would keep the Ox in the yoke, plowing the fields. The Ox needs the support of her mate to aim for the stars.

The Ox's opposite mate is the Sheep, but she can also have a Horse or a Monkey for a partner.

The Ox and the Sheep

The Sheep needs be victorious in life and show the Ox how to be a winner. The Sheep needs to show the Ox how to be discriminating and stay with relationships that encourage her to grow into her full potential. The Sheep who feels victimized will only keep the Ox yoked to the plow.

The Ox and the Horse

The Horse needs to bring a heart full of love to the relationship. In finding a mate with whom she feels she truly belongs, the Horse will allow the Ox the freedom to imagine and create great things. The Horse who is out of touch or self-absorbed, will keep the Ox working in the fields, trying to fulfill the Horse's needs.

The Ox and the Monkey

The Monkey needs to have faith in what the Ox seeks to accomplish. It's tempting for the Monkey to jump in and try to control the master plan. But the Ox seeks a higher order and needs to know that everything is unfolding in a divine order. If the Monkey is full of faith, he can be a terrific partner who can be the business head who will take the Ox a long way in her bid for success. The Monkey, who has to control the relationship, will ultimately find an Ox who throws over the traces and goes off on her own!

The Tiger

The Tiger needs to feel her full power. She needs to voice her opinions and feel the recognition that she is heard and respected for who she is and what she has to say. The Tiger needs to be recognized and her ego needs to be built up. She needs people around her who are proud of her accomplishments and encourage her to be in the spotlight. She dreams expansive dreams and needs to have partners who support her in making her dreams come true.

The Tiger's opposite mate is the Monkey, but she also can have a Sheep or a Rooster as a partner.

The Tiger and the Monkey
The Monkey needs to recognize the Tiger as an individual being who knows what she's doing. He needs to have faith in her ability to do things right and be successful. The Monkey can be a terrific partner if he truly sees the Tiger for who she is . . . and loves her for who she is. The Monkey who must control the Tiger may find she has "left" spiritually and emotionally and that only a mask of the person remains.

The Tiger and the Sheep
The Sheep can do wonders for a Tiger when the Sheep is discerning and can lead the Tiger through the land mines of experiences. The Sheep can admire the Tiger and work for her tirelessly. The Sheep who feels victimized, however, can thwart her at every turn and crash her dreams upon the rocks.

The Tiger and the Rooster
The Rooster needs to provide the Tiger with a "wake-up call" to see where her life is going and what she should do to change it for the better. The Rooster's work ethic will do wonders for her if she will emulate it and put in the hours that will bring her the true recognition she seeks. The Rooster who frets and wrings its feet (it doesn't have hands!) over every little thing will just make the Tiger feel anxious and doubt her own ability.

The Cat
The Cat has issues with being clean enough. Notice how a cat cleans and cleans and cleans his body. The Cat is correlated to the large intestine, which controls defecation. The Cat needs a partner who will tell him how valuable he is, what his good points are, and look up to him, not down on him. Any mate for a Cat needs to point out why it's so good having him in her life. When the Cat knows he's worthy, he'll do anything in the world for her. The Cat generally has a Rooster for a mate. But it can also have a Dog or a Monkey.

The Cat and the Rooster

The Rooster is hypervigilant, always looking for something to go wrong, while the Cat is insecure. To compensate, the Cat has a certain calm aloofness that the Rooster admires. At its best, the relationship has the potential for the Cat to allay the Rooster's fears and bring peace, by exuding the self-confidence that will make the Rooster feel everything is okay. When the Rooster comes from a state of peace, she can help the Cat to realize its true worth.

The Cat and the Dog

The Cat and Dog are natural enemies, yet when they can lie down together and see each other's finer qualities, this can be a good twosome. The Dog has the potential to bring an intimacy to the relationship that the Cat has never known before. Being truly loved, the Cat can find her own sense of sacredness and feel worthy. But the Cat can have self-esteem issues and the Dog can be inhibited, getting territorial and barking when emotions get too intense. The Cat can figure it's all his fault, when the Dog simply has to come to terms with her sexuality.

The Cat and the Monkey

The Cat is rather particular and the Monkey tends to be a more primitive type. The Cat doesn't like to admit to bodily fluids, and the Monkey can be in denial, so the two may not be looking at their relationship clearly. The Monkey can get irritated with the Cat's incessant need for cleanliness, and enjoy messing up their place just to get her reaction and open her up a bit.

The Dragon

The Dragon needs to be fed. There are seeming unquenchable fires in the belly that need to be assuaged. The Dragon needs a mate who will help him see that, while it's great to create an identity of husband/father/provider/lover, his real identity is a soul evolving and identities are just roles we play. The Dragon has high expectations and needs someone who will help him make his dreams come true.

The Dragon has a Dog for a mate, but can also have a Rooster or a Boar.

The Dragon and the Dog

The Dragon can be "larger than life" and be a bit intimidating for the Dog. The Dragon has such a huge appetite for everything, including sex, that the Dog may back off and bark, keeping the Dragon at bay until she feels comfortable enough to let him into her space. The Dragon is so charming, however, that, when he wins her over, she can open up and become his sexual equal.

The Dragon and the Rooster

The Dragon tends to be a high roller, looking for the fun in life, and the Rooster can be a good mate to help the Dragon realize there is work to be done and tasks to accomplish. The Rooster can help the Dragon fill his tummy by promoting the work ethic. The Rooster who nitpicks and pecks (henpecks?) her mate too much, will find the Dragon off in his dreamworld, doing magic with the kids.

The Dragon and the Boar

The Dragon has high expectations and can be disappointed easily if the world doesn't live up to them. The Boar needs to see the hope in every situation and help the Dragon to make his dreams come true. The Boar who is sinking in the bog will only confirm the Dragon's underlying feeling that he can "expect" his expectations to not come true.

The Snake

The Snake needs to bond; it needs to be one with her mate. The Snake needs a lover who will give her the reassurance that all is well in the relationship and he will stay. The Snake needs to feel significant and know that her partner values her above others. The Snake will frequently test a relationship to see how much the other will take to know where her boundaries are. The wise mate will recognize this and allow her to test the waters, showing her where his line is without tearing the relationship asunder. Then the two can live quite happily within those perimeters.

The Snake has a Boar for a mate, but can also have a Dog or a Rat.

The Snake and the Boar

The Boar who is optimistic and positive will allow the Snake to feel secure. The Boar will appreciate and admire the way the

Snake can move around so quickly and be so flexible. The Snake likes the predictability of the Boar and the fact she can count on him to be right where he's suppose to be. The Boar who is feeling futile can bring the Snake right down into the bog with him.

The Snake and the Dog

The Snake and the Dog can have some problems, because the Snake is always sensing rejection and the Dog can have a fence around her keeping the Snake at a certain distance. The Dog needs to come to terms with her sexuality, to allow her innocence and loyalty to reach out to the Snake without barking. The Snake needs to realize that, when the Dog has put up its boundaries, it is not necessarily rejecting the Snake; the Dog just needs to deal with its own feelings about intimacy.

The Snake and the Rat

Here again, we have natural foes. The Rat needs to provide the Snake with a place of unconditional love so that she will trust that this relationship is going to last and she doesn't have to look for a problem around every corner. The Rat who has experienced abandonment may not be the correct mate for the Snake who senses rejection . . . it may be just a matter of who can back out the door first!

The Horse

The Horse needs to belong. She needs a mate who truly loves her and makes her feel cherished. She needs someone who likes to touch and is touchable. The Horse enjoys being in a relationship and wants someone who likes to do things together. The Horse needs to be passionate and believe in her partner.

The Horse has a Rat for a mate, but can also be married to a Boar or an Ox.

The Horse and the Rat

The Horse can be very good for the Rat, and vice versa because the Horse loves to love and the Rat needs to be adored. The Rat needs to reflect that Horse's love and reciprocate to the same degree. As long as these two look at each other with eyes of love, they can be a very happy duo. The Horse can be shattered by a Rat who betrays her.

The Horse and the Boar

The Boar who lives out the positive can be a source of inspiration for the Horse who is always searching for the meaning of life. The Boar who is pessimistic, however, can increase her own insecurity.

The Horse and the Ox

The Ox can be very imaginative and reach for the stars, and the Horse can get caught up in the inspiration of it all. The Horse is a good mate for the Ox, because she can be a true helpmate. The Ox who is angry and frustrated might break the Horse's heart.

The Sheep

The Sheep needs to be discerning in the mate he chooses. Too frequently, he can make a decision that he may soon regret. A Sheep needs to take his time, date a number of people, and be able to compare and decide just who is right for him and who isn't. The Sheep ultimately needs a mate who will see him as a victor in life and encourage him to be so. The Sheep needs to define his responsibilities in a relationship and see clearly which are his and which are his mate's. It's too easy for him to blur them and try to do more than he should.

The Sheep has an Ox for a mate, but can also have a Rat or a Tiger as a partner.

The Sheep and the Ox

The Ox needs to show the Sheep its potential. The Ox can see the bigger picture and see what's possible. The Sheep needs to "color outside the lines" with the Ox and know they can transcend the mundane together. The Ox who feels repressed by life can enhance the Sheep's victim side.

The Sheep and the Rat

The Rat can aid the Sheep to come into victory by adoring the Sheep and making him realize how wonderful he is. The Sheep wants to gravitate to the victor's side and win, and the Rat can help him get there. The Rat who has been abandoned can abandon in return and cause the Sheep regret.

The Sheep and the Tiger

The Tiger is good for the Sheep in showing him just what being a winner is all about. The Tiger has ego issues and the Sheep needs to strengthen his own ego and acknowledge it as positive. The Sheep can learn the art of winning by being alongside the Tiger. The Tiger who has had his ego crushed by life will only show the Sheep the other side.

The Monkey

The Monkey needs a mate who will gently let him know that it's okay to let down a bit—that he doesn't need to be in charge every minute of the day, that there are other things in life more important than duty. It can be a little disconcerting to the Monkey at the outset, when she isn't intimidated and can see right past the rigid demeanor to the core person inside. The Monkey needs his faith increased and a mate who will make it safe for him to crack open the world he's so deftly constructed, and allow him to be who he truly is.

The Monkey is mated to the Tiger, but can also have a relationship with an Ox or a Cat.

The Monkey and the Tiger

The Monkey can have a "tiger by the tail" when he meets up with his Tiger. He can try to control her all he wants, but the Tiger won't have any of it. She has a jungle to run and won't brook much interference. The Tiger can be of great benefit to the Monkey if she can ignore his trying to control her and just love him instead. The Tiger who has lost her dreams will allow the Monkey to take over.

The Monkey and the Ox

These two are formidable energies, and neither one is going to "give in" any time soon. The Ox can show the Monkey the benefits of having faith and letting go, if the Ox has been allowed to reach the full potential of life . . . or at least a big chunk of it. When the Monkey can see the larger picture, he's more willing to entertain the idea that the universe just might know what's right after all. The Ox who has a yoke around its neck and is plowing the field without looking either way may be just what the Monkey is looking for, because he can be in control and she won't challenge him.

The Monkey and the Cat

The Cat who has a sense of his own value can show the Monkey what it's like to walk with confidence and know he has a place on this Earth. The Cat who is worried about looking just right and measuring up will be constantly in the Monkey's shadow. The Monkey can then manipulate the Cat through feelings of unworthiness.

The Rooster

The Rooster is looking for someone who will allay her fears; someone with whom she can find a safe haven and find some peace. The Rooster is willing to work and delay meeting her own needs as long as there is a greater goal to be reached within the partnership. However, she can get caught up in the machinations of the partner to the extent that her needs are never met, and then she can lose her chi—life-force energy—and not see a way to get out of it.

The Rooster has a Cat for a mate, but can also connect with a Tiger or a Dragon.

The Rooster and the Cat

In order for the Rooster to stay on top of things and not dive into fear, it must find a Cat who has a sense of self-worth and can go out and tame the world. The Rooster can see worth in the Cat that the Cat might not see in himself. However, if the Cat scurries to the confines of the home for safety and can't get out again, the Rooster is left fending for itself.

The Rooster and the Tiger

The Tiger can do a lot for the little Rooster to show it how to really get out there in the world and conquer it. The Rooster needs a strong mate who can be an ally and friend and give it a strong shoulder to perch on to see the larger picture. The Tiger who has lost her dreams may only enhance the Rooster's fear.

The Rooster and the Dragon

Here, the Rooster has a strong ally in the Dragon. The Dragon can protect her and give her peace of mind when he feels fulfilled. The Dragon who hungers and needs to overcompensate by buying too much or drinking too much, etc., can give the Rooster real fears about paying the rent.

The Dog

The Dog needs a partner who will lead it gently past her issues with intimacy and help her connect with the ecstasy of love. She needs someone who will not be turned off by her barking and trying to scare him away, but allow her this time to shake off the fear and find out that he is a nice guy after all—and maybe someone she can be with who will prove that all these bugaboos she's run from all these years are simply perceptions she's created in her own mind. When she finds the right man to do this (or the right gal for the guy with Dog placements), she'll wonder why she did all that barking for so many years and lost out on so much.

The Dog has a Dragon for a mate, but can also have a Cat or a Snake.

The Dog and the Dragon

The Dragon can be the perfect one to lead the Dog down the road of myth and magic to see what a wonder the path of love reveals. The Dragon is also big enough to shelter the Dog from all she fears (barks at). If the Dragon overshadows the Dog and tries to protect it too much, the Dog can feel suffocated.

The Dog and the Cat

Now here are two natural protagonists! The Cat and Dog just can't resist hissing and barking at each other. If the Cat has developed a strong sense of self-esteem and the Dog is ready to play, they can live in harmony together. But the Dog has natural resistance to people until she's comfortable, and, if the Cat suffers from esteem issues, the two of them can be chasing each other for years.

The Dog and the Snake

Of the three potentials, the Dog and it's opposite, the Dragon, works the best. With the Dog and the Snake, the Snake needs to get by her knee-jerk reaction of rejection when the Dog barks. If the two can get past their normal reaction patterns, this pairing can work—but the Snake can't reject when she thinks the Dog's barking is rejection, and the Dog can't withdraw into her haughtiness of inhibition when the Snake hisses. Both animals have natural reticence and only time will get them past their natural defenses.

The Boar

The Boar needs a mate who is positive, "up," "high on life"; someone who will keep the Boar out of the bog and expecting the best. The Boar tends to be slow and sluggish and can get dour very easily. He needs his "other half" to keep both of them looking at life from a positive perspective.

The Boar has a Snake for a mate, but can also have a Dragon or a Horse as its shadow.

The Boar and the Snake

The Snake who has bonded with the Boar will provide the foundation for the Boar to see life from a positive perspective. The Boar needs the solidarity and the constancy of the Snake that the Snake will provide when she feels safe. The Snake who hisses and rejects will send the Boar into a deeper mire of depression.

The Boar and the Dragon

The Boar needs the Dragon to show him the wonders of the universe. The mythical Dragon caught up in the magic of what can be, might be the best antidote the Boar can have to restore that glimmer of hope. The Dragon who feels that expectations are never fulfilled, will only confirm what the Boar feels he already knows.

The Boar and the Horse

The Horse wants to merge. The Horse can see the potential in the Boar and nuzzle him to do better. The Horse can be ready for marriage from the beginning, but the Boar may be too caked with mud from the bog to move as quickly; he'll need some coaxing to find hope in a union. The Horse who is jealous and self-absorbed will probably not stay around anyway.

Your Children

Our children are our future, our potential. They show us our sense of fun and childlike innocence. It is our responsibility to teach them the positive attributes of their archetypal animal, and support them to move away from the negative. When we understand our children's hopes and fears and feed the positive, we raise strong human beings that expect the positive, which then manifests in their lives.

In this chapter, I will speak about your children in general, and your first child in particular. You will see certain traits that apply to all your children, and yet your oldest will reveal them most specifically. Once again, your first child may actually be the archetypal animal described, but it is more common for the child to simply express that energy to you (and they may have that energy prominently somewhere else in their chart). Your mate will experience that child from their own perspective, so you can synthesize the two to see how best to raise them. If you are born in the even-numbered hours, look to the reading above and below yours and synthesize them to get a more accurate picture.

The Rat

The Rat has Dragons for children. It is the Rat's duty to see that the Dragon's inner needs are met. These are babies who can't be fed by the clock, but must be fed when hungry. The Dragon child needs to learn how to get his own needs met and his expectations realized.

The first child in particular is larger than life, loves to perform, and has a gnawing hunger inside. He can have an insatiable appetite for things as well as food. You might have problems with them "taking" things that don't belong to them. Some feel like the world owes them a living. Sometimes their expectations are that their expectations are never realized and feel deprived.

This Dragon can have "tummy aches" when he wants to stay home from school. He can also have allergies and food addictions, as well as being a clothes horse or having gambling issues. Or, in contrast, the Dragon child can sometimes overcompensate for his hunger and squirrel away for a rainy day.

The Ox

The Ox has Snakes for kids. It is the Ox's responsibility to recognize that this is a very sensitive soul who seeks perfection and always feels that she comes up short. She has a deep need to bond and to know she is special in her parents' lives. She is a worrier, and feels rejection keenly. The Ox needs to create an atmosphere where she understands that not everyone gets along, but it's no one's fault. You do the best you can, but some people cause friction in your life for other purposes.

Snakes are testers. These kids will test and test and test, to see how far you will go. When you finally yell "Halt!" they shrug and walk off. They've found your line, and now they know where not to tread again. Somewhere in their young lives a lie leads to a perception they can build their life upon if not caught early.

Snake children love sugar, but are sensitive to it. They probably shouldn't be denied it, for they will feel it's the ultimate rejection, yet it should be monitored, for they are more prone to sugar imbalances.

The Tiger

The Tiger has Horses for children. It's the Tiger's task to make the Horse feel she belongs from the very beginning. She needs to have a reassuring touch that is calm and tender. The Horse child needs to be handled gently and never broken or "saddled" too early with burdensome responsibilities. The Horse child feels vulnerable and the Tiger, Mom or Dad, needs to protect her gentle heart from harm.

The Horse child can be "hard-hearted" if she's abused. She'll shut down and not allow herself to be vulnerable again. In the extreme, it's hard to reach her.

Horse children need to have an open, flowing heart that gives to others, so as not to incur heart problems along the way.

The Cat

The Cat has Sheep for children. The Cat's responsibility here is to develop a sense of victoriousness in his child. The Cat needs to allow the Sheep child to win as often as he possibly can—to solve problems and find answers to his challenges. The Sheep child knows what he should eat, and should be encouraged to listen to his inner self for guidance. Battles of will will only make the Sheep child feel like a victim and create problems down the road. The Sheep child has an inner sense of refinement that should be encouraged.

The Sheep child raised in a negative atmosphere tends to blame others (bleat?) for their own mistakes in life.

The Sheep takes his experiences into his small intestine, which chooses what is healthy and discards what is not. The Sheep child who practices this inwardly and outwardly will be successful.

The Dragon

The Dragon has Monkeys for kids. It's a good thing the Dragon is larger than life, for maybe he's the only one who can stand up to these adorable Monkeys—who get their way, regardless. The Dragon needs to instill cooperation in his Monkey child and help him observe what happens when he doesn't throw a monkey wrench into his life. The Dragon needs to provide an atmosphere where the Monkey child doesn't have to make the decision to control.

The Monkey child tends to take control early, and Dragon parents will feel something of this energy in all their kids, but the first one will demonstrate it most succinctly. The Dragon needs to teach his Monkey magic and myth and the fantasy of life, so that he can see how expansive and creative he can be when he understands how much larger the universe is and the power it has to create good in his life.

Monkey children are prone to problems with their bladders and may wet the bed as youngsters if they feel "out of control."

The Snake

The Snake has Roosters for kids—the type of children who are up just as the Sun dawns and don't give up until they're exhausted. If their chi is low, however, they'll cock a weary eye at the rising Sun and go back to sleep. The Snake needs to recognize this child's inherent fear of life in general, and help her to live in peace.

The Rooster child tends to be a worrier, always afraid something bad is going to happen, so she doesn't risk very often. The Snake parent needs to carefully move her one step at a time to show her there is nothing to fear and allow her to develop a consciousness that is based on a sense of peace about her personal safety.

The first child can have kidney problems and perhaps fertility issues as an adult. The kidneys can be strengthened in order to neutralize some of this tendency.

The Horse

The Horse has Dogs for children. The Horse is the perfect parent for a Dog. The Horse should be full of love and open to show the Dog that love and intimacy are a beautiful part of life. The Horse who has shut off, however, can only enhance the Dog's native sense that intimacy is something from which to shy away.

Dog children are reticent and usually marry later than others. Horse parents can look bewildered at their Dog children, who tend to be conservative and so much more reserved and shy than they are.

Dog children have cold hands and feet and are modest and shy; finding it hard in school to circulate and become one of the group. They are usually loners who prefer to be by themselves, unless the Horse parent has really done her job and has provided an unconditional atmosphere for the Dog to open up and include others.

The Sheep

The Sheep has Boars for children. Sheep parents need to present a positive posture for the Boar child that this is a glorious world with all sorts of potential. Otherwise, the Boar has a natural tendency to be down and depressed, with a heavy energy that finds it hard to be optimistic. The Sheep parent needs not to blame, but always to encourage his Boar child to do the best he can; to set realistic goals that the Boar can achieve.

Boar kids can be overweight, with metabolic problems. They can flush and be embarrassed easily. Boar kids can get into trouble as teenagers if they have been dealt with harshly, and feel there is no hope.

The Monkey

The Monkey has Rats for children. Rats need to be adored, to feel they are the center of their universe, and the Monkey parent who makes them march to his tune can create a child who feels abandoned. The Monkey parent needs to "put a lid on" his penchant to control and allow the little Rat to express himself—standing back and observing what the child would do if left to his own resources. While the Monkey parent may never feel that what the Rat does on its own is good enough, the child will be less likely to develop a deep anger for this parent if allowed to express himself and be given credit for what he does right.

Rat children will take care of other children in school, and will give up their lunch if need be to help someone else.

Rat kids can have trouble digesting fats and should stay away from fried foods. They also tend to have headaches and leg pains.

The Rooster

The Rooster has Oxen for kids. The Rooster's fear can rub off on them. Rooster parents tend to be "smother mothers" who continually feel something awful may happen to their child at any second. So they tend to overprotect them and keep them from experiencing life. Hence the little Oxen grow up angry and "liverish" at being held back for so long. They also can be immature, because they haven't experienced things in a sequential process like other kids.

Rooster parents need to allow their kids to take risks and see what life is all about. They need to encourage them to step out and test their mettle.

Oxen children tend to have refined motor skill problems and get irritable and impatient. They get angered easily and, as mentioned earlier about Oxen, can do a really good "Incredible Hulk" impersonation.

The Dog

The Dog has Tigers for kids. Dog parents who tend to be uptight and morally righteous will create problems for the Tiger child, who needs to develop a healthy ego and "roar" at life, living it to the fullest and absorbing all the tantalizing elements at her disposal.

Dog parents needs to examine their attitudes about sexuality and, if they serve them, be open to a child who needs to be far more open and expressive than they are.

Tiger kids need to challenge their egos, and yet have parents who encourage their need to be proud of what they do. They need to be recognized and allowed to be the leaders and shakers of this world.

Tiger children are prone to bronchitis and other lung problems when they are overcontrolled and feel their dreams are ridiculed.

The Boar

The Boar has Cats for kids. The Boar parent needs to carefully nurture this child's self-esteem. They need to see the Cat child's worth and cultivate it at every opportunity. The Cat child needs to know from birth that he's the greatest experience that ever happened to his parents. The Boar parents who are pessimistic and see the Cat's flaws and imperfections and play them up only succeed in developing a personality who feels defective and can never be valued.

The Cat, while loving its home, may leave early to get away from this influence, or conversely, it may stay home long past the time it should leave, because it doesn't feel good enough to exist in the outside world. The parent who wishes his child would "get a life" needs to look at what self-esteem skills they did—or didn't—instill in their child.

Minor Characters

Mom, Dad, and Mate represent the three most powerful relationships with which we deal in our lifetimes. They show us our challenges and our shadows in our evolution of becoming. Whether we "choose" them or not is debatable, but they are the people who help to sculpt and define us during the course of our lives. Our children, too, are great dispensers of wisdom to help us on our path.

However, it doesn't stop there. There are any number of minor characters who enter and leave the scene at various intervals who make an impression along the way.

In the following paragraphs, you can see how other people play out in the lives of the animal archetypes. Remember, if one doesn't seem "right on," look to the corresponding section for the animal above and/or below the animal in question. And, once more, they can be, but don't have to be, the exact animal to reflect this energy to you. It can come from elsewhere in their chart. In this section, you should use the animal for the hour you were born, as you did for Mon, Dad, and Mate. But it's also useful for the year you were born as a general tendency.

The Rat

Siblings: The Rat has Tigers for siblings, particularly the first one after him. Tigers yearn for the spotlight and may leave the Rat in the shadows. Tiger sibs can have lung problems and depression in their lifetimes.

Employers, employees, coworkers: The Rat has Snakes to cohabit with in the workforce. The Rat needs to curry a win-win situation where he works, so the natives don't get restless and slither away. Snakes are testing all the time. The Rat needs to draw his line so they know their limitations with him. Snakes have sugar imbalances.

Ministers, priests, coaches, mentors: The Rat has mentors and religious leaders, as well as sports coaches, who tend to be dogmatic and live by one rule . . . their own! They are Monkey types who need to honor their religious upbringing and trust in a supreme being. They place duty above all.

Friends: The Rat has friends who are Dogs. In order to have the adoration he so desires, the Rat needs to attract friends who are loyal and friendly, like puppy dogs. Territorial dogs that bark need not apply.

Animals for Other Minor Players in the Rat's Life

CHARACTER	ANIMAL		CHARACTER	ANIMAL
Mom's mom	Horse		Mom's dad	Rat
Dad's mom	Rat		Dad's dad	Horse
Dad's 2nd wife	Snake		Mom's 2nd husband	Boar
1 sibling older	Dog	→	This sibling's mate	Dragon
1 sibling younger	Tiger	→	Sibling's mate	Monkey
2 sibling older	Monkey	→	Sibling's mate	Tiger
2 sibling younger	Dragon	→	Sibling's mate	Dog
2nd child	Horse	→	Child's mate	Rat
3rd child	Monkey	→	Child's mate	Tiger
4th child	Dog	→	Child's mate	Dragon
1st grandchild*	Monkey	→	2nd grandchild*	Dog
1st grandchild**	Dog	→	2nd grandchild**	Rat

*first two children of first child
**first two children of second child

The Ox

Siblings: The Ox has Cats for siblings, and the first one in particular. The Cat is elusive and much more agile than the Ox. The Ox envies the Cat's independence. The Cat needs to feel superior and can make the Ox feel inferior. The Cat gets constipated.

Employers, employees, coworkers: The Ox has Horses in the workplace. Horses buck and whinny and can have heart problems —physical or emotional ones. They continually talk about their relationship problems. The Ox's coworkers can have hearts as large as all outdoors, or may have shutdown and seem hard-hearted.

Ministers, priests, coaches, mentors: The Ox has Roosters as religious leaders, as well as sports coaches who are cautious and preach conservatism and playing "by the book." It is these ministers who instill "the fear of God." These people often have kidney problems.

Friends: The Ox has Boars for friends. These two really need some energy from another archetype to keep them moving. It's too easy to sink into a complacent friendship that doesn't go anywhere. These friends tend to be pessimistic and have metabolism problems.

Animals for Other Minor Players in the Ox's Life

CHARACTER	ANIMAL		CHARACTER	ANIMAL
Mom's mom	Sheep		Mom's dad	Ox
Dad's mom	Ox		Dad's dad	Sheep
Dad's 2nd wife	Horse		Mom's 2nd husband	Rat
1 sibling older	Boar	→	This sibling's mate	Snake
1 sibling younger	Cat	→	Sibling's mate	Rooster
2 sibling older	Rooster	→	Sibling's mate	Cat
2 sibling younger	Snake	→	Sibling's mate	Boar
2nd child	Sheep	→	Child's mate	Ox
3rd child	Rooster	→	Child's mate	Cat
4th child	Boar	→	Child's mate	Snake
1st grandchild*	Rooster	→	2nd grandchild*	Boar
1st grandchild**	Boar	→	2nd grandchild**	Ox

*first two children of first child
**first two children of second child

The Tiger

Siblings: The Tiger has Dragons for siblings and the first one after him specifically. Tigers and Dragons have strong egos and are competitive. Tigers need to be recognized and Dragons need the spotlight—a tough twosome. The Tiger's sibling can go far. He also can have problems with allergies and addictions.

Employers, employees, coworkers: The Tiger works with Sheep. Hmmm. That might be like being in the cat-bird's seat for the Tiger. Here the Tiger rules supreme—but the Sheep may have some tricks up his sleeve.

Ministers, priests, coaches, mentors: The Tiger has Dogs for mentors, ministers, and coaches. They can come across as best friends or good buddies, always a laugh and a song. Or, they can be

straight-arrow types who have intimacy problems and preach absti-
nence. They tend to wrap themselves up in the flag or get morally
righteous about sexually explicit material in the media. These people
tend to female problems for women and prostate issues for men.

Friends: The Tiger has Rats for friends. They can count on the
Rat to be there in times of trouble. The Tiger and the Rat play
hard, and are extremely emotional about each other. Sometimes
the Tiger feels the Rat is too subjective. These friends tend to
have migraines or sciatica.

Animals for Other Minor Players in the Tiger's Life

CHARACTER	ANIMAL		CHARACTER	ANIMAL
Mom's mom	Monkey		Mom's dad	Tiger
Dad's mom	Tiger		Dad's dad	Monkey
Dad's 2nd wife	Sheep		Mom's 2nd husband	Ox
1 sibling older	Rat	→	This sibling's mate	Horse
1 sibling younger	Dragon	→	Sibling's mate	Dog
2 sibling older	Dog	→	Sibling's mate	Dragon
2 sibling younger	Horse	→	Sibling's mate	Rat
2nd child	Monkey	→	Child's mate	Tiger
3rd child	Dog	→	Child's mate	Dragon
4th child	Rat	→	Child's mate	Horse
1st grandchild*	Dog	→	2nd grandchild*	Rat
1st grandchild**	Rat	→	2nd grandchild**	Tiger

*first two children of first child
**first two children of second child

The Cat

Siblings: The Cat has Snakes for siblings and the first one younger
in particular. The Cat and Snake can toy with each other. The Cat
finds his siblings are sensitive and can be hurt easily. The Cat
needs not to be so independent, but include his siblings in his
plans. Siblings can have diabetes or other sugar imbalances and
should stay away from the sugar bowl.

Employers, employees, coworkers: The Cat has Monkeys for
coworkers . . . no one needs to tell the Cat that. Monkeys can be
fun to play with and comedians, but they can also be controlling
and dogmatic in their approach to work. Those in the workforce
with the Cat tend to have bladder control problems.

Ministers, priests, coaches, mentors: The Cat has Boars for mentors and ministers. They can be expansive and see a glorious vision for the future, but they tend to have a "doom and gloom" attitude that the end of the world is near. Boars do not make good coaches unless they are really operating from the positive. These people struggle with weight problems, and could have had a traumatic shock somewhere in their lives.

Friends: The Cat has Oxen for friends. These people are honest and true and steadfast and sturdy. They can be counted on in a pinch. They can also hold a vision for their friend or keep them from moving forward in their love and professional life.

Animals for Other Minor Players in the Cat's Life

CHARACTER	ANIMAL		CHARACTER	ANIMAL
Mom's mom	Rooster		Mom's dad	Cat
Dad's mom	Cat		Dad's dad	Rooster
Dad's 2nd wife	Monkey		Mom's 2nd husband	Tiger
1 sibling older	Ox	→	This sibling's mate	Sheep
1 sibling younger	Snake	→	Sibling's mate	Boar
2 sibling older	Boar	→	Sibling's mate	Snake
2 sib younger	Sheep	→	Sibling's mate	Ox
2nd child	Rooster	→	Child's mate	Cat
3rd child	Boar	→	Child's mate	Snake
4th child	Ox	→	Child's mate	Sheep
1st grandchild*	Boar	→	2nd grandchild*	Ox
1st grandchild**	Ox	→	2nd grandchild**	Cat

*first two children of first child
**first two children of second child

The Dragon

Siblings: The Dragon has Horses as siblings and expresses in the first one after him specifically. The Horse is full of love and can be the one who tags along and looks up to this older Dragon sibling who seems so magical. The Dragon and Horse can get along well, but the Horse can also be self-absorbed and the Dragon can do all his magic without making an impression. This sibling can have heart issues.

Employers, employees, coworkers: The Dragon has Roosters in the office environment. These people can be whistle blowers, but they surely are the ones who arrive early and leave late. They also tend to fret and worry over every little thing and wonder why the Dragon is so laid back. Office people in the Dragon's world tend to have stress and the effects of too much fear.

Ministers, priests, coaches, mentors: The Dragon has Rats for mentors and ministers. These Rats can be there simply because it's the right thing to do, no strings attached. They see a need and fill it. They are also hotheads and can blow up at the slightest provocation. These people tend to have headaches and problems digesting fats.

Friends: The Dragon has Tigers for friends. When their Tiger friends are strong and in their power, they can be great allies for the Dragon. Tigers can also be sad and depressed, grieving over the past. Tiger friends heave great sighs and suffer from bronchitis and other lung issues.

Animals for Other Minor Players in the Dragon's Life

CHARACTER	ANIMAL		CHARACTER	ANIMAL
Mom's mom	Dog		Mom's dad	Dragon
Dad's mom	Dragon		Dad's dad	Dog
Dad's 2nd wife	Rooster		Mom's 2nd husband	Cat
1 sibling older	Tiger	→	This sibling's mate	Monkey
1 sibling younger	Horse	→	Sibling's mate	Rat
2 sibling older	Rat	→	Sibling's mate	Horse
2 sibling younger	Monkey	→	Sibling's mate	Tiger
2nd child	Dog	→	Child's mate	Dragon
3rd child	Rat	→	Child's mate	Horse
4th child	Tiger	→	Child's mate	Monkey
1st grandchild*	Rat	→	2nd grandchild*	Tiger
1st grandchild**	Tiger	→	2nd grandchild**	Dragon

*first two children of first child
**first two children of second child

The Snake

Siblings: The Snake has Sheep for siblings and the next youngest in particular. The Sheep yearns for a life of refinement and to be distinguished in his profession. The Snake needs to take a hand in the Sheep's upbringing to ensure that the Sheep feels he can win in life, and not sabotage the Snake with his maneuvers. The Sheep can blame the Snake for all his problems in life.

Employers, employees, coworkers: The Snake has Dogs to work with on the job. The Snake tends to be pretty fluid and easy-going, and enjoys playing with the open, friendly puppies. But she can be rankled by the uptight religious types she deals with on occasion. These Dogs have intimacy issues and can hide behind their religious indignation.

Ministers, priests, coaches, mentors: The Snake has Oxen for mentors. These are "shoulder-to-the-wheel" types who preach the work ethic and the value of working hard and not expecting much more. The Ox who has taken off the yoke and has moved beyond this has a true vision and creativity that can't be matched. These Oxen tend to have vision problems and anger easily.

Friends: The Snake has Cats for friends. They may skirt each other and check each other out, but they can be great friends. The Cat can sacrifice in relationships, however, and the Snake has to make sure that she doesn't become too strong, so that the Cat always defers. The Cat's home tends to be cluttered or extremely neat—nothing in between.

Animals for Other Minor Players in the Snake's Life

CHARACTER	ANIMAL		CHARACTER	ANIMAL
Mom's mom	Boar		Mom's dad	Snake
Dad's mom	Snake		Dad's dad	Boar
Dad's 2nd wife	Dog		Mom's 2nd husband	Dragon
1 sibling older	Cat	→	This siblings's mate	Rooster
1 sibling younger	Sheep	→	Siblings's mate	Ox
2 sibling older	Ox	→	Sibling's mate	Sheep
2 sibling younger	Rooster	→	Sibling's mate	Cat
2nd child	Boar	→	Child's mate	Snake
3rd child	Ox	→	Child's mate	Sheep
4th child	Cat	→	Child's mate	Rooster
1st grandchild*	Ox	→	2nd grandchild*	Cat
1st grandchild**	Cat	→	2nd grandchild**	Snake

*first two children of first child
**first two children of second child

The Horse

Siblings: The Horse has Monkeys for siblings and particularly the first one born after him. The Horse is spirited and doesn't want to be "broken" by a Monkey who needs to run the show, even if he is younger. The Monkey needs to respect the Horse and allow her to be unfettered. Monkey sibs tend to have bladder problems, particularly when not getting their way.

Employers, employees, coworkers: The Horse has Boars to work with on the job. The Boar who is pessimistic tends to bring down the Horse, who dreads going to work every day. There is usually one Boar who drains the Horse's energy by looking at the bleak side of life. Boar women tend to have a harder time with menopause, because their hot flashes seem to be more intense.

Ministers, priests, coaches, mentors: The Horse has Tigers for mentors and religious leaders. These Tigers usually have large egos and are known for their oratory. Occasionally, Horses draw in Tigers who are melancholy and never seem to get beyond their grief over some loss.

Friends: The Horse has Dragons for friends; people who will open the Horse up and draw her out and help her to see the magic in this wonderful world. These Dragons can also have strong appetites and addictions and turn to the Horse for a loan . . . and she's always a soft touch.

Animals for Other Minor Players in the Horse's Life

CHARACTER	ANIMAL		CHARACTER	ANIMAL
Mom's mom	Rat		Mom's dad	Horse
Dad's mom	Horse		Dad's dad	Rat
Dad's 2nd wife	Boar		Mom's 2nd husband	Snake
1 sibling older	Dragon	→	This sibling's mate	Dog
1 sibling younger	Monkey	→	Sibling's mate	Tiger
2 sibling older	Tiger	→	Sibling's mate	Monkey
2 sibling younger	Dog	→	Sibling's mate	Dragon
2nd child	Rat	→	Child's mate	Horse
3rd child	Tiger	→	Child's mate	Monkey
4th child	Dragon	→	Child's mate	Dog
1st grandchild*	Tiger	→	2nd grandchild*	Dragon
1st grandchild**	Dragon	→	2nd grandchild**	Horse

*first two children of first child
**first two children of second child

The Sheep

Siblings: The Sheep has Roosters for siblings. The Rooster can ride herd on the Sheep, particularly when the Rooster wakes up so bright and perky and nudges the Sheep until it wakes up. The Rooster freaks and peaks over the news and the decay of society and can develop hearing problems, or have bone/structure issues.

Employers, employees, coworkers: The Sheep has Rats in the workplace—hopefully the high type of Rat who will help the Sheep on his rise to success. There can also be Rats who work behind his back. These rats will be angry individuals who see him as an obstacle to their success.

Ministers, priests, coaches, mentors: The Sheep has Cats for mentors. High-type cats will encourage the Sheep to attain his full potential; low types can belittle and motivate from criticism.

Friends: The Sheep has Snakes for friends. Snakes are always looking for signs of rejection and, if the Sheep is the type who blames, then the relationship has its problems. The Sheep needs to find a win-win playing field in his friendships.

Animals for Other Minor Players in the Sheep's Life

CHARACTER	ANIMAL		CHARACTER	ANIMAL
Mom's mom	Ox		Mom's dad	Sheep
Dad's mom	Sheep		Dad's dad	Ox
Dad's 2nd wife	Rat		Mom's 2nd husband	Horse
1 sibling older	Snake	→	This sibling's mate	Boar
1 sibling younger	Rooster	→	Sibling's mate	Cat
2 sibling older	Cat	→	Sibling's mate	Rooster
2 sibling younger	Boar	→	Sibling's mate	Snake
2nd child	Ox	→	Child's mate	Sheep
3rd child	Cat	→	Child's mate	Rooster
4th child	Snake	→	Child's mate	Boar
1st grandchild*	Cat	→	2nd grandchild*	Snake
1st grandchild**	Snake	→	2nd grandchild**	Sheep

*first two children of first child
**first two children of second child

The Monkey

Siblings: The Monkey has Dogs for siblings and particularly the first one born after him. The Monkey, who may have been victimized and now needs to control his life, often can't understand the Dog, who is detached and seemingly unaffected. The Monkey may resent the Dog.

Employers, employees, coworkers: The Monkey has Oxen who work with him. These Oxen can be highly creative, artistic people with great vision, or they can be pretty "by the book" types and the Monkey can take charge. Oxen can revolt, however, when they get mad enough.

Ministers, priests, coaches, mentors: The Monkey has Dragons for mentors. The Dragon type has a huge appetite for knowledge and can express the glory of the past, in religion and pagentry. Coaches tend to be loud types who exhort their charges to victory. The one thing they can't abide, however, is being ignored.

Friends: The Monkey has Horses for friends. The Horse is more than willing for the Monkey to take the lead, as long as it gives her a long rein. The Horse wants to be one part of a twosome and will allow the Monkey his control as long as he provides what she needs in the relationship. The Monkey, however, always seems to know that she looks right through him and has seen his soul, and knows this macho act is just so much bravado.

Animals for Other Minor Players in the Monkey's Life

CHARACTER	ANIMAL		CHARACTER	ANIMAL
Mom's mom	Tiger		Mom's dad	Monkey
Dad's mom	Monkey		Dad's dad	Tiger
Dad's 2nd wife	Ox		Mom's 2nd husband	Sheep
1 sibling older	Horse	→	This sibling's mate	Rat
1 sibling younger	Dog	→	Sibling's mate	Dragon
2 sibling older	Dragon	→	Sibling's mate	Dog
2 sibling younger	Rat	→	Sibling's mate	Horse
2nd child	Tiger	→	Child's mate	Monkey
3rd child	Dragon	→	Child's mate	Dog
4th child	Horse	→	Child's mate	Rat
1st grandchild*	Dragon	→	2nd grandchild*	Horse
1st grandchild**	Horse	→	2nd grandchild**	Monkey

*first two children of first child
**first two children of second child

The Rooster

Siblings: The Rooster has Boars for siblings. This can be frustrating for Roosters, who are so wiry and interested in all sorts of things. Boars can bring the Rooster down if they are depressed. The Rooster needs constantly to herald the dawn and show the Boar the gloriousness of life.

Employers, employees, coworkers: The Rooster has Tigers to interact with on the job. Often the Rooster doesn't know what to make of these Tigers, because of the mask they wear so others won't know what's going on inside. Tigers often try to run roughshod over their little Rooster counterparts, because they are so much bigger. But the Rooster has the last laugh—if she doesn't watch the clock and keep everything organized, the whole place can fall apart.

Ministers, priests, coaches, mentors: The Rooster has Snakes for mentors. They will always test the mettle of the Rooster, sometimes with a critical tongue to exact the perfection they seek. They can also motivate by withdrawal. The Rooster needs to know the Snake's Achilles' heel. They need approval above all.

Friends: The Rooster has Sheep for friends. The Sheep are perfectly willing for the Rooster to take the lead. The Rooster needs to stay positive and not exhibit any fear they might have, for it will only undermine the Sheep in the long run.

Animals for Other Minor Players in the Rooster's Life

CHARACTER	ANIMAL		CHARACTER	ANIMAL
Mom's mom	Cat		Mom's dad	Rooster
Dad's mom	Rooster		Dad's dad	Cat
Dad's 2nd wife	Tiger		Mom's 2nd husband	Monkey
1 sibling older	Sheep	→	This sibling's mate	Ox
1 sibling younger	Boar	→	Sibling's mate	Snake
2 sibling older	Snake	→	Sibling's mate	Boar
2 sibling younger	Ox	→	Sibling's mate	Sheep
2nd child	Cat	→	Child's mate	Rooster
3rd child	Snake	→	Child's mate	Boar
4th child	Sheep	→	Child's mate	Ox
1st grandchild*	Snake	→	2nd grandchild*	Sheep
1st grandchild**	Sheep	→	2nd grandchild**	Rooster

*first two children of first child
**first two children of second child

The Dog

Siblings: The Dog has Rats for siblings. They have intense feelings about one another. The Rat can have hurt feelings if the Dog is territorial; but if the Dog is loving, there is nothing the Rat will not do for her.

Employers, employees, coworkers: The Dog has Cats for coworkers—a sure sign of contention. These people will look askance when the Dog enters the workplace—do you feel out of place here, Ms. Dog, with all these cats around? The Dog needs to show those he works with that they can coexist in harmony, but she has to win them over.

Ministers, priests, coaches, mentors: The Dog has Horses for mentors. They can wear their hearts on their sleeves and think she's just the greatest, or they can be untouchable when she asks for assistance.

Friends: The Dog has Monkeys for friends. They like to be in charge in the relationship, and at some point the Dog needs to stand up for herself and demand equality in order for the relationship to continue . . . something the Monkey may or may not be willing to do.

Animals for Other Minor Players in the Dog's Life

CHARACTER	ANIMAL		CHARACTER	ANIMAL
Mom's mom	Dragon		Mom's dad	Dog
Dad's mom	Dog		Dad's dad	Dragon
Dad's 2nd wife	Cat		Mom's 2nd husband	Rooster
1 sibling older	Monkey	→	This sibling's mate	Tiger
1 sibling younger	Rat	→	Sibling's mate	Horse
2 sibling older	Horse	→	Sibling's mate	Rat
2 sibling younger	Tiger	→	Sibling's mate	Monkey
2nd child	Dragon	→	Child's mate	Dog
3rd child	Horse	→	Child's mate	Rat
4th child	Monkey	→	Child's mate	Tiger
1st grandchild*	Horse	→	2nd grandchild*	Monkey
1st grandchild**	Monkey	→	2nd grandchild**	Dog

*first two children of first child
**first two children of second child

The Boar

Siblings: The Boar has Oxen for siblings. These sibs can be "liverish" and irritable; the Boar never knows when they will get angry and explode. The Boar who has creative Oxen in his life, who have grown to their potential, will have delightful companions throughout their lives. These two tend to be slow prodders, however, and need someone to spur them on.

Employers, employees, coworkers: The Boar works with Dragons. They can be voracious and try to get all the plum jobs for themselves. The Boar can work in the background while the Dragons take center stage. The Boar dreams of a day when he can leave it all behind and branch out for himself if he's full of hope.

Ministers, priests, coaches, mentors: The Boar has Sheep for mentors. The Sheep who has reached this position should be operating from a sense of having overcome his challenges and emerging the victor. A mentor who has mastered his demons can show the Boar how to overcome his pessimism and depression. Sometimes the Sheep hasn't succeeded and can victimize the Boar.

Friends: The Boar has Roosters for friends. They are always needling him, always pushing him, nudging him out of his doldrums. Boars need Roosters to help them see life's plusses, but should not be pulled down into the Rooster's fears.

Animals for Other Minor Players in the Boar's Life

CHARACTER	ANIMAL		CHARACTER	ANIMAL
Mom's mom	Snake		Mom's dad	Boar
Dad's mom	Boar		Dad's dad	Snake
Dad's 2nd wife	Dragon		Mom's 2nd husband	Dog
1 sibling older	Rooster	→	This sibling's mate	Cat
1 sibling younger	Ox	→	Sibling's mate	Sheep
2 sibling older	Sheep	→	Sibling's mate	Ox
2 sibling younger	Cat	→	Sibling's mate	Rooster
2nd child	Snake	→	Child's mate	Boar
3rd child	Sheep	→	Child's mate	Ox
4th child	Rooster	→	Child's mate	Cat
1st grandchild*	Sheep	→	2nd grandchild*	Rooster
1st grandchild**	Rooster	→	2nd grandchild**	Boar

*first two children of first child
**first two children of second child

Case History: Michaela

One of the ways astrologers interpret a chart is to "Turn the Wheel." Since the 4th house represents mother, for example, if we "turn the wheel" and make the 4th house the 1st house for Mom, we can "read" her characteristics from that perspective. Since the 10th house represents Dad, if we turn the wheel and make the 10th house the 1st for him, we can read him around the client's wheel as well. In fact, we can do that by turning the wheel for any family member, friend, boss, or others in our lives just by finding that "house" and turning it. Since Mom is the 4th house, and we turn it and make it the first for Mom, then by counting over, we find that house 7 in a client's chart becomes Mom's 4th house and represents her mother, the client's grandmother.

Children are represented by the 5th house, and that is where the first child resides. The second child appears in the 7th house. So, the 7th house not only represents the client's mate, it is where Mom's mom and Dad's dad (because the 7th house of the client's is 10 away from Dad's house) appear, and is also the energy for the second child. You'll often find you relate to your mate and your second child in a similar fashion, i.e., the dynamics of the energy are the same.

To give you an example of how all this works in an individual's life, we will consider the astrological chart of Michaela, born June 30, 1958, at 12:00 noon, PST in Concord, California.

As I write this, Michaela is a 40-year-old single working mom who was born in the Year of the Dog, the Month of the Cat, the Hour of the Horse, and the Minute of the Rat.

Being born in the Year of the Dog, Michaela is reserved and shy. She has a refined sense about her, and some people can see her as aloof. Once you've proven yourself to her, she'll be the most generous, kind, giving, caring person you'll ever meet; but you'll not know that on first meeting. It's hard for her to be spontaneous. In fact, when she's in a group of gregarious people, her reserve is almost painful to her, although others may just think she's shy . . . and wonder if she's judging them.

The Dog is the archetype for the Circulation-Sex meridian, which is also called the Pericardium. This is the membrane sac that protects the heart, taking the poundings of emotion first, so the heart doesn't get bombarded. So, too, does the Dog energy protect Michaela from emotional relationships. The problem is, however, that, at times, the Dog's "barking" keeps everyone at bay, and the Horse (Heart) feels alone and lonely because the Dog is doing too good a job and not allowing the Horse to experience the merging with another and loving someone that she wants so dearly.

Michaela was born in the Month of the Cat. In this system I've developed, relating the animals to the meridians, the Cat relates to Cancer, and, for the correlation with the Sun sign only, we use the animal related to the astrological sign, not the meridian it's in.*

As a Cat, Michaela enjoys her home. She's not averse to traveling, but prefers to come home after a day's trip and sleep in her own bed. When she was four, her mother and grandmother took her and her siblings on a car ride some twenty miles away— her first trip that far away from home. After a while, Michaela started getting upset. "I want to go home," she cried. For some reason her little heart felt that they would never find their way home again. To this day, she's anxious when she moves beyond the perimeters she's established for herself. She feels guilty that she doesn't see as much of her family as she should, but, with work and kids, as a single mother, there are just so many hours in the day. She also has this "cleanliness" thing that sometimes drives her kids wild, which takes up the rest of the time.

Born in the Hour of the Horse**, she has a heart as big as all outdoors. She can wear her heart on her sleeve and wants more

---

* The bulk of everyone born in the United States has their Sun sign in Large Intestine (the Cat). Capricorns have their Sun sign in the Stomach area (Dragon, also some Sagittarians and Aquarians), and Cancers have their Sun sign in Lung (Tiger, also some late Geminis) due to the angle of the Sun in relation to Earth. So most of us have issues around self-esteem and self-worth. Because of this, it wouldn't be enlightening to use the meridian in this instance.

** Some may wonder why we don't use the animal of the astrological sign during the hour of birth. In our example of Michaela, she was born at 12:00 P.M. and this gives her a Libra rising. In this instance, the sign and the animal are the same—the Horse "rules" Libra. But if we had someone born at 7:00 A.M. on a different day, say with Aries rising, we would use the information regarding the Dragon (Stomach meridian) because Dragon time is 7–9 A.M., rather than the Rat (Gallbladder), since we're referring to the Chinese system. However, that doesn't keep you from synthesizing some Rat information for the Aries rising as well. Melding these systems works very well.

than anything to love and be loved. Yet she has a sensitive soul and can back off if her feelings aren't reciprocated. She desires to be in relationship (even if she says she doesn't at times). Michaela can be complacent and let things slide, waiting for the universe to provide. She wants "only one," you see, and she'll wait for him to come along . . . for surely, her first husband, Art, was not "the one" to her mind. Yet, at one point, she realized that nearly ten years had slipped by since she had been married to Art, and she had become really gun-shy about walking into another relationship that might fall short again. No one has ever quite measured up to her standards.

About this time, Michaela dug into the energy of her "shadow," the sign opposite hers (the Rat/Gallbladder) and got angry enough to move forward and answer some of those personals ads. Sometimes, one needs a little kick in the pants from Rat energy to get going again and do something rather than waiting for it to happen. She's met some decent guys, but hasn't found the right one yet.

At the outset, she was rather full of herself, realizing she could actually talk to a stranger on the phone and go out to a restaurant and talk comfortably without her heart pounding wildly. But after she established that she could do that, she got a little weary of standing in restaurants and hotel lobbies trying to spot the guy she agreed to meet and not feel like a hooker . . . and at a certain point her Dog energy reasserted itself, and she decided that was enough of that.

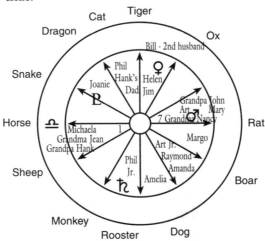

Figure 16. Michaela:
June 30, 1958, 12:00 P.M. PST, Concord, California.

Born at 12:00 noon, Michaela's animal for the minute of birth resides in Rat energy. Here we have issues around abandonment and betrayal, looking for trust and unconditional love—proffering many times, and wondering why it isn't reciprocated. And good ol' Art was just the guy to act out this energy pattern for her (more about him later).

If we only worked with her animal totem, we would see that Michaela is shy and territorial (Dog) because she wants so much to be loved and become one with another human being (Horse), and yet her experiences have taught her that she doesn't receive the trust that she confers (Rat), and so she draws back, wondering if its her fault (Cat). She wonders what she has done to bring this upon herself (Cat), and so decides that, to protect her tender heart, she'll not step lightly into a relationship for a long time (Dog).

The second totem to look at are the animals on the 1st house (self), 4th house (home and mother), 7th house (mate), and 10th house (career and father). The animals/meridians here will show us our vulnerability to stress and dis-ease.

Predisposition to Dis-ease

Born in the Hour of the Horse (Heart), Michaela needs to be heart-wise and heart-healthy. This doesn't mean that she'll necessarily have problems with her heart, but it's something she needs to be aware of and keep healthy and strong. Exercise is important for her, as well as developing her upper body strength to keep her heart healthy. Between ages 16 and 24, Uranus (the planet of electrical instability) went through the heart area of her chart and she experienced some palpitations. But she was young and in good health, and the period passed without incident. Even so, the family remembers it well.

Michaela tends to have cold hands and feet and be reserved in social interaction (Dog). She has some deep, unexpressed anger (Rat) that she has never explored. She tends to feel poorly when she eats too much greasy food, and certainly had a lot of migraines when she was married to Art (Rat). The migraines have pretty much gone away since she's been on her own with her kids, and she sometimes worries if they'll come back with a new relationship.

Michaela never realized how, even though she's very close to her dad, he has a way about making her feel inferior (Cat). She always feels "not good enough" around him and strives to please him. She'll often come back from a family visit constipated and wonder why.

Along with bringing her anger to the surface and dealing with it, Michaela's quest in life is to deal with her need for approval (Pluto in Virgo in Snake/Spleen energy). She fears rejection and has always tried to be "the good girl." Now, as she approaches 40 and has experienced her "Pluto Square" (to itself)—a time for empowerment—she pretends to gag as she realizes how that sweet saccharin facade affected her life. Her self-approval is the only one she needs now.

Family

Michaela was born in the Hour of the Horse. Family members that mirror this energy to her, among others, are her grandparents; her dad's mom and her mom's dad. It was their responsibility to pass down to Michaela a sense of love and trust and give her confidence to become a beautiful racehorse, who has the strength and stamina to make it to the finish line of health, happiness, and success.

Michaela's Grandmother Jean (her dad's mom) really loves her. She knows she can turn to her whenever she needs her. Grandma Jean has an open heart for all her grandchildren, but there seems to be a bond between her and Michaela that she can't quite explain. The moment she picked up baby Michaela at birth, she knew there was an unspoken connection that would never be broken.

Grandma Jean is a warm, open being, but it wasn't always that way. She remembers when she was shy and retiring like Michaela (dog energy in her 4th house); when she held back and rehearsed everything she was going to say. She liked the TV show, "Who's the Boss?," and asked at some point as she got into menopause, "When did I go from Angela to Mona (the sexy mother)?"

Grandma Jean is currently living with her second fella since her divorce, and doesn't give a hoot about what President Clinton is up to. Secretly she sort of enjoys a president breaking the taboos of a puritanical country after all the shenanigans in the White House for decades, to which the media turned their backs. "Even Paula Jones admitted he told her he wouldn't force her to do anything she didn't want to"—that's good enough for Grandma Jean. Her daughter-in-law Amelia shrieks in horror about this, and Michaela has some reservations about it as well.

Speaking of Mom, Amelia is represented in Michaela's chart by the 4th house, down at the base of the chart—the foundation—and the meridian overlapping is Circ-Sex (the Dog). Being born in the Year of the Dog, and having it as the foundation of her life, gives it even more credence. Traditionally, the Rooster would be on the 4th house cusp, but this is a good example of how the animal sign can shift because of the distortion in the sky.

Amelia has always been a bit uptight—"Down right frigid," hurumphs Grandma Jean. "I mean, I went through that phase, but I got beyond it," she says with a certain amount of pride. Amelia, however, is rather prim, and both her husband's mom and her daughter wonder sometimes if Michaela and her siblings weren't immaculate conceptions. She is a loyal, loving person, but there's just this reserve that's hard to penetrate at times. She's a fierce defender of her daughter and will go to bat for her at a moment's notice when her tender heart has been crushed. But in her own life she prefers to wear unisex clothes and sensible shoes and a no-nonsense hairdo that eschews any sense of sexuality. She abhors what the president is alleged to have done, is appalled at Grandma Jean's acceptance, and wonders why she doesn't stand up for womanhood. Grandma Jean, on the other hand, rolls her eyes and says something to her that makes her blush, bringing some heat to an otherwise cold body, for Amelia has circulation problems and her hands and feet are always cold . . . something Amelia's husband, Phil, is more than aware of.

Phil is everything that Michaela aspires to be. He's a larger-than-life character (Tiger) whom Michaela looks up to. He is represented in her 10th house of career and the power animals are the Tiger and the Cat (Lung and Large Intestine). Phil has a strong need to stand out and be recognized (Tiger). He's made a lot of money in real estate and likes to live the good life. He has a natural tendency to draw attention to himself, and Amelia sniffs and adds, "Sometimes he thinks bad attention is better than none at all." He tends to smoke too much and Michaela is always urging him to quit. "I will someday, honey," he tells her, but in his heart he knows he probably won't. Phil is in his 60s now. He used to jog to keep in shape, but his hamstring got him one day and he hasn't really gotten back into it. As he gets older, he has started to be persnickety about things, such as checking out the kitchens in restaurants before he'll eat anywhere (Cat), which drives Amelia crazy.

When they met, Amelia was young and pretty and dazzled Phil. They were engaged before they knew it, and married shortly thereafter. Amelia's hormones were "raging" (as they said in those days) and she wanted to have a baby more than anything, so whatever reservations she had about sex at that time were overridden by her desire to procreate. Joanie was born first, and then Michaela, and next came Phil Jr. By the time the third baby was born, Phil noticed that Amelia was making excuses more and more about being busy with the kids and being too tired to slip away to the bedroom for the sexual adventures he thought they both used to enjoy. She got pregnant again with Amanda, as she seemed to enjoy being pregnant and it was an excuse not to have sex.

Amelia and Phil actually divorced at one point. The lustiness of the Tiger couldn't understand what had happened to the passion in their marriage. He married Margo (represented in Michaela's chart by the 6th house and the Boar/Rat energy). If she was passionate and a "hot mama" (a term he used to describe her that angered Michaela) to Phil, she was a bit of a bore to Michaela, and reminded her a bit too much of Art. (Gallbladder/Rat energy overlapping from the 6th house of stepmother to the 7th house of mate). Eventually, Margo did betray Phil and leave him, and, after a while, he started seeing Amelia again. She might not be as uninhibited in bed, but Phil always knew Amelia was the love of his life, and that she would always be there for him. Actually, with the children now grown, and after listening to Grandma Jean for over forty years, Amelia is retrieving some of the passionate intimacy she had enjoyed with Phil.

Siblings
Joanie is Michaela's older sister (11th house of one sibling older) with Dragon (Stomach) and Snake (Spleen) energy. It so happens that the planet Pluto is located here, and Michaela finds Joanie hard to deal with. Joanie has always "lorded" it over her and tried to manipulate her. Joanie's a maverick (Uranus is in this part of the chart, too) and goes her own way, yet expects everyone to follow her. She's carved herself an identity as "oldest sibling" and feels as if she's the third member of a parenting triumvirate— something Michaela refuses to acknowledge.

Joanie's married to Raymond (5th house opposite the 11th, with the Boar energy there), a somewhat dour individual who allows Joanie to set the pace. It so happens that Michaela and Raymond dated at one point (5th house being her boyfriends' as well as the house for older sib's mate) and she remembers him as a much more ebullient person. Joanie moved into the picture and "took him away" from Michaela, in a seeming power grab, but there wasn't a lot of spark there, so Michaela soon let him go. She sometimes wonders if Raymond would be able to see a brighter future if he had made other choices.

Phil Jr. (represented in the 3rd house with Saturn there and a Rooster/Kidney overlay) is a respectable businessman. He travels a lot, and, because of Rooster energy, he always buys the maximum flight insurance . . . "just in case." He's taken the safe path in life, afraid of what might be around the next bend. He's been kidney deficient for a long time, as Michaela will tell him, being an acupuncture aficionado, and she thinks she's just about got him convinced to see her acupuncturist. Those aching feet of his are worrying her.

Phil's wife, Helen, is just the opposite of Phil. (Well, why wouldn't she be? The mate is always represented in the house opposite, in this case, the 9th.) She's much like Phil Sr., with Tiger energy. She's open and expressive and she's continually pulling Phil Jr. out of his fear-induced "paralysis." Once she's gotten him beyond his fear, Phil Jr. finds an exhilaration he's never known before . . . which is why he's so devoted to her.

Michaela's sister Amanda and Raymond are very much alike (because they both represent 5th-house energy, along with her first child, Art Jr., whom we'll discuss momentarily).

Amanda has always been on the chubby side. She's laid-back, and abhors the idea of exercise. Her family is always on her to get outside and burn off some of those excess pounds, but she really hasn't much impetus to do so. She lays around the house and watches TV a lot. A doctor told her once she had thyroid problems, but she never took the thyroid pills for very long. She has a curiosity about death and dying that few other people in the family understand. While never being truly suicidal, she understands how people get to that point. While truly not eating a lot, she has metabolism problems that keep her from losing much weight.

Family Dynamic

It was Amelia's responsibility (because the Dog/Circ-Sex energy is at the base of her chart where Mom's energy is described) to give Michaela a healthy sense of sexuality, to allow her to be authentic and not fear how her words would be taken.

Phil Sr. was given the area of preparing her for relationships with men and working confidently in her career. He needed to show her that to be a woman in a man's world was to be recognized and appreciated for her dedication, that she should have men in her life who would see her talents and reinforce her self-esteem, showing her how much she's valued at the firm.

Phil Sr., for all his endearment to Michaela, does have a slight misogynist tendency (Cat). He will cut down the women he loves, fearful that they will leave him, which only serves to make them accept jobs and assignments they shouldn't for fear of losing their jobs. Michaela has gotten on to him in recent years, and, while she loves her dad with all her might, she doesn't let him get away with those "you" statements anymore.

Grandma Jean (Phil's mother) and Grandpa Hank (Amelia's dad), represented in the 1st house, were assigned the responsibility of teaching Michaela to lead with an open heart, to be loving, forgiving, and passionate about life (Horse/Heart energy). Grandma Jean got past her reticence, but Grandpa Hank expresses the other side of the energy.

Part of Amelia's inhibition comes from her father being undemonstrative. He closed down years ago, being self-absorbed in his business. His dad (10th house with Cat overlay) was very critical of him, and disappointed that he chose a career that was not to his dad's liking. He has a lot of bitterness toward his father, which he expressed to his children.

The mates of these grandparents, namely Grandma Nancy (Hank's wife) and Grandpa John (Jean's ex-husband)—both rats—represented in Michaela's 7th house, were given the task by the universe of adoring Michaela as much as a loving God would, and instilling in her a sense of trust that could never be assailed, a sense that God is a loving God who will never abandon or betray her. They were suppose to teach her how to make wise choices and judge from a place of love. Grandpa John had split with Jean before Michaela was born, and she never remembers seeing him. "Just as well," Grandma Jean snorts, still feeling betrayed.

Grandma Nancy tries her best. She's always volunteering and sharing what she has with the world. You'll find her down at the church mailing flyers, volunteering at the bookstore, ushering at services. She feels the love of God smiling upon her at all times . . . and secretly hopes one day Hank will feel it, too.

Michaela's Husband

Of course, we can't forget Art. Since Michaela experienced a "mixed bag," as it were, from her grandparents expressing the energy of the Rat (in the 7th house), Michaela didn't have a firm concept on which to base the selection of an ideal mate.

Art was young and impetuous. He was a go-getter and Michaela enjoyed being his partner, his mate, and his support system . . . for a spell. With Mars in Aries in the 7th house in Michaela's chart, an astrologer told her early on that Art would be a handful for her. Mars is the planet for the Aries sign. She was sure to draw in a man who was eager to challenge and confront and who needed to be first. And so, when Art appeared in her life, she had the perfect mirror in which to look at her "shadow" elements (the 7th house also representing our shadow).

On top of Aries energy appearing in her 7th house of mate, the Rat (Gallbladder) energy is there. As it relates to grandparents Nancy and John, it also relates to Art, as well as their second child, Mary.

Art was loving, emotional, and adored Michaela. He was also angry and abusive. He always said he loved her more than anything, but he was jealous and, when triggered, he'd lash out emotionally, often not being able to control his actions. Michaela took it for quite a few years, but, when Art picked up Mary, the baby, and nearly threw her in a fit of rage, Michaela took the children and got them out of the relationship.

Art was served with a restraining order, but eventually went into military service, which has helped to straighten out his life. No wonder Michaela hesitates getting into a new relationship!

Michaela's Children
Art Jr. is her first child, who shows up in the 5th house in her chart, along with her sister Amanda, and brother-in-law, Raymond (Boar energy). He tended to be a serious, dour child, and Michaela took the lead from these adults and checked with a doctor to see if his thyroid was functioning properly and his metabolism wasn't sluggish. Since the Boar energy is expressed in her 5th house, it is her duty to show him that there is always an answer to every problem, to make him see the most positive side of every situation so that he can visualize a positive future. Because she did this, when Art Jr. became a teenager, he escaped the drugs and fast cars that were part of his peer group. He's now in college studying to be a filmmaker.

Her second child, Mary (7th house, Rat), is a teenager now, and Michaela finds herself going toe-to-toe with her a lot. They adore each other, and yet they can get into some rip-roaring donnybrooks. They have a very subjective relationship. Mary is headstrong and Michaela is more yielding, yet Michaela has learned to hold her own. Because they've gone toe-to-toe so often (and Michaela has gotten to see her shadow more acutely), they have a history and connection that she really doesn't have with the other two, however much she loves them. Mary says she'll never marry anyone like her mother at times (with a sly grin to get her goat) and yet Michaela knows from a reading I gave her that the second child will marry someone exactly like the mother (actually a composite of both parents), so Michaela may have the last laugh.

Michaela has yet to marry for the second time, but, if we look at her chart, we can see the potential for the second mate in the embodiment of her third child. The energy for the second mate and third child resides in the 9th house and, in this instance, the meridian overlay belongs to the Ox (Liver) and Tiger (Lung).

The planet Venus (in Gemini) is located in Michaela's 9th house, so the people represented in this house have a strong affection for her and she for them. She gets along very well with her third child, Jim. He's a little immature because she's protected him a little too much, but he's good-natured and doesn't realize that, at some point, he'll get frustrated at not doing things the other kids in school get to do. He's quite a bit like his Grandpa Phil, since the Tiger energy spans the 9th house (Jim) and 10th house (Phil Sr.). Michaela can tell that Jim's going to be a "chip off the old block," as she sees her dad in many of Jim's movements and attitudes. Right now, she's learned to squash any tendency Jim has to put people down.

As for Michaela's second husband, we can project that his energy will be a lot like Jim's. Because of the Venus energy, she's bound to find someone for whom she really has an affection. This man will have some of the elements of her father (Tiger), yet he'll be a rock for her, giving her the security she never had (Ox). He may have asthma (Tiger/Lung), and he can have some type of liver problems, but Michaela isn't worried about that. She knows she can provide him with the opportunity to take bupleurum, milk thistle, and dandelion, which will help those liver issues immeasurably. She needs to make sure that the man who is drawn into her life to express this second-husband energy and the Ox has his sights set high and has developed his creative abilities and talents in order to be a healthy, artistic, creative individual who reaches for the stars. When Bill walked into her life recently, she knew she had found the right guy for her, and a fantastic role model for her fatherless children. As her lonely nights turned into a fulfilling, satisfying experience, she soon stopped rehearsing and editing herself, and became a far more open, spontaneous, and authentic person. She now realizes what a wise woman Grandma Jean was after all.

Advanced
Techniques

When you have read this book, at some point the concept will become clear and you'll be able to figure out other people in your life and how they express as animal archetypes. You can also shift to some advanced work. As a teaser, I'm going to give you the "next step" and you can take it from there.

Most of this book is based on the hour of birth. That is where different people in your life will reflect most specifically for you in their corresponding areas. However, you can also combine the animals for your year, month, and hour to get a deeper picture. Take your children for example. Say you were born in the Year of the Horse. Look up the Horse's children and how they act in the Horse's life. The Horse has Dogs for kids.

Next, say this Horse was born in the month of Virgo, and is thus a Snake. Look up the Snake's description of it's children. The Snake's children are Roosters. Let's assume this Horse was born at the time of the Rooster. Look up the Rooster's description of it's children. The Rooster has Oxen for children. You now have a pyramid of the different aspects of your children.

Synthesizing these issues, you can see that a Virgo Snake, born in the Year of the Horse and in the Hour of the Rooster, has children who tend to marry later and be shy and modest dealing with the opposite sex (Dog). They have a lot of fear issues to get beyond, and often find it hard to take risks (Rooster). So, the reason they are angry is that they feel stifled and repressed by these energies that keep them from being in the mainstream (Ox).

You can do this with any relationship to see more facets of the personality with which you are interested in learning how to more successfully interact.

Advanced Example

Every person who was born in the Year of the Horse has children who reflect aspects of the Dog; shy or territorial, loyal and loving, or barking. How are those children different from others? The month the Horse was born in refines it a little more. A Horse born in Virgo with Snake energy, finds that the Rooster adds an aspect of fear vs. peace to the mix. These children find it difficult to approach others because of the fear aspect. (A Horse born in the sign of Aries would have Dragon children. Here, the Dog child would be fleshed out with the elements of the Dragon: searching to fill real or imagined hungers, needing to be content in a relationship.)

These children are further defined by the hour in which the Horse was born. In this example, the Horse was born in the Hour of the Rooster, hence the children pick up the elements of the Ox: because of the fear (Rooster) over intimacy and connecting with another individual (Dog), these children are angry because they were deprived of experiences that would have allowed more freedom of expression and interaction with a mate (Ox).

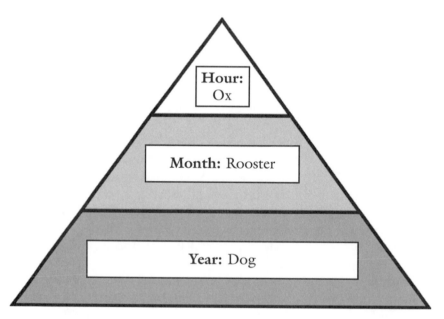

Figure 17. The Horse's children, first child in particular.

Part IV

Celebrities as Contemporary Gods and Goddesses

Celebrity Archetypes

When the O.J. Simpson debacle occurred, pundits were quick to point out that we should be careful of the heroes we make. Too often, they pontificated, we glorify those who eventually show their imperfections to the entire world.

What they didn't take into consideration was that, in this day and age, we don't have gods and goddesses as the Greeks and Romans did. Our celebrities are our archetypes, and they simply reflect the society in which we live. If we were heroes, our celebrities would be heroes. Since they display their vulnerabilities and frailties on a grand scale, we are able to see what is wrong with our value system and life in general. We choose these very heroes with feet of clay in order to project onto them what we won't look at in ourselves.

The relationships of our celebrities—whether it be on the political scene, in the entertainment field, or in sports—can give us graphic descriptions of how this energy works in our lives and make it become more real for us.

Here we will look at the lives of Bill and Hillary Clinton, Prince Charles and Princess Diana, O.J. and Nicole, and Richard and Pat Nixon. In these four instances, the man is the dominant figure in public life, and so we will look at the public stance of these couples from his chart. In the case of a couple such as Elizabeth Taylor and Larry Fortensky, we would look at Liz's placements to see how they are mirrored as archetypes.

Bill and Hillary Clinton

Bill Clinton is reported to have been born on August 19, 1946, at 8:51 A.M., CST, in Hope, Arkansas. He was born in the Year of the Dog, the Month of the Dragon, the Hour of the Dragon, and the Minute of the Tiger.

Born in the Year of the Dog, Clinton has a reserve, even shyness, that he has had to move beyond in being president. The Dog has to develop an intimacy with his audience in order to be able to get up and speak effectively—something he has had to do over the years and that probably was not easy for him. Intimacy can very well be an issue, as Dogs who have not connected sex with love can develop the problems he is perceived to have as a womanizer.

Leo equates to the Dragon, and Clinton was also born in the Hour of the Dragon, indicating that he has large appetites and high expectations that obviously got him all the way to the White House. He dreams in a grand style and sometimes reality doesn't match his vision. Obviously, Bill Clinton's concept of the White House experience has been attacked by the reality of the situation. The fact that he is a double Dragon should help him to rise above the posturing of his opposition. The Leo/Dragon energy is open, gregarious, warm, and oppulent, but the Dragon also has its own demons. This is a person who can be addicted to food, sex, or power. This doesn't mean it's bad, but when other needs aren't met, he can look to overcompensate with compulsions when his life is not working—displaying a kind of "I'll show you" attitude.

Born in the Minute of the Tiger, Clinton won't be ignored. Do anything you will, but ignore him you won't. The Tiger relates to the lungs, and this expresses in his oratory ability and the power of his stamina to prevail. He has a large nose, which is an indicator of the Lung meridian, which the Tiger rules.

The animals/meridians at the base, or foundation, of his chart are the Monkey and the Rooster. The 4th house of family ruled by the Monkey shows his mother was obviously a very strong woman, who chose to control her reality and set that belief in Bill. She modeled, by word or deed, that to be a woman was to be in control and, certainly, when he took a wife, he chose someone who was as strong or stronger, than Mom. However, it was probably Mom's concept of reality that kept the family together. She would not have wanted to hear anything that was not what she constructed. And yet, because the Rooster's energy is part of his foundation, too, there are nagging fears instilled early with which he always has to battle.

We don't know very much about Bill's father, but from Clinton's perspective (chart), his dad reflects the energy of the Ox. He may have felt he was on a road to nowhere, plodding through each and every day. Since his father died before he was born, Bill had no role model. He has had to carve that identity for himself. He had no one to emulate. In order to reach the heights of your career, you need to look at what Dad did right and copy that, and do the opposite of what he did wrong. Bill Clinton took the qualities of the Ox, hard work, patience, creativity, and mental dexterity, to reach his full potential. As reflective of his career, the Ox energy can continue to plow straight ahead, or it can choose to move out of that rut and create something entirely different and creative with a vision of the future. It also indicates that in his career, he can be stifled and repressed and not allowed to do what he set out to do.

Hillary Clinton is represented in Bill's chart by the Dog as well as the Boar being in his 7th house of mate. As we have learned, the Dog is fiercely territorial and will defend what it has laid claim to. Hillary, in fact, was born at the Hour of the Dog, and she reflects the cool, reserved, even shy, elements of the animal. Hillary is a Scorpio and Scorpios have found their sex drive was blunted during the 1990s, so her energies were seemingly put into the power of the presidency and the legacy they would leave behind.

Yet, hidden, there are also elements of the Boar in her relationship with Bill. The Boar can get mired in the bog and do self-destructive things when she feels life isn't going her way. She needs to stay in complete optimism and hope to move beyond her critics. Certainly, as the Clinton presidency progressed, she had plenty of opportunity to feel the hopelessness of the Boar's personality and the need to know there is always a light at the end of the tunnel.

O.J. and Nicole Simpson

Interestingly, O.J. Simpson has a similar animal configuration to Bill Clinton. O.J. is reported to have been born on July 9, 1947, at 8:08 A.M. PST in San Francisco, California. He is a Boar, born in the Month of the Cat, the Hour of the Dragon, and the Minute of the Boar.

Born in the Year of the Boar, he also has the Boar as the power animal for his minute of birth: his Achilles' heel. The Boar, remember, in its animal state, has a natural bent to suicide—or, more specifically, a self-destructive bent gauged by the function or dysfunction of childhood. When the media interviews the populace and they wonder aloud why someone with his position and money would allegedly do something so heinous, we only have to look at the Boar to realize the potential involved.

Born in the month of Cancer, the Cat is a nocturnal animal that likes to prowl unobtrusively in the dark. His quest is for self-love, and, when it is lacking, he will seek to project it onto other people, ever searching for that elusive perfect relationship. The degree to which he was criticized as a child reflects on his sense of self, and he can become obsessed with cleanliness.

He and Bill Clinton were born during the Stomach meridian hours. O.J., too, has a larger-than-life appetite for the good things. He seeks fulfillment and the trappings that it provides. He can also have compulsions, addictions, and be prone to excesses.

O.J. has the Monkey/Bladder energy at the base of his chart, too. Again, this suggests Mother was a controlling figure. One can find that comforting to a degree, or chafe at the inflexibility. Monkey/Mom can also be in denial, and construct a world that meets her needs, and mustn't be challenged.

We have a father who seems to be absent or not a primary figure in the man's life—again, liver energy. There can be anger over the lack of a father figure in his life to establish a role model to aim for in his life. Here we have the same decision—to play it safe and go the father's way, or turn it around and make it totally opposite. O.J. had to carve his career for himself, creating a new path where no pattern had been established.

Female relationships are found in the Boar/Triple Warmer energy in O.J.'s chart. It would say that, either he's self-destructive over marriage, or that his wives can have elements of self-destructiveness. Nicole was actually born in the Year of the Boar; so she reflects this energy specifically, even though she was the second wife. Certainly, she was depicted as feeling hopeless in the situation.

In 1994, Pluto, the planet of subjective power, moved into O.J.'s 4th house of home/mother/foundation and the Bladder meridian. It made that energy more volatile and combustible. When a person is born with Pluto in the Bladder meridian, it intensifies the need for control. These people can really be what we term "control freaks." When Pluto moves into the Bladder area by transit, it strengthens and intensifies the need for control. There's an element of payback in the Bladder emotions, needing to be in control or get even. If we go back to the three forms of denial, on a subconscious level, O.J. was willing to deny himself the life that he lived, in order not to deny himself being in control of Nicole's life, rather than leaving it up to God/universe.

While sometimes our mates don't actually have the animal of the mate position as primary in their charts, but reflect it from elsewhere, actually Nicole was born on May 19, 1959, at 4:44 P.M. CET in Frankfurt, Germany, in the Year of the Boar. She was born in the Month of the Ox, late in the Hour of the Monkey (making the Rooster the primary animal), and the Minute of the Horse. Being born at the time of the Monkey, she was a strong personality as well, creating her own life. Yet, with the Rooster there in the 1st house of self as well, there was a lot of fear of being victimized.

Two beautiful people, having it all, slowly self-destructed together.

Prince Charles
and Diana

We have seen in the fairy tale on page xiii that the animals of our celebrities speak eloquently of their personalities.

Prince Charles of Britain was born on November 14, 1948, at 9:14 P.M. GMT in London, England. He was born in the Year of the Rat, the Month of the Sheep, the Hour of the Boar, and the Minute of the Rat.

Rats are altruistic people who deal with abandonment and betrayal in their lives. Remember, the Rat can be very subjective and "lose it" when his will isn't obeyed. This is Charles' base for the year he was born, and it's also his Achilles' heel: that which he needs to heal in this lifetime.

Charles was born in the Hour of the Boar, which reflects in his dour visage to the public. Moving rather slowly, not one to show emotion, much less affection, the Boar is implacable and not easily moved. Having reached middle age and not being allowed to be king, he might be seeing a gloomy future. Again, we have a Boar with self-destructive tendencies. It's becoming clear why these people self-destruct in public. The Boar seems to be prominently placed in their charts. Should a person born in the Year, Month, Hour, or Minute of the Boar give in to these sabotaging tendencies? Of course not. The celebrities are living out these traits on a large scale, so Boar people of any persuasion can see what happens when one is drawn into this negative path instead of taking the high road. The Boar who sees the positive, who is full of hope, can take their energy to the heights, and transform into a beautiful, graceful swan.

The traditional mate for the Boar is the Snake, but, because London is quite a distance from the equator, the distortion brings Charles a Horse, with elements of the Sheep, as his mate. Interestingly, the Snake falls into the area of "love affairs," so that Camilla, as his potential true mate, from the standard perspective, becomes his lover instead, and may never be able to be much more than that.

In the area of career, we find the Monkey/Bladder: control, denial, and duty above all. This is reflected in the energy of Prince Philip as the expression of the career house, as well as Queen Elizabeth, because the Moon is posited therein, showing that good ol' Mom is the power house here. Duty, duty, duty; "stiff upper lip." The Monkey/Bladder is the seat of the emotions, something that is hard to access or tolerate. It must be denied in the face of duty. But what did that do for the beautiful princess and her beloved sons?

Certainly, one could sense in Diana the spiritedness of the Horse, looking for love, seeking to belong. Yet there is an element of the Sheep there, too. Diana certainly exemplified the energy of seemingly being victimized by an unrelenting press and overbearing family, and yet she was shrewd enough that, being taught "the system" while she lived there, she used it to her own ends when she went public, and assumed her short-term victory on pretty much her own terms.

Diana was born on July 1, 1961, at 7:45 P.M. GMD, in Sandringham, England. While assuming the energy of the Horse/Sheep for Charles and England, in actuality, she was born in the Year of the Ox, the Month of the Cat, the Hour of the Dog, and the Minute of the Tiger.

Diana exemplified even more of the quiet, shy reserve of the Dog as the power animal of the hour in which she was born. She needed a certain fence around her that no one could enter unless invited; and anyone was certainly barred at the gate if they came in too loudly, too fast, or lacking refinement.

She was born in the Minute of the Tiger, so, much like Pat Nixon, she had dreams that were undoubtedly crushed when marrying the future King of England and becoming Princess did not turn out to be the fairy-tale life she might have dreamed it would be. The Tiger, remember, hates being ignored, and, in her own way, she made her wishes known and made sure that she got out of the marriage what she needed.

But Diana, as Princess of Wales, was Charles' "Horse." She was hard to tame and chafed at the reins. After the accident that took her life, they battled to save her heart and keep oxygen going to her brain . . . both Heart-meridian ruled. The rose is a transformative symbol for the Horse, and her funeral procession was filled with roses. Elton John changed his song to "England's Rose."

In his eulogy, her brother, Charles, mentioned that being named after the goddess Diana, she was the most hunted woman in the world. And we are also advised that Tigers in this world are being hunted and killed at an alarming rate. The late Unity minister, Rev. Carol Ruth Knox, stated that we go from victim to victor to vehicle. Diana's life certainly exemplified this axiom.

Richard and Pat Nixon

Former President Richard Nixon was reported to be born on January 9, 1913, at 9:35 P.M. in Whittier, California. He was born in the Year of the Ox, the Month of the Rooster, the Hour of the Boar, and the Minute of the Tiger.

The Ox and the Boar together give one a very heavy energy. The Ox is a large, heavy animal, and so is the Boar. If the Ox has a yoke around its neck and is plowing the field, and the Boar is mired down in the bog . . . that's pessimism. It is certainly a combination where, if one wasn't born surrounded by optimism, a one-note outlook could result.

On top of that, Nixon was born in the Month of the Rooster . . . fear. Here we have someone who was probably held back in some way as a child, not allowed to do what other kids did, had a fearful, conservative bent, being a Capricorn, and then had to fight his demons of self-destruction. When he said, after he lost the California gubanatorial election, "You won't have Dick Nixon to kick around anymore," that was certainly a Boar-pessimistic evaluation. Yet, he came back to fight another day. When the Boar moves through his doubt into a state of certainty, he reaches a state of hope that can't be assailed.

Nixon's Achilles' heel lies with the Tiger energy. He had a strong desire to be recognized, and feared being ignored. That drive for recognition undoubtedly pushed him past much of the pedantic energy of the other animals in his chart. He was annoyed because Henry Kissinger got a lot of the credit in his presidency. In fact, with Clinton and Nixon having the Tiger as their Achilles' heel, one wonders if that's a prerequisite for the presidency: a desire to be recognized at the highest level.

Nixon had the Cat (Large Intestine) energy at the base of his chart. In his strict Quaker upbringing, he may not have had much reinforcement of his value and worth in the family structure. Here, his foundation is based on sacrifice and not thinking of one's self, or getting what he truly needed, always putting the needs of others ahead of his own.

His father energy was represented by the Monkey, undoubtedly a no-nonsense controlling figure who had tight control of his family. On top of that, Pluto is in this Monkey/Bladder area of his chart in the 10th house of father and career. It has been written that Watergate (which occurred at his Pluto square for those knowledgeable in astrology) was handled much in the way he had survived his father, by passive-aggressive stonewalling. That is certainly a Bladder proclivity, made even worse with Pluto there to add domination and power. When Watergate happened, Pluto had moved to his 1st house and the Boar/Triple Warmer energy, so that he self-destructed through his use of the control he was used to exerting. Pluto always breaks down in order to create something new. If the Republican contingent had allowed the universe to play out the election without allegedly trying to throw a monkey wrench into it, history might have had a different story to tell.

Pat Nixon is represented by the Snake in Nixon's chart. The Snake wants to be perfect and be the proper wife for a president. She can choose to marry someone who will be faithful to her, with whom she won't have to worry about any rejection issues, and yet could have found that playing it safe had it's own problems. In her own chart, she was born in the Hour of the Tiger, which is Nixon's Achilles' heel. It would seem that Nixon's ambition to be president eclipsed her own dreams, and she settled for putting on "a face" to the public to get through it, being erroneously called "Plastic Pat" because of it. (Note: she's a Pisces, which is ruled by Neptune, which governs oil, which makes plastic). Mrs. Nixon reportedly died of lung cancer (the meridian of the Tiger).

The United States of America

If we can relate the power animals to people, can we do so with governments? . . . with our own U. S. of A? Of course we can!

There are a number of "birth" times attributed to the United States, but using 2:17 A.M., which is frequently shown as the official time, it dovetails quite well with the power animals attributed to its signs.

The United States was born in the Year of the Monkey, the Month of the Cat (Rabbit), the Hour of the Ox, and the Minute of the Monkey.

The Monkey, you'll recall, has problems with "live and let live." The Monkey needs to throw a monkey wrench into the natural order of things and control it's actions and the actions of others. Certainly, the United States, throughout history, has seen fit to move in and affect the destiny of other countries and inflict our standards on to them, right or wrong.

The Monkey tends to have a dogma by which it lives and doesn't stray too far away from it. It needs to be in control and doesn't like to be denied anything. And yet, it will deny itself something it wants to secure a greater subconscious goal. The Monkey believes in duty, and will deny himself his own personal needs to live up to it.

Born in the Month of the Cat (Rabbit—see explanation on page 265), we are homebodies, who can travel around the world, but always find that the best place is home in the good ol' U. S. of A. We have magazines that are always talking about self-worth and self-esteem, and encouraging us to be more assertive. We are bombarded with ads about cleanliness and cleaning agents that other countries look at curiously—all qualities of the Cat and the Large Intestine meridian. Living in the land of opulence and abundance, we still are stricken with conscience, wondering if we deserve it.

Born in the Hour of the Ox, we are a country of violence. Uranus, the planet of rebellion, is right at the hour in which we were born. We feel stifled and repressed and want to lash out and be autonomous and free, sometimes at any cost. The instability of Uranus causes irritation in the liver consciousness, and continually keeps our autonomous nervous system on edge. Any attempts at curtailing our freedom causes us to lash out, angry at the thought of being held back from attaining our inalienable rights.

The violence in our country is partly because the country was born at Liver time, and partly because Uranus is there to keep it unstable and volatile. With the Ox/Liver at the hour of our birth, we tend to be an angry culture, resenting the lack of progress we have made toward attaining our goals. We stated we had an inalienable right to the pursuit of happiness (and happiness is a Liver emotion). Maybe we shouldn't have made it a futuristic concept, but said "attainment" of happiness. The subconscious takes things very literally, so that we have created an inalienable right to "pursue," but not necessarily attain, and yet we feel curtailed when we don't reach that level of attainment.

The United States was born in the Minute of the Monkey, as well as the year. A double Monkey is going to have lessons around letting go and letting God/universe do its perfect work, rather than trying to be the policeman of the world.

As an added note, the planet Pluto, which signifies transformation, evolution, and soul growth in a chart, was in the Circulation-Sex area of the national chart at birth, or the meridian of the Dog.

Dog people, as we have seen, can have problems with intimacy and sexuality. In its negative, they see sex as dirty and something to be avoided. This is our stigma in this culture, and other countries around the world wonder why we are so puritanical and uptight over sexuality. With Pluto in Circ-Sex, as a nation, we need to move beyond viewing sex as a purely physical act and alchemize it with love. Until we do, we will continue to polarize between fantasizing over romance novels, while pornography proliferates. At the same time, we continually titillate the public with an advertising media that uses sex to sell everything.

Bill Clinton, our 42nd president, shows up in the Circ-Sex, or Dog, area of the national chart. We could say that his comportment is a mirror of our own repressed sexual issues. The media event might have happened to show us, pro and con, where we stand, and hopefully move us to a more healthy psychology about sex. It was heartening to me to see that the populace has finally grown up and can take a rational position. Maybe we're finally reaching a maturity about sexuality, and are now truly alchemizing sex with love.

Our politicians, celebrities, and sports figures are archetypes of our population. If they have sexual issues, it's because we have sexual issues. They are playing out on a large stage what we play out in our daily lives. If we want the people who run our nation to be circumspect, then we have to create that energy for them to mirror. We will probably look back on the end of the 1990s as the unlocking of sexual repression in this country and the beginning of a more healthy approach to sex and love. It's time this country recognized that there are the three Ps: "Politics, Power, Penis"* and that they are all part and parcel of one another. The most powerful man in the world must have a healthy libido or risk being emasculated in his duties (the Ox is an emasculated Bull, after all). If we are sexually healthy as a nation, then our president will be able to have a healthy sexuality as well.

It has long been privately accepted that a politician quite often marries the "proper" woman to present to the world and has his private passions. There is a big difference between sexual harassment and consensual liaisons. It is hoped we are moving to a more European view of sexuality.

---

*Phrase coined by author.

Part V

Chinese Power Animals and Health

Chinese Power Animals and Illness

As we've discovered, the time you were born is very crucial in working with the power animals and their meridians. Your body will be inclined to take its experiences—positive and negative—into the organ or process that was in residence at the time you were born. It is known that, by simply smiling, you are aiding your liver, while frowning stresses it. That's one reason why you should keep a smile on your face! But, there are also other sensitive areas set into motion at the time of birth.

Figure 15 (see page 142) also reflects the meridians that are primary in an individual's life process. While the power animal and its meridian at the time of birth is the organ in focus, the animal/meridian at the base of the circle is not only mother, but your foundation—the belief structure from which you function. This animal/meridian/organ is also a powerful archetype in your being. It reflects your root philosophy. These two should always be taken into consideration as the two primary animals to work with to keep in balance and health.

In tandem with these two are the animals/meridians on the other two angles: the 7th and the 10th—the areas of mate (shadow) and father (career). While you take the brunt of your experiences in the meridian/organ in residence at the time you were born, your primary relationships (mother, dad, mate), and the areas they cover (home, relationship, career) create the four major areas where stress and illness are more likely to occur in your life—the emotions and organs you need to keep positive, where you get your predispositions, the illness these people are likely to exhibit, and/or the dis-ease in your body you generate contending with them.

As always, we are talking about the extremes of the polarities: what can happen if we stay in the negative, and what we need to do to move into the positive and create health. Some people do live in the extremes, but most of us dip back and forth into each polarity to varying degrees according to the function or dysfunction of our families of origin. You will know as you read the following pages where you stand in relation to them. (You can also use these pages for the year, month, and minute you were born, but it is most specific to the hour.)

The Rat
Gallbladder Meridian

> • **Gallbladder** • **Large Intestine** •
> • **Heart** • **Kidney** •

Born between 11 P.M. and 1 A.M., as a Rat person, you wear your heart on your sleeve. You are instinctual and often motivate from your reptilian brain, the core of the brain that deals with survival instincts. The Rat is emotionally on the edge most of the time. You have fierce passions and get emotionally aroused easily. You will never be accused of being too detached or remote. The Rat jumps in head-first and is very subjective about life and how it is lived.

Because of this, you get angry—angry at the injustices of the world, angry at your own injustices in life, angry just to be angry sometimes. Where the Ox/Liver gets angry, the Rat acts on it, or more precisely, reacts on it. You can fly off the handle, "lose it," and will provoke altercations. You view remarks as personal affronts that need to be handled . . . now!

You see, the Rat has issues with abandonment and betrayal, and you can lash out whenever you feel you're going to be hung out to dry again. Being reactionary, you can be inflamed by other people to hop on a bandwagon or other just or unjust causes. Because of this, you can have migraines, sciatic nerve pain, and gallstones, as well as digestive issues around the gallbladder's ability to process and break down fats.

In his fury, the Rat can have constipation or diarrhea issues, holding on or letting go. You have a lot of self-worth issues that continually plague you that can be at the core of your insecurity. When abandonment or betrayal occurs, there can be a bottom line subconscious "agreement" that you really aren't worthy. Colitis and other intestinal problems can show up when your foundation is tested. You can be ridden with guilt, wondering if you precipitated the betrayal in any way. Sometimes you feel unclean, and develop neuroses around cleanliness as a way to justify the betrayal; you just weren't good enough.

The Rat can almost literally have its heart broken in relationships. You want to love, to belong. You want to merge with another individual . . . and yet that abandonment issue is always there. Can you trust again? Can you put your heart on your sleeve and love again? Can you believe in a love that will be constant and true? The Rat can have palpitations and heart issues over relationships.

Why does a person get angry? Because they're fearful. As a Rat person, you have fears on the job of whether you're good enough, whether you're ambitious enough, whether you can make it or not—fear of what happens when you're out in the cold, cruel world. So the Rat puts on a brash facade, appearing tough enough to handle what this harsh ol' world has to dish out. Sometimes, the Rat will not take risks and play it safe and choose a job that has security and longevity instead of getting what might be the perfect job. Inside, that makes you angry that you won't take risks because of the fear and the abandonment issues.

 **In a nutshell:** To be a healthy Rat, you need to feel adored, i.e., loved by a God/universe that supports you in accomplishing whatever it's in your heart to do. With the aid of gallbladder-calming herbs such as milk thistle and bupleurum, you can shift into a much smoother mind-set where every action is not a need for reaction on your part. By working on your self-worth and seeing the sacred person that you are, opening your heart to others, and not being afraid of getting it hurt, you can move out of fear and into a peaceful place where you can allow the world to play out in front of you and not feel it is attacking you.

The Ox
Liver Meridian

> • Liver • Stomach •
> • Small Intestine • Circulation-Sex •

Born between 1 A.M. and 3 A.M., as an Ox you are angry a lot of the time. You really resent the yoke around your neck and being set to the plow, walking up and down those rows (ruts) . . . back and forth, back and forth. Sure, because of the Ox, seeds are being planted and new growth happens, but do you get to enjoy it? Not really. You just go over to another row and start plowing, up and down, back and forth . . . and, in the process, you get angry—angry at being stifled, angry at having to do this same monotonous thing every day, year in and year out. As an Ox, you were born with so much creativity and potential, and here you are, plowing up and down the rows, in the rut of life. Why won't your "farmer" let you free to go out into the meadow and enjoy life, much like Ferdinand the Bull? Now there was an animal who knew what was important in life! . . . to sit in the meadow with the flowers and see the blue sky and envision what life could be.

The Ox needs to be free and independent, and when you are held back and not able to live up to your potential, you can develop liver problems. One of them may come from drinking, because you may be trapped in a go-nowhere job, which leads to cirrhosis of the liver. The Liver meridian also has a connection to the autonomic nervous system, so a frustrated Ox can have refined motor problems and not have the patience to do nitty-gritty detail work when frustrated. You can have vision problems because you may, symbolically have "blinders" on. Because the Ox feels stifled, there's an immaturity about you simply because you haven't had a lot of life experiences. Your early childhood could well have been sheltered, and you longed to do what the others kids were doing.

There's sugar in alcohol, and sugar is numbing. You began life with visions and dreams of what life held in store, and if those dreams weren't realized, you can fall prey to addictions and compulsions in order to compensate for an unexpressed life. When life doesn't live up to those expectations, disappointment can set in. Disappointment can lead to eating more and more . . . and then the vicious cycle begins. The more weight the Ox puts on, the less desirable you feel, the more you stay home and don't experience the glory life has to offer, the more stagnant you feel . . . and the cycle keeps repeating itself. Stomach problems can ensue as well as allergies that can "protect" the Ox from the outside world.

At this point, you can feel victimized by life. The Ox can draw in victims who will mirror this shadow element, who will only reinforce these feelings . . . or you can, in the extreme, become a perpetrator, feeling justified in getting even for past treatment. Sometimes the "poor me" persona emerges, finding "perks" in this victim role, and yet it can take over at some point where you can seemingly be unable to get out of that rut and turn life around. Intestinal problems can occur.

Withdrawing can then become a way of life. Retreating from society, falling into the trap again. Justifying this stance by embracing highly moralistic judgments about more moderate, open types in order to feel comfortable. Prostate problems can occur in men, and frigidity in women. Hands and feet can feel cold. Problems with circulation can be experienced.

In a nutshell: To be a healthy Ox, you need to throw over the traces, unlock the yoke, and get out there and experience life! Sure it's going to be scary. Take it one step at a time, but life is to be lived, not endured. As an Ox, you need to know that you are a spirit evolving, glory in all that life has to offer, and not get caught up in the role of victim. You need to find fulfillment in living out the dreams you dared to dream as a child. The Ox needs to be responsible and see what a vicious cycle is operating. See how you created it, don't blame the outside world for what has happened. Take responsibility, and pick yourself up by the bootstraps and turn life around. Then the Ox will feel free to connect with others, to warm up to a more friendly world, and, by interacting and networking, reconnect with those dreams that were thought long-forgotten and unattainable.

The Tiger
Lung Meridian

> • Lungs • Spleen/Pancreas • Bladder •
> • Thyroid/Metabolism •

Born between 3 A.M. and 5 A.M., the Tiger is mainly concerned with lung issues. Asthma, bronchitis—simply having sufficient lung power to breathe can sometimes be a problem. The Tiger has the tendency to be depressed. A quick remedy for that is deep breathing. The more depressed we get, the more we have a tendency to breathe shallowly. By practicing deep breathing and expanding the breath, you get more oxygen circulating and, among other things, your depression can lift.

Because you were born in Tiger time, you also have sensitivities with the Spleen/Pancreas, the Bladder and the Triple Warmer (which governs thyroid, weight, and metabolism, among other things), as well as the lungs.

Because the Lung and Triple Warmer each have issues with depression, being born in these two time periods (3 A.M.–5 A.M. and 9 P.M.–11 P.M.) can give Tigers and Boars more problems than others fighting mood changes.

As a Tiger, you deal with pride and life-and-death issues, and become depressed because you fear rejection. Even though you have the pride of the Tiger, inside you may suffer from feelings of insignificance. You mope around because you fear rejection, and can jeopardize relationships precipitously, creating scenarios around perhaps innocent interaction that you perceive as rejection. There is the possibility that you never bonded with your mother as a child, and the rejection complex stems from that connection never being truly made. Blood problems can occur, and sometimes you can literally "reject" yourself. There can be elements of self-hate, as if somehow it's all your fault. As a Tiger, when you feel rejected, you can head for the cookie jar to make you feel better.

So, what do you do when you fear rejection? Your pride can get the best of you and you can decide to control the issue. Better not put yourself out there again. It's better to put on a few extra pounds (or more than a few) or shy away from people so you put yourself in a position where you aren't rejected by anyone . . . except maybe yourself.

Pride is a tricky emotion. We need it to develop self-esteem and have confidence and self-worth, and yet, as the old saying goes, "pride goeth before the fall." Sensitivity and pride can lead you to create a world for yourself that is safe . . . safe from rejection, safe from sadness and grief, safe from everything, unfortunately. Because in insulating yourself from the bad, you frequently block out the good as well. Then you can have bladder-control problems, or bladder infections.

And when you get stuck in this world, then what happens? You feel despair and "what's the use?" because you can't move beyond it. Down deep inside you realize that by keeping the bad out you are also keeping the good out, and you get depressed. The world turns gray and you feel bogged down. Your metabolism gets sluggish as you slog through the mud. You may have thyroid problems.

In a nutshell: To be a healthy Tiger, you need to be surrounded by people who recognize your talents and worth and who encourage you to go higher and higher. You need to be appreciated and to develop a healthy ego that prides itself on accomplishments so you can have justifiable pride in what you do. You need to bond with a healthy female figure (man or woman Tiger) who can be a surrogate mother and let any feelings over bonding issues go. You need to know it wasn't a personal thing and release feelings of not being good enough. You need to stop and "take a beat" and let people reveal themselves to you, so you can make accurate decisions on who is good in your life and who isn't. You need to love yourself. You need to let life play itself out and not throw a monkey wrench into the fray, and experience what happens when you don't. As a Tiger, you need to walk and exercise and take action to get out of the doldrums and give life meaning again.

The Cat
Large Intestine Meridian

> • Large Intestine • Heart • Kidneys •
> • Gallbladder •

Born between 5 A.M. and 7 A.M., the Cat has issues about self-esteem and guilt. You need to love yourself in order to have the relationships you desire. If you have a lack of self-esteem, to whatever degree, you can move into relationships that are not good for you. You generally seek partners who are beneath you so you can feel superior . . . or, at the very least, stay at the level of your self-esteem.

For the Cat, the hamstrings can be a problem, as well as the sacrum. The sacrum relates to sacrifice, and the Cat will often find himself sacrificing for the sake of others, putting himself last. Sometimes the Cat can put on a false front and be that supercilious, superior Cat who pretends he doesn't care, preening and strutting around, oblivious to everyone else. It's just a protection, of course, for his sensitive feelings.

As a Cat child, you could have taken on the responsibility for the family and felt that everything you did was wrong and felt guilty that you couldn't be better so that the family could be happy. You are a child who can feel responsible when parents divorce.

When the Cat takes everything into the intestines, you can have low-back problems associated with the sacrum, as well as colitis, etc. When there is a sudden attack of diarrhea or constipation, there are self-esteem issues at hand.

The Cat has self-worth issues because the family home may not have been warm and cozy. There may have been distance from family members, particularly Mother. The Cat longs to be held, to be loved, to be touched, to be part of a whole instead of feeling isolated. Because the Cat is self-effacing, he can give too much of himself, and may reach a time when he shuts his heart down, because this hasn't been reciprocated, and he just can't do it anymore. The Cat's life is based upon a need to find a sense of reality and belonging. Any heart ailments, a weak voice, blood-pressure problems, etc., stem from dealing with your home environment. As a Cat, you may have reached out for love and found it wanting, so you created an air of detachment, much as cats do, about being touched again.

The Cat can be reticent and timid because of fear . . . fear of loss of love, fear of not being good enough, fear of life, fear of sex. As a Cat, when your fear takes over, you can feel paralyzed and impotent. This can cause fatigue, malaise, and a general loss of chi (life energy). The kidneys and adrenals can act up, and you can have low-back pain.

If alienated as a child, the Cat gets angry over past transgressions and can lash out at the family, hissing and scratching because of the lack of love and attention. You have little tolerance of your father, and react in kind on the job, suspecting betrayal at every turn.

 **In a nutshell:** To be a healthy Cat you need to be around people who see you as "sacred space," as a person who is very special. Belonging is the Cat's desire and you need to find a home where you feel you fit in. As a Cat you need to tap into your sexuality and become secure in who you are and draw in someone who is going to make you feel safe. Anger can be a good thing when it's used constructively. It's a healthy anger that can turn things around when you decide you don't want to live in a state of malaise anymore and take action to make your life meaningful.

The Dragon
Stomach Meridian

> • **Stomach** • **Small Intestine** •
> • **Circulation-Sex** • **Liver** •

Born between 7 A.M. and 9 A.M., the Dragon deals with a stomach that can cause you to breathe fire when you take your experiences into that area of your body. Your expectations are high and often life doesn't measure up. Changes in your lifestyle can cause the stomach to churn. As a Dragon, you create an identity for yourself and define yourself by who you are—provider, mate, lover, parent, etc. When life spins the wheel and a new phase commences, and you must leave an identity behind, as a Dragon, you don't do well. You can develop stomach ulcers, anxiety attacks, and/or butterflies when you embark on a new phase of life.

The Dragon has so many identities that you try hard to fulfill. Somewhere, you lost the identity of who you truly are . . . and that's who you're searching for; not the person who has tried to live up to everybody's expectations, but the person you are inside.

As a Dragon, when you are stressed because the world is whirling too fast and life is not living up to your expectations, you can escape by overindulging in food, sex, gambling, or other compulsions and addictions. Stomach ulcers can result or you can find yourself vomiting because you "can't stomach it" anymore. You can get disgusted and have resentments that make your stomach turn.

The stomach is the seat of nourishment . . . the rest of the body depends on it for life. The right food needs to be eaten in order for the body to be properly nourished.

The Dragon needs to be valued and, when you aren't, you can feel victimized. That stomach needs to have food coming at regular intervals and, when it doesn't, the Dragon can take a "poor me" stance and complain that life leaves you with less. The Dragon is the epitome of "more," and less feels bad. It's as if you feel you should be special and should be above the mundane, that life should treat you better, but when the prince becomes the pauper, you're left with feelings of "why me?" Then you can mope around like a sad dragon, berating a world that would do this to you.

When this happens, you become haughty and withdrawn, put yourself above the fray, becoming isolated, perhaps, finding it hard to sleep and finding you have emotional problems dealing with others. You're protecting your heart, you see, from once again another seeming degradation. Ailments like arteriosclerosis, headaches, and skin problems can occur.

Then the Dragon gets angry. The frustration at falling from your pedestal can cause you to take it out on the people at work. You were worthy of that promotion, weren't you? Sure you were. Why aren't you in that role of supervisor or manager . . . or CEO? That frustration can lead the Dragon person to hit the bottle, or otherwise commiserate with others over his fate. When his vision is blocked, the Dragon can lose the mythical wonder and magic that keeps it alive.

In a nutshell: To be a healthy Dragon, you need to be valued for who you are and what you do. But more importantly, you need to see that you aren't what you do. You need to be responsible for your actions and find win-win situations in your daily affairs. You need to be a discriminating person who chooses your associates wisely: people who are healthy, mentally and emotionally, and who provide wise counsel. You need to ignite the fire inside into love and find glory in sexual experiences, drawing in someone who is equally passionate. You need to open up and connect with others and be more egalitarian. It doesn't hurt to take your crown off and be one of the guys periodically. Then you can follow your ideals, and be the person you always dreamed you'd be, living the life worth living and being the mythical, magical animal you are.

The Snake
Spleen Meridian

• Spleen • Bladder •
• Weight-Metabolism • Lung •

Born between 9 A.M. and 11 A.M., as a Snake your are concerned with perfection and you worry a lot. You can assuage your feelings with sugar when you feel attacked. You need to feel that you have the approval of the group wherever you go. Too often, like the real Snake, you feel rejection, even if it isn't there. The Snake has problems with bonding and can slither away if it feels rejected. To the extent that you didn't feel loved as a child, you will turn to the sugar bowl for comfort. The perfectionist in you needs to be right, and you can cross your arms in front of you and not pay attention to any counterthought.

The Snake is rooted in denial. You have certain things that you want and you can sacrifice other things to get them. You can mope and pout and bemoan your fate, that you aren't getting this or that, but in reality your subconscious is happy just the way it is. Being perfect is sometimes more important, and creating the perfect world can be really exhausting over time. It is the Snake personality who will decide when the relationship starts, when it ends, and how long it will endure. You may complain because you don't have many relationships in your life, but one day you'll realize you're perfectly happy with this on a subconscious level. Too many people create a chaos they can't control and it's hard to keep all those plates twirling at one time, like a circus act. You can become a worrywart and be stressed out a lot of the time, trying to keep your world from falling apart. You can be the true codependent (along with the Sheep), trying to maintain that perfect facade, while your world is falling apart on the inside. Diabetes is a possibility, as well as vomiting and muscle spasms being experienced, and hemorrhoids.

As a Snake you need to look hard in the mirror and recognize that the person you've drawn in represents your deepest fears. Your mate may be self-destructive and be mired down in a sense of hopelessness. The spouse (or even a roommate) may be eating themselves into destruction or be addicted to drinking, drugs, or other forms of spiraling despair. If so, this can bring the Snake down even further, because, to you, it's another form of rejection. Why aren't you perfect enough to make this person happy? In your zeal for perfection, you can slip into a space of imperfection to justify what you don't have in life. That, too, is a variation of control. In your despair, you can become depressed and feel it's all hopeless; how can you keep your world together when these people won't do what you tell them to? Thyroid issues, embarrassment, and problems with the endocrine system can result.

Life would be so great if people recognized the great person that you are, and appreciated all you do. To get the accolades that you richly deserve would be the crowning achievement. But you can be afraid of success at the same time. You'd rather toil behind the scenes than be singled out. With this confliction, you get down and depressed, and mourn the life you aren't living. Your depression mounts as your stress increases. In all the scenarios, you need to gauge where you fall in the spectrum between healthy and unhealthy.

In a nutshell: To be a healthy Snake, you need to be open to bond with another and not sense rejection at every turn. You need to hang tight and let the universe provide the most perfect turn of events and not control the situation by manipulating it. As a Snake, you need to have faith in a perfect universe that knows what is right for you and is on your side, and allow life to present the perfect solution to any problem. You need to exercise and get out of your own way, in effect. Keep your spirits optimistic and see the bright side of life to make the right choices. You need to appreciate the limelight and not shrink from it. You need to stand in the spotlight and realize the heat will not burn, but will enhance your life.

The Horse
Heart Meridian

> • Heart • Kidney •
> • Gallbladder • Large Intestine •

Born beteween 11 A.M. and 1 P.M., you are a Horse, and you have a big heart and are willing to do for everyone . . . until you get exhausted, always putting yourself last. At times then, you will turn around and appear hard-hearted, or self-absorbed, because you've shut down and cut off your emotions in order not to lose your heart again in a relationship in which you don't receive the appreciation and support for who you are and what you do. "Don't touch me" can be the Horse's cry, because you don't want to get in touch with your emotions and the feelings that continually assail you. As a Horse, you can have problems with your heart or nervous system if you wear yourself out. You can have speech problems and stutter.

You can become a workaholic to forget the lack of connection with a special someone. You work to forget how lonely you are at times. Getting lost in your job can make life more tolerable. As a Horse person, you can have sexual hangups or fertility problems, and can fear the relationship you want most. Backaches, cystitis, tinnitus, and impotence are some of your issues.

Because of this, there can be a simmering rage beneath the surface, because you fear getting out there and experiencing love . . . experiencing the give and take between two individuals.

As a Horse, you are never detached about your mate, second child, Mom's mom, Dad's dad. These relationships are always fraught with emotion and intrigue. You can have internal rage from interacting with them over the years and feel betrayed at various times. Mention any one of these people to you and you respond with a subjectivity that surprises others. Although a mild-mannered person normally, you will brook no nonsense from these people in your life and the continual anger stewing inside can create gallbladder problems—sciatica, migraines, gallstones, etc.—as time goes on.

The Horse has self-esteem issues that can keep you from breaking the plowhorse mold and becoming a thoroughbred racehorse. Your angst over your own worth and your feeling that "if I can do it anybody can" can lead you to undervalue yourself. You can sacrifice for the sake of others and then wind up with hamstring problems, as well as colitis or appendicitis. You can find it hard to live up to the conditional standards of others. You can have problems with your intestinal track and have diarrhea or constipation when dealing with people on the job. You can feel guilty and try to be everything to everybody.

 **In a nutshell:** To be a healthy Horse, you need to know you are a thoroughbred and not a plowhorse. You need to feel the love and adulation from "the crowd" (collective consciousness), allow your heart to be open, and let people back into your life. As a Horse, you need to take action to change your life and not get stuck in keeping life safe from harm. You need to come to terms with key people in your life and find the adoration within to love them from a God place and literally "let go" of it. You need to value yourself and your sacredness and know that you're special and deserve the spotlight—it's okay to have more than others and not feel guilty about it. Each one of us has a different path to take, and you needn't feel guilty if yours is better than someone else's.

The Sheep
Small Intestine Meridian

> • Small Intestine • Circulation-Sex •
> • Liver • Stomach •

Born between 1 P.M. and 3 P.M., as a Sheep, your four major areas of the body concern the small intestine, circulation and sexual issues, the liver, and the stomach. This combination can manifest generally as stomach problems, because the small intestine and liver affect the way we process things and affect, in a psychological way, the stomach.

As a Sheep, you need to discriminate and not be with people who can put you in a victim position. You need to recognize your part in any given circumstance, so that you don't blame others for your fate. You need to choose to associate with those who will empower you, not set you up for failure. As a Sheep, you have issues with the small intestine and processing food.

The Sheep's foundation is the Circ-Sex meridian, so you have issues around sex and socializing. You can be withdrawn and prefer your own company to that of others. You may be awkward or even anxious in a social setting. In a sexual encounter, the evolved Sheep will have ignited the flame that connects love with sex and be open and intimate. The unevolved Sheep will see it as an "icky" thing and become inhibited. The Sheep's mother set this pattern, and her sexuality will create the foundation whether the Sheep, man or woman, has a healthy sexual experience or not. Because of this you can have circulation problems, cold hands and feet, arteriosclerosis, blurred vision, and emotional disturbances.

A Sheep can feel victimized and get territorial and keep people away. You get angry inside for letting this happen and the liver acts up. The liver houses the soul and governs the eyes. You get angry when your mate mirrors to you precisely those areas of your life that you'd prefer not to deal with, thank you very much. But that's what the mate is there to do. The Sheep's shadow deals with repression, being held back from experiencing life. The Sheep can feel the mate holds him back, or that the mate's lack of experience is a repressive factor in their relationship. The Sheep gets angry when he sees himself in this mirror.

The Sheep's stomach can churn when you go to work. You can have high expectations about what you want to accomplish, which, at times, are not met. Or, you can find that you created a role for yourself that you now find confining, yet you may not know how to get out of it. You need to find your true identity and be authentic to yourself in order for your stomach to calm down and let you "digest" the fruits of life. The Sheep's father set the pattern of how the career will go. If your father let you know that he was proud of you and that you met all his expectations (i.e. lived up to the role), it is more than likely that you will be successful in this lifetime. If, however, you never seemed to measure up, no matter what you did, your stomach will churn as you live your life trying to appease your father and live up to this role . . . and the dragon in your stomach will breath fire.

In a nutshell: To be a healthy Sheep, you need to be true to yourself, becoming a social person who has ignited the flame of sexuality (Circ-Sex) and is determined to proceed on the creative path to wholeness (Liver). You can see in this combination that there is a lot of withdrawal and repressed energy that needs to be overcome. When the Sheep is authentic to self, when you are socially and sexually open and "hibited" (as opposed to "<u>in</u>hibited"), and experience life in all it's glory, then you will be victorious in life.

The Monkey
Bladder Meridian

> • Bladder • Triple Warmer •
> • Lung • Spleen •

Born between 3 P.M. and 5 P.M., most Monkeys have decided, on some level, to whatever degree, that they have to take control. Faith is a dicey thing. As a child, you might have felt you were tossed about by fate, and determined that wasn't going to happen again. You surmised that the way people treated you was due to fate or God, and decided that you had to take control to be sure life was safe. Because of this, you can become inflexible and rigid, with a body that reflects this attitude. You may have armored your body with stiffness, or, if you've held tight for too long, your body can let go, having muscle-control problems like multiple sclerosis—you just can't control your life (or your body) anymore. On a lighter level, you can have bladder infections, hemorrhoids, nosebleeds, and ear problems. You see life as a dangerous place and look to keep yourself in a zone where you play not to lose, rather than playing to win.

As a Monkey, you have bouts of depression, because on a deep, subconscious level you know that you are keeping yourself from really living. You may not be losing, but you certainly aren't winning, either. This "lock" you have on your universe can make you feel hopeless and, when that concept settles in, you can have thyroid problems, hypothalamus issues, and weight problems because you feel so "weighted" down. This depression can set you up for a spiral of self-destruction—eating too much, drinking too much, putting duty above you own needs, or, conversely, being the teetotaller who doesn't drink or smoke, who won't indulge in anything that will take you "off duty" in anyway.

And, when you are in this depression, you grieve and mourn for the life that was lost. You have a strong drive for recognition and hate to be ignored. As a Monkey person, when you mourn the life you should have lived, you can get bronchitis, pneumonia, and other lung disorders, because you didn't speak out when you should have. Then, you can put on a face to the world that masks what you truly believe.

The Monkey is also sensitive to sugar imbalances. Hypoglycemia and it's opposite, diabetes, are part of the Monkey's need to control and to create boundaries in your life. You need to draw the line in your relationships, particulary at work. As a Monkey, you will test the waters to see just how far you can go. When you find "the line," then you have to make the decision as to whether you want to stay within it or not. When the Monkey feels rejected, you can find yourself with sugar imbalances that can lead to diabetes or other sugar problems when you go to either extreme—either setting too many boundaries and walking away before things get too sticky, or not having any boundaries and doing the proverbial "Do not cross this line!" Then, when that line is crossed, you may move backward and again decree, "Do not cross this line!" The Monkey needs to discern when boundaries are healthy and when they are stifling.

 **In a nutshell:** For the Monkey to be healthy, you have to be flexible and fluid, you need to have faith and let life flow. To do this, you need to develop a positive attitude that sees the world as a glorious place that sustains and supports you on every level. You need to set appropriate boundaries and know when to insist upon them or let them down. Of the four in this set, the Monkey is the one who really needs to take a look at how boundaries aid or hinder his life. When the Monkey is optimistic and sees the full potential of life (Triple Warmer), when you're recognized and appreciated for who you are (Lung), and approved of and feel significant (Spleen), then you will move into the fullness of your life and live with a proud sense of who you are and what you contribute. Then is when you will be loose, fluid, and flexible to flow with life.

The Rooster
Kidney Meridian

> • Kidney • Gallbladder •
> • Large Intestine • Heart •

Born between 5 P.M. and 7 P.M., as a Rooster, you are fearful. You cock your head around from side to side, always looking for something or someone who's going to do you in. Quite often, you must admit, you're running around like "a chicken with your head cut off," because you're flitting from one thing to another, trying to keep yourself distracted, and not really dealing with what is at hand. As a Rooster, you can have fertility problems and may suffer from chronic fatigue or have other "tired blood" issues.

Why is the Rooster fearful? Because your foundation is often rocked by abandonment. The cocky little rooster is angry inside because of real or perceived betrayals early in life. Can you trust the universe not to abandon you? Can you ultimately trust God not to betray you? "God," in this instance, is life, fate. So you become hypervigilant and the muscles in your neck (trapezius) become rods of steel as you try to keep up with everything. As a Rooster, you read the newspaper, watch the news from 4 P.M. to 7 P.M., and then catch the 11 o'clock news just to be sure nothing important has happened in the interim that might adversely affect your life.

The Rooster has very subjective feelings about home and family. You can have migraines, and sciatica when dealing with the family. When the Rooster is drawn to french fries and chips, it's a good bet issues around childhood are up for you. You may have inadvertently been left behind at school or on a vacation, and have felt a sense of abandonment ever since.

The Rooster has real issues about productivity and how she is perceived. As a Rooster, you can be a workaholic, trying to show people your worth and value. You can develop intestinal problems when self-esteem is not what it should be. This includes colitis, appendicitis, and other illnesses associated with the large intestine. You may feel guilty because you feel you didn't do enough to keep the family from betraying you.

Part of the Rooster's fear is based in wanting to belong. You frequently feels like the "odd man out," that no one really wants you there—almost like a duck out of water. In order to please, you work hard and seek to make people love you by what you're able to do. You need to love yourself and insist others love you for who you are, not what you do. As a Rooster, you need to have an open heart and forgive your family for whatever betrayal you feel you've experienced at their hands.

In a nutshell: To be a healthy Rooster, you need to get in touch with your sexuality and recognize how vital it is to a functioning adult to belong, to be in relationship, to be one with someone. You need to welcome the idea of procreation and know you can be a good parent. As a Rooster, you need to know that you're adored by a loving universe that wants the very best for you and supports you in attaining it. Rooster people need to cultivate a sense of self-worth and self-esteem, to stop sacrificing for the sake of others, and draw in someone who reflects your own level of worthiness. As a Rooster, you need to be full of love—love for yourself, love for those you work with, and love for what you can become. Forgive the past and let it go.

The Dog
Circulation-Sex Meridian

> • Circulation-Sex • Liver •
> • Stomach • Small Intestine •

Born between 7 P.M. and 9 P.M., the Dog is shy and tends to put up a wall in a group setting. Self-conscious, you try to hide behind someone else and not be noticed. As a Dog, you have issues with cold hands and feet, because of circulation problems. Male Dogs can have prostate problems, and women, yeast infections. There are psychological issues with sex and intimacy and Dog persons can create reasons for not facing their fears in that area. Because you view sex apart from love, until you alchemize the two, you can retreat into religion as a safe haven that gives you justification for your reticency. You bark and growl ferociously about the decline of moral values in society and can have a "holier than thou" attitude about indulging in such behavior. Some Dogs become zealots in their need to justify their views.

If you reach a point, however, when the spark is ignited that unites sex with the power of love, then you can move mountains. All that hell and damnation stuff is soon forgotten. In the meantime, being inhibited and withdrawn causes problems in relation to circulation and sexual intimacy.

As a Dog, you can be remote and shy because you were held back as a child . . . perhaps "smother love" would be a good description. You feel you didn't have the experiences in life you should have in your early years to cope with being an adult. You have a lot of anger over this, which erupts from time to time and surprises those around you. You can have liver issues and problems with your eyes. The Liver meridian relates to the pectoralis major sternal muscle across the chest and involves the breasts.

Somewhere along the way, something happened that altered your life experience. Everything was going along fine, and then all of a sudden, *Clang!* It was a clinker, something you hadn't expected, and you've been looking for something to happen in any situation. You can't quite believe anything perfect could be just that—something's sure to go wrong somewhere, and you're always on the lookout for it.

The Dog's stomach will become agitated as you seek—sometimes desperately—to create an identity for yourself as the mate, or live-in friend, in a relationship. You need the fulfillment of a relationship and yet you can fear one. You go toward it and run away from it at the same time. You will not feel complete unless you're attached, and yet the whole idea can smack of "smother love" again, based on your upbringing. So you bark and run away. But when you do, you feel hungry and empty for that loving relationship that you know you want, that could move you past your intimacy fears into a place of love and contentment.

Part of the Dog person's apprehension over relationship stems from your inherent need to discriminate . . . not in a bad sense. Coming from a place of refinement, it's hard for you to let go and be passionate in a physical relationship until you have ignited the connection between sex and intimacy. If your father was uptight emotionally and sexually, it may be that, in trying to be the "good child" for Daddy, you can't acknowledge your sexual needs. In dealing with the opposite sex, you can feel victimized, which only enhances your need to keep the opposite sex at bay.

 **In a nutshell:** To be a healthy Dog, you need to ignite the fires between love and sex. You need to stop looking for the clinker and enjoy the totality of the symphony of life. You need to take yourself by the bootstraps and go out and experience life and relish all the beauty and glory about it, knowing you are victorious in this life's adventure and refusing to allow any sense of victimization to enter your head. In relationships, you need to get beyond the idea that your sense of identity comes from being with another, and find contentment within yourself. This is when you can open up to someone freely when they enter your life. For the Dog not to wind up with genital problems, the quest is to move beyond intimacy fears and feelings of victimization and let down the fence that blocks you from relationships, to stop barking and growling and become the open, friendly, loyal, puppy dog who loves adoringly and unstintingly and will jump up and get in someone's aura and lick their face with love.

The Boar
Triple Warmer Meridian

> • Thyroid/Metabolism • Lung •
> • Spleen • Bladder •

Born between 9 P.M. and 11 P.M., the Boar tends to plod along. Even though you're part of the fire element, your metabolism can be sluggish, and you just don't burn off those calories as you should. You frequently have problems with your weight, and can have other problems with metabolism related to thyroid if it isn't functioning correctly. As a Boar, you can fret continually about your self-image, wishing you were as graceful as a gazelle, but finding you feel like a bull in a china shop much of the time. You tend to be pessimistic, which brings your energy level down, so you can get depressed, and this becomes a vicious cycle. Pretty soon, you're sinking deeper into the bog, becoming a couch potato with a bag of chips on your belly, watching TV, feeling hopeless about life, and feeling that life justifies your perception. (Once in a while, the metabolism runs amok, and you're skinny because it burns too hot.)

The Boar feels this way because, at some point, your dreams were shattered. You had to give up on a career or family or something that was important to you. When the Boar is simply existing instead of living, here lies the core of your physical complaints.

It's rather obvious, then, that if, as a Boar, you aren't exercising much, you shouldn't indulge in sugar. But that's exactly what you tend to do. You fear rejection in relationships, and yet can create a body that justifies rejection, to your way of thinking—"If I were 30 pounds thinner, I could have any girl I wanted." But what if you were 30 pounds thinner and you still didn't have a relationship? There could be a million reasons why, but you aren't going to look at it that way. So you better you have a reason why this isn't happening, a reason that will give you the power you need to change it any time you want to.

There's a "who's going to reject first?" component to your relationships. You attract people who fear rejection, which causes your own rejection complex to rear its ugly head. So, instead of enjoying each other, it's a constant game of chess to see who's going to make the first move out the door. Of course, in any relationship like that, someone is actually going to close the door first. Either way, as a Boar, you will turn to sugar to make yourself feel better, to numb your hurt feelings. You have a perfectionist strain in you that feels that, if you can't have perfection in a relationship or in your life, you've somehow failed. You can also draw in a mate who is critical and a perfectionist and always finding fault with you.

Because of all this, somewhere along the way, as a Boar, you've dug in your heels and you "ain't movin'." Life isn't fair and, by golly, you are going to throw in a monkey wrench whenever need be to make life work to the extent you want it to. You sit back and seek to control this life—perhaps as you watched Dad control his life when you were a child. You've never learned to let go and watch the magic the universe can perform when it's left to its own resources. The Boar can have bladder problems associated with his career, or gravitate to people in the career arena who are controllers.

It's not hard to deduce, then, that, as a Boar, when you aren't living a constructive, hopeful life, you can get into self-destructive habits. The Boar has to fight continually to see the positive side of life, and you need to surround yourself with people who are upbeat and who keep you from being dour.

In a nutshell: To be a healthy Boar, you need to get up and start walking, exercising, doing something, anything, to get yourself going. Then the endorphins will kick in and you won't be quite so depressed. Your lungs might not have been expanded in years, so it can take some time and you need to go at a casual pace at the beginning. One trick from kinesiology is to take two fingers and press at the base of the larynx and then every ½ inch down to the sternum. That helps the lungs to expand just a little bit more. When the Boar's mental state starts to improve, then you can start implementing a dream. When you come into a state of certainty and confidence about yourelf, and you see life as positive and full of hope, then you'll stop controlling and manipulating and find a reason to live a more healthy lifestyle and let life flow again.

Case History: Michael J. Fox

So far we have used the Chinese Time of Day Wheel to show how the meridians and animals relate to our personalities and emotions. But, the wheel is also a vehicle to pinpoint the reason for illness and disease. By placing the Time of Day Wheel over the astrology wheel, we can determine the emotions/organs/meridians from which each planet is operating.

The preponderance of dis-ease has its roots in the emotions and events of the past that are still held in the body. As I've explained, emotional joy and trauma don't just go into the body willy-nilly. Organs/meridians react to specific emotions. By using this system and overlaying the Time of Day Wheel on the astrology chart, we can find the underlying issues that are manifesting today.

We will look at the chart of actor Michael J. Fox, who first appeared on our TV screens as Michael P. Keaton on *Family Ties*, and then was successful in the *Back to the Future* films. In November of 1998, he announced that he has had Parkinson's disease since 1991. At the time of the admission, he was starring in *Spin City*.

In 1998, the second solar eclipse of the year occurred on August 21st, at 28 degrees of Leo, activating any planets we might have in the vicinity. For Michael, the Sun and Moon passed over Uranus at 22 degrees of Leo, just before creating the eclipse. Uranus triggers exposure, among other things. We usually see the results from an eclipse approximately 90 days later, in this case, November 21st. On November 25th, Michael announced he had Parkinson's disease. It had started in 1991 while he was making Doc Hollywood. He had noticed a little twitch in his pinkie finger.

It is rather uncommon in a young man, but it became steadily worse. In March of 1998, he had brain surgery to relieve major tremors. Prior to that, it was reported he had the driver of his limo circle the Golden Globe Awards ceremonies three times before he was able to enter without drawing attention to himself.

Parkinson's disease is a degenerative neurological disorder that destroys brain cells that produce dopamine, a chemical important to movement, tremors, and difficulty moving and/or controlling movement.

To see how this occurred in his life, let's take a look at his Western chart, with the Time of Day Wheel overlaying it, showing us which emotions/events were triggered.

Michael J. Fox was reported to have been born on June 9, 1961, at 12:15 A.M., in Edmonton, Canada. His totem animals are the Ox, Cat, Rat, and—if the minute of birth was accurate—the Sheep.

Everyone born in 1961, in the Year of the Ox, has issues about being independent and free, expressing oneself autonomously, breaking out of preconceived ruts, and reaching for the stars. To the extent that energy is curtailed, they are frustrated and angry at not experiencing enough of life or perhaps being smothered as a child.

Born in the Sun sign related to the Tiger, Michael has a desire to be recognized and appreciated, to feel proud of who he is and what he's accomplished. If that energy is repressed, his ego can be deflated, and he can mourn what might have been.

So, generally speaking, all Geminis born in 1961 have these needs to be met and realized. To find how we specifically act out this energy to heal and come into our most positive expression, we look

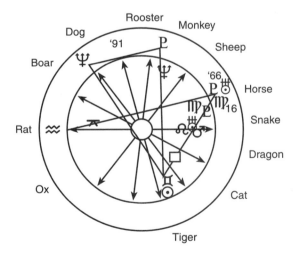

Figure 18. Michael J. Fox:
June 9, 1961, 12:15 A.M. MST, Edmonton, Canada.

to the hour and minute we were born. In this instance, Michael J. Fox was born in the Hour of the Rat. It is said to be 12:15 A.M. The Rat's hours span from 11 P.M. to 1 A.M. standard time.

The Rat looks to have trust in his fellow man, to love and be loved unconditionally. He lives by the golden rule: "Do unto others as you would have them do unto you." He'll do what he sees is necessary without a hidden agenda. His trust is broken at times, because he has issues with abandonment and/or betrayal. His faith can be shattered by those who don't stand by him. A deep, subconscious anger then swells inside. He can have subjective views and wonder, as others do, why he can't be objective about certain people or events. Then, he can sometimes lash out uncontrollably. For Michael, born during Rat (Gallbladder) time, you can see his altruism in coming forward with information that might help other people.

When I first heard Michael had Parkinson's disease, I immediately felt he had some type of imbalance in the Heart meridian. Getting an accurate time of birth is often difficult. As this has become his Achilles' heel and is life-threatening, I would suggest we might very well rectify his time of birth to somewhere between 12 A.M. and 12:10 A.M., rather than 12:15, placing the minute of his birth in the Heart meridian sector of his chart. Our key challenges in life often occur in the meridian/organ where our minute of birth resides.

The Heart meridian rules the heart organ, but also the brain function. Interestingly, the Heart meridian begins in the armpit and works down the arm to the little finger (pinkie).

Being born near the half-way mark during the Rat (Gallbladder) hours, the natural shadow partner in the 7th house opposite should be the Horse (Heart meridian). But because he was born in Canada, quite a distance from the equator, some meridian houses are wider than others (we know that, in Western astrology, some houses can become very wide, encompassing a sign and a half or even two signs when we are born far north or far south of the equator, and it is so with the meridian wheel).

Michael has Uranus (electrical instability as well as exposure of secrets) and Mars (surgery) at 22 and 18 degrees of Leo, on the cusp of the 7th house, and Pluto in Virgo in the 7th. The Snake and the Horse rule the 7th house of partner/shadow issues from the meridian overlay wheel.

Pluto is in his 7th house, at 5 degrees of Virgo, as the Snake/Spleen energy ends and the Horse/Heart energy begins, at his birth.

In 1966, when Michael was 5 years old, we had a big phenomenon in the sky as Uranus caught up to Pluto at 16 degrees of Virgo. This occurred in Michael's 7th house of partners, in the Heart meridian overlay, and squared his Sun at 18 of Gemini in the 4th house of his foundation and roots (which is the area the Lung meridian—recognition, appreciation—covers). The conjunction of Pluto and Uranus, two mighty outlying planets that create evolution and change on fundamental levels to the masses, also inconjuncted (150 degrees) his Ascendant at 18 degrees of Aquarius on a personal basis. An inconjunct is a power point, and often relates to health issues. Uranus by itself, moving through the Heart meridian overlay on the chart, sometimes can cause heart palpitations or brain irregularity because of the instability of the electrical energy associated with Uranus/Aquarius, in this area of heart and brain.

Finger of God
Natal Uranus and Mars in Leo oppose Michael's Ascendant in Aquarius, so when the Uranus-Pluto conjunction happened in 1966, it semi-sextiled natal Uranus-Mars, which caused these two latter planets to become the trigger of the "Finger of God" to the Ascendant when some lighter-weight planet moved over the midrange of Cancer, which very well could have been Mars or the Sun itself. The inconjunct, remember, is a YOD, and is called the "Finger of God" because it points to the "answer," as well as shows to whom or what the energy is directed. Overlayed by the Rat (Gallbladder) energy (anger and rage over some betrayal, needing unconditional love) in the 1st house of self, and squaring his Sun sign of Gemini with Lung (grief, sadness) energy, I would suggest here that something might have occurred when he was 5 years old that had a profound effect on him. The force of the YOD was directed at him.

I work a lot with the major YOD in this century of Neptune and Pluto. These two planets with separate orbits (Pluto taking 247 years to orbit the Sun; Neptune taking 156) have been 60 degrees apart, give or take a few degrees, for almost 60 years. They create their own "Finger of God," which is a primary evolutionary soul-growth experience for everyone born in this time frame. Whenever I couldn't figure out what was going on in a person's chart, the answer became this YOD that was showing the way, if we could only decifer it.

For those born in 1961, the YOD power point 150 degrees on the other side of the chart from Neptune (in Scorpio) and Pluto (in

Virgo) was in Aries, with an Ox (Liver meridian) overlay. The Ox, remember, is also the animal for the year of his birth. Ox people need to take off the yoke and rise to the top of their creative potential. When they are held back, they get angry and repressed and it can affect their autonomic nervous system.

By 1991, the year Michael's pinkie started twitching, this "Finger of God" point had moved as the Neptune-Pluto sextile moved, so that Pluto, at 18 degrees of Scorpio, and Neptune, at 18 degrees of Capricorn, shot the YOD down to a power point at 18 degrees of Gemini—Michael's Sun sign position. This triggered the energy of his Sun sign. YOD points touching off a planet can create times of movement and change in one's life; times when you remember your life taking a definite shift. It can also trigger energy to bring events to the surface to be healed. Remember, this is in the Lung meridian, which grieves and mourns over past traumas. At this point, Michael's subconscious may have brought up whatever occurred to him at age 5, when the Uranus/Pluto conjunction happened.

The Ox (Liver) energy doesn't want to be suppressed and held back, and when the Ox gets angry (and the Liver gets frustrated), the Rat (Gallbladder) can see the abandonment/betrayal issues.

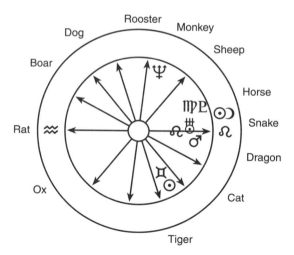

Figure 19. Solar Eclipse 8/21/98.

7th House of Shadow Partners

The 7th house, with Pluto there, refers to a number of people who mirror that energy. Most prominently, it is one's mate. But it also reflects the second child, and after that comes the third sibling born after and the third sibling born before the person who's chart you're looking at. It also relates to grandparents—Mom's mom and Dad's dad. It would say that, perhaps, one of these older mirrors could have been very domineering and overpowering.

In 1998, as Uranus in Aquarius was completing its trek through Michael's 12th house of the subconscious, this hologram from thirty years before was being brought to the surface, as Uranus was moving in to conjunct his Ascendant at 18 degrees of Aquarius and oppose Mars and Uranus at 18 and 22 degrees of Leo. An opposition brought closure to a series of events.

As a hypnotherapist using guided visualization, I would ask Michael who was the "snake in the grass" (Snake/Spleen), who may have rejected him, who then broke his heart (Horse/Heart) in 1966, causing him grief and sadness and depression (Tiger/Lung) to his Sun sign, Gemini in the 4th (at home, in its roots and foundation), which caused him to feel betrayed and abandoned (Rat/Gallbladder Ascendant), so that he became so enraged on a subconscious level that he literally couldn't control himself. I would work with him to bring up those issues in and around 1966 and use the energies of the Rat, the Horse, the Snake, the Tiger, and the Ox as metaphors in guided visualization to come to a healing place.

Again, our celebrities are our mirrors, acting out on a grand scale what we deal with in our personal lives. For someone who has given so much enjoyment and laughter to the world, one hopes that, by the time you are reading this, a cure has been found for him.

 **In a nutshell:** By looking at Michael J. Fox's Western astrology chart and overlaying the Time of Day Wheel of the Chinese five-element system, I can see that some event probably occurred when he was about 5 years old that hid in his subconscious until 1991, when it started to emerge. Because the Heart (Heart relating to the brain as well) and Gallbladder (subterrean rage) meridians were involved, there may well be deep-seated anger that can no longer contain itself.

Part VI

Healing Therapies for the Power Animals

Chinese Power Animals and Bach Flower Essences

Pamela Galadrial, D.D., Bach Flower Practitioner

Bach Flower Essences work on the emotional/spiritual condition of individuals, and thus are natural healing modalities when working with the emotions of the meridian system and the power animals. According to Dr. Bach, each essence has a specific emotional healing effect. Because the flowers are distilled into a concentrate, only a drop or two is needed and placed under the tongue at intervals, to create a shift on the emotional plane. Bach Flower Remedies can be used undiluted, a drop at a time, in an emergency. However, 2–3 drops can be put into a one-ounce dropper bottle filled with clean, distilled water and a drop of vodka or brandy as a preservative, and used for convenience—carried in your purse or briefcase.

Each power animal has at least one Bach Flower Essence that will aid in transforming the negative energies. You can look to the animal for recommendations for your primary totem, or you can see what might be appropriate at the present time for what is going on in your life in relation to the emotions you are experiencing.

The Rat

Because the Rat is prone to emotional outbursts, Cherry Plum is a natural antidote. Sometimes the Rat can feel as if he is about to explode and Cherry Plum is an effective calming agent.

Impatiens is much as it's name implies. It is good for impatience, irritability, and temper flareups.

Sweet Chestnut speaks to hopelessness and despair, which relates to the Boar, but it also addresses a feeling that God has forsaken us. When abandoned, we often feel it is beyond the person who has offended us, but goes back to a far greater betrayal.

The Rat is concerned with making wise choices and clear decisions, yet, at times, can feel uncertain about which way to go or the best course to follow. Wild Oat aids in clearing the mind to see the proper road to take.

The Ox

When we feel frustrated and repressed, we often have the feeling of being put upon, held back in some way, and Willow is for those who feel short-changed by life. They look at others' good fortune and are irritable that it hasn't happened to them.

The Tiger

The Tiger masks its anxieties. Tigers can feel lonely and apart from others, and Agrimony is a good essence for this. If you wake up between 3 A.M. and 5 A.M., this is a good antidote.

Honeysuckle is for those who are grieving, and who tend to live in the past. It is for those who don't want to look to the future, but get stuck in the memory of better days.

Wild Rose is for resignation, when we have let go of our dream and are resigned to our fate, making no attempt to change things, feeling it is too hard to do so, since it "wouldn't do any good anyway." Resignation is slightly different from hopelessness, which resides with the Boar.

The Cat

The essence Crab Apple is to cleanse mind and body. It is for those who have a sense of uncleanliness, who have problems loving themselves.

Pine is for those who feel guilty and deal with self-reproach. Self-sacrifice resides here as well, so it is perfect for the Cat, or someone with Cat issues who needs to know how special they are.

Vervain is recommended for those with tension and hyperactivity, for those who are high strung (as in cat gut for violin strings?).

The Dragon

Chicory sounds as if it should be for the Monkey/Bladder, as it helps with behaviors involving control and manipulation. But here it is more for those who crave attention or are domineering parents.

Scleranthus helps indecision, which can be applied here to identity—which way should I go? One road will lead to one identity, another

to something else altogether. What do I want to be? Where do I want to go?

Again, when looking at Vine, we can attribute it to Monkey as well as Dragon issues. This is for someone who yearns for power, almost greedily. Use Vine to move from control to a wise, loving, leader.

Walnut is for people experiencing life's major changes, and Dragons are more prone to identity crises than others. "Who am I?" is a constant question they ask themselves.

The Snake

Beech is for those who are critical and intolerant, who analyze and obsess over an issue. It is used for people that need to be right. Stiff necks and shoulders are a result of this uptight attitude.

Red Chestnut is for anxiety, which is slightly different from the Rooster's fear. This essence is particularly helpful for those who need to care for others with a more detached attitude.

White Chestnut is for worriers, those with "brain chatter" that seems impossible to stop. It aids concentration and the Snake's meridian, Spleen, deals with concentration and memorization. It helps us to live in the present.

The Horse

Centaury speaks to those who are out of touch with their own sense of self. They need to be in touch with what they want and how they can get it. Centaury helps here. It helps those who are quiet and passive.

Heather is for the Horse who is self-absorbed, who has drawn into herself and is preoccupied with her own problems to the exclusion of others.

It always surprises me that Holly is for hatred and jealousy—such hard words for the Horse! But its opposite is love, and that's where it fits. It's also for those who lacked for love as a child, and closed their hearts somewhere along the way.

The Sheep

Cerato is the essence for those who don't trust their own instincts, but seek advice from others and are misguided. They can be caught up in the strength of the herd and not go their own way when necessary.

Oak is for those who overwork, who struggle, and who may plod along.

Rock Rose is for a crisis, brief but intense. Shock is attributed to the Triple Warmer and the Boar, but it can also pertain to being victimized in some way.

Willow helps those who perceive themselves as victims, and who, when ill, hesitate to see any improvement.

The Monkey

Chestnut Bud is for fear of failure, and can be a contributing factor to the Monkey's need for control. When one is in denial, one will continue to make the same mistakes over and over.

Chicory is an antidote for those who need to be in control, and who manipulate in order to maintain it. Genuine love is sometimes hard for them to express because they did not have any role models in childhood.

Rock Water and Vine are two different essences for slight variations of inflexibility. They help those in denial and self-repression. It is for those who can be self-dominating, which is a form of self-denial. They tend to have a dogmatic approach to many subjects. Their bodies can be rigid, reflecting their mental rigidity.

The Rooster

Aspen works on fears that are free-floating and have no known origin. It can help those who are suddenly gripped by fear. Mimulus is for fear of things that are known: large dogs, spiders, earthquakes, etc.

The Rooster tends to be a workaholic. Once in a while, they can be suddenly overwhelmed by all they've taken on. Elm addresses this issue.

Gorse helps those with dark circles under their eyes, which is a Rooster trait. Hornbeam helps procrastination.

Olive is for exhaustion, when you sleep but don't seem to get any rest.

The Dog

Water Violet aids those who are aloof and shy and tend to withdraw. They may seem emotionally frigid, and can appear cold to others.

The Boar

Clematis is used for those who would rather be lost in their own world than face reality. There are a lot of remedies here for different aspects of hopelessness. Gentian is used for those who are negative and pessimistic. Gorse is for those who are discouraged and despondent. Larch aids those who lack confidence and Mustard is for those who suddenly go into a black depression, which lifts just as quickly. Rock Rose is for shock, and Star of Bethlehem is for the aftereffects of shock. And, finally, Sweet Chestnut is for that hopeless despair for those who have reached the end of endurance.

Pamela Galadrial, D.D., is a minister who founded "Fellowship of the Heart." She is a glorious singer, actress, and composer who has written music for selections from "A Course in Miracles." She is an intuitive counsellor and Bach Flower practitioner. She tours the country, lecturing, singing, and conducting playshops. Her book, *We Never Left the Garden,* is a popular item, along with her music cassettes and CDs. You can reach Pamela at **mceligot@usa.net.**

Chinese Power Animals and Essential Oils

(Aromatherapy)*

Essential oils were once considered to be as valuable as gold. They were used as currency in many cultures. Actually, spices and herbs were better than money! We all know that the wise men took frankincense and myrrh with them as presents when they visited baby Jesus. Throughout the ages, essential oils have been used as healing agents. In today's world, with its concrete structures and paved roads, we do not dwell where there are a lot of natural scents that would automatically act as balancing agents as we go about our daily activities. We look to essential oils today to bring order and balance back into our world and enhance our lives by bringing calm and healing through their aromatic essence.

As a general practice, if you take a whiff of an aroma and you really love it, it really speaks to you, then you are in a place where you are healing those issues the oils address. You look to it as something you can use in meditation or before a stressful event to bring you into a place of peace and healing. Conversely, if you can't stand the smell, it's reminding you of issues you have "successfully" tamped down, and you don't want to deal with them at this time.

You can use essential oils in many ways. Put a drop or two on a lightbulb so that the essence fills the room. Or put a couple of drops in 2 tablespoons of massage oil and massage your body. (If you don't like a scent but realize you need to use it to get to the issues involved, rubbing it on the bottom of your feet will get the desired effect without having to deal with the scent until it shifts.) It's also a good way to test out the oil to see what your reaction is. It is always good to work with an aromatherapy practitioner to help you move through the emotions that may arise.

The following guidelines outline the essential oils that are beneficial for issues which concern the power animals.

---

*My thanks to O'Hara Beals, aromatherapist and owner of Laguna Beach Botanicals, for her aid on this chapter. Email her at oharabeals@yahoo.com.

Fire

Horse • Dog • Boar • Sheep

The animals of the fire element—the Horse, Dog, Boar, and Sheep—are concerned with relationship issues. The Horse relates to the heart, and perhaps being heartbroken. The Dog has intimacy issues and can be shy in front of people. The Dog seeks to "circulate" easily and relate comfortably (the Circulation-Sex meridian). The Boar addresses humiliation and ridicule, and searches to find the positive in relationships. The Sheep needs to discern who is good to befriend, and who would victimize him. The following are the aromatherapies that benefit these four.

Black Pepper is a very hot and passionate oil used in many of the different disciplines to "burn through" a block; it also aids food and digestion.

Rosewood is difficult to find; Bergmont is often used instead. Rosewood is an antidepressant. It has a calming effect that reasons with the heart.

Jasmine has been mentioned in relation to the prostate in men, which is a Circulation-Sex, or Dog, issue.

Angelica is frequently a balm for Boar people, as it can lift their mood and create a more positive outlook.

The fire element focuses on emotional issues, specifically relating to others. You have to have a heart that's working and strong, and for that you need oxygen. Using black pepper in massage oil would give you more confidence and well-being. It also helps in finding a direction. Fire people can be overly passionate or passionless. There are fire people who burn passionately and then there are others who withdraw, like the Dog, and need to get in touch with their passion again.

Earth

Dragon • Snake

The earth element addresses issues of power, ego, and money. The body organs are the stomach and spleen. The animals are the Dragon and the Snake. The Dragon seeks to be content and fulfilled; the Snake wants to be perfect. In that quest, they may find their expectations not met or they may fear the possibility of rejection. Obsessions and compulsions may result.

Sandalwood is one of the more expensive oils. It is made from a wood that has to be at least 30 years old before it can be extracted. The oil is mature by the time it is used; it's not a young oil. It imparts a sense of paternal protection. It is a very golden oil. Sandalwood is warming. It has been used since antiquity for barter as gold. It is a good "grounding" oil. Good Sandalwood is hard to find and varies in price.

Vetiver is an oil that has a really earthy smell to it; it is also very grounding. It is uplifting and comforting, and can relax deep fears of insecurity.

Myrrh is another oil used in antiquity. Remember the wise men brought gold, frankincense, and myrrh to the stable when Jesus was born? Myrrh is also used to counteract the addiction to sweets that Dragon and Snake people usually have. Myrrh has been used in the past for gum disease (the gums are the province of the Stomach meridian).

Bergamot helps deal with compulsive behavior, including eating disorders.

Earth relates to issues of money and finance; in essence—survival. Being out of balance with your earth energy can lead to love and sugar addictions. Frequent disappointments and disapproval often stimulate identity crises and ego issues. Using essential oils when you think someone is about to reject you can keep you from "jumping the gun" and rejecting that person first. Make sure that the other person isn't just having a bad day before you walk away.

Metal

Tiger • Cat (Rabbit)

Tigers and Cats are mental types who need to get in touch with their emotional natures. They need to be acknowledged and appreciated for what they do. The following are among the essential oils that address these issues.

Patchouli is a good oil to expand joy and freedom. Patchouli is usually associated with the 1960s; the decade of abandonment and sexual freedom, which is exactly what Patchouli is used for—to find personal identity and move away from conditional authority figures. Patchouli expands the joy and freedom of life. We can look to the 1960s to see how, in that decade, we had the support to tell the outer male, the authority figures, they no longer controlled us. Patchouli supports us to find a balance within ourselves, to find our inner authority. This is good for Cats who need to build self-esteem.

Palmarosa is a good oil for metal types, for it brings refreshing qualities and relieves dryness. It is used on the skin. The skin is considered the "third lung" because it breathes. Palmarosa is used for stress reduction and nervous exhaustion.

Frankincense is a small tree that grows in Yemen and Somalia. It is good for lung and genito-urninary complaints, which fits perfectly in this Lung/Large Intestine element.

Basil is a familiar herb that translates well into an aromatherapy oil. Basil helps rattled nerves, mental fatigue, and helps develop positive thoughts.

The Tiger and the Cat benefit from oils that move them out of their heads and settle their nerves.

Water

Rooster • Monkey

In the water element, the Rooster and Monkey have issues around fear and holding on too tightly. They don't know how to let the universe express itself through them. In this element, oils such as clary sage, peppermint, and fennel, along with ylang ylang are very healing.

Clary Sage is a good oil for acne, or skin that is out of control. It has an estrogenic action and aids the adrenals, which are related to the kidneys. It also helps paranoia.

Fennel is an herb that helps obesity and water retention. It is good to take when we want to counteract sugar and alcohol; as an aroma, it strengthens resolve. It also helps the adrenals.

Labdanum aids inflamed kidneys and helps brighten the emotions.

Peppermint is a an uplifting and heartening aroma. Peppermint lifts the mood, so while there isn't an aroma here for fear, peppermint will help take people's minds off problems, and perhaps bring them to a more objective place to find answers.

Ylang ylang aids fear, tempers jealousy and anger. The bladder (Monkey) houses the "seat of the emotions" and ylang ylang will help to bring us more objectivity.

The water element relates to emotions. And remember, emotion is "energy in motion." When we get too damp and watery, we get stuck in our emotions and are not able to think clearly or see things as they truly are. When we get into "fear," we often move into control in order to keep our world safe. Picture driving from one state to another!

Wood

Ox • Rat

The wood element looks for autonomy and freedom. The Ox longs to throw off the yoke to be independent, while the Rat seeks unconditional love and acceptance. In Chinese lore, the Liver and Gallbladder meridians relate to wise decisions and excellent excution. Wood must be in balance so that we don't get frustrated and lash out.

Rosemary was traditionally used by Indian women in their moon huts during their menstruation. It was put around the perimeter to keep out evil spirits and protect them, because they felt psychically open during this time of the month. They would have deep, prophetic dreams. Rosemary helps us feel anger but not have it close in on itself. It helps to hold a safe place while we are processing the anger. Rosemary is used for remembrance, being able to remember resentment and anger but in a way that aids us in processing it. The Liver meridian is related to PMS and menstruation.

Fennel helps release toxins, which is always good for the liver and its meridian. Fennel helps us find our motivation so we can move independently. It can also brighten our personality.

Ylang ylang adds a touch of humor, it is an antidepressant, a lighthearted energy. It will take us to the issues of the root chakra—fear and anger. It is a personal power plant that washes away impurities of thought and judgment and gives us the inner confidence to stay centered.

The Ox and Rat can often let frustration and anger get the best of them. These aroma oils can help keep this energy in a focused, directed space.

Tarot Cards of the Chinese Power Animals

The years assigned to the power animals can be reduced to a single number, i.e., 1967 = 1 + 9 + 6 + 7 = 23 = 2 + 3 = 5. There are three patterns of three numbers, which the years represent. These numbers can be related to the major arcana in the tarot card system. Use the tarot card for the year of your birth as a meditative tool to come into alignment with its universal principles.

Numbers: 1 4 7
Rat • Cat • Horse • Rooster

1 - The Magician or the Magi. Communication is a major part of your personality. Writing and speaking effectively are among your skills, being able to say the right thing at the right time for the best result. If you feel you aren't in tune with this energy, in meditation, ask Mercury, the winged messenger, for guidance.

4 - The Emperor. You are a solid member of the community, creating a solid foundation on which to develop your world. The Emperor speaks to you about personal power. He helps you to learn to be assertive and set appropriate boundaries. If you are having trouble speaking up, use the Emperor card, and ask him in meditation what you need to do to come into your power.

7 - The Chariot. You are able to let go of the reins and let the energy carry you to where you are to go. It is the card of change. If you find that change brings something worse into your life, use the Chariot card to tap into the wisdom of how to access change that alters your life forever for the good.

Numbers: 2 5 8
Ox • Dragon • Sheep • Dog

2 - The High Priestess. The card encourages you to be self-resourceful, to be independent and trust in yourself. She calls you to tune in to your intuition and react to life from a higher level. When you aren't working easily and effortlessly, ask the High Priestess in meditation how you can change your life.

5 - The Hierophant. You are a life-long student who becomes the wise teacher. This education usually comes from the family matrix. Born under the auspices of this card, you can use your knowledge to manifest what is important for you. If you find you aren't producing this in your life, access the Hierophant in meditation for your answers.

8 - Adjustment. This is the card with the scales of justice on it. Most times, they are balanced, but in some decks they are shown askew. This card asks you to come in to harmony and balance, to cut through any illusion and see clearly. If you aren't expressing this in your life, ask the goddess Maat, as depicted on the Crowley-Toth deck, for guidance.

Numbers: 3 6 9
Tiger • Snake • Monkey • Boar

3 - The Empress. The Empress is the earth mother and calls to you to nurture humankind. It is the card of giving and receiving love unconditionally, as a mother would. If your mothering instincts are not producing what you wish, access the Empress in meditation for the healing solution.

6 - The Lovers. This card represents the merging of the masculine and feminine, of becoming one. It encourages the formation of relationships with the skills to act effectively within them. If you feel split down the middle and not "together," ask the Lovers archetype in meditation what you need to do.

9 - The Hermit. The 9th card in the deck, the Hermit represents completion. The Hermit asks us to complete past karma and make way for a new beginning. If you find you are too involved in issues of the past and aren't making progress, access the Hermit in meditation for the answers to resolve past actions that are cropping up in this life.

Colors of the Power Animals

Be aware of the colors in your world: the ones to which you are drawn, or the ones which you avoid. What colors do you frequently wear? Which ones would you rarely or never wear? By simply looking at these colors and deciding to which you are drawn, which you really don't like, and which are neutral at the time you are viewing them, can tell you a lot about what is in balance and what is out of balance in your life.

Fire:	Red
Earth:	Yellow
Air (Metal):	White
Water:	Blue and Black
Wood:	Green

You might even start your day by looking at the five colors and seeing which of them "speaks" to you and which don't. If you are really drawn to a color or really detest a color, look to see which animals represent that color and dialog with them a bit, much as you did with your personal power animals, to see where they are today, and what they can tell you about how to successfully proceed with your day.

If you find yourself wearing a particular color frequently, or decorating your home with one, you can be assured that this is a healing balm for you at this point; you need it to sustain the imbalance you are feeling in the element it represents. Also, be aware of when colors change favor in your life, and examine what that means in relation to your personal healing and soul's growth.

As an example, Amy had her house decorated in powder blue. It was a natural color for her to pick from her point of view, and she was surprised when other people took pokes at it; most people do not decorate predominantly in blue, she discovered. As she came into an awareness of colors, she saw that she was dealing with water-element issues and that it was supporting for her to be "in" the color blue so much of the time. When I checked in with her recently, the blue had been replaced with a marshmallow white. It was obvious that her Kidney/Bladder issues were nearly resolved, and she no longer needed the assistance of the blue color in her home to soothe her imbalanced water emotions.

Your Power Colors
Do you know which colors are your power colors? If you look at the colors for your power animals/elements, you will find the color combination that you can use to best advantage.

The color for the fire element is, quite appropriately, red. Earth's color is, not green or brown, as you might expect, but yellow. The metal (air) color is white, while the colors for water are blue and black, interchangeably. Finally, the color for wood is green.

So, go back and check out the element under which your animals rule. If I look at mine, the Horse is the power animal for the Heart meridian and the fire element. The Snake, for my Sun sign, Virgo, represents the Spleen meridian and the earth element, while my rising sign's power animal is the Rooster, and that falls under the water element. The Tiger and the metal element represent the minute I was born. Hence, my colors are red for the Horse, yellow for the Snake, blue for the Rooster, and white for the Tiger. Red, yellow, blue, and white are my power colors.

For example, my son James was born on January 4, 1967, at 5:55 P.M. He was born in the Year of the Horse (because it didn't change until February 9th that year), the Month of the Rooster, the Hour of the Rooster, and the Minute of the Tiger. The Horse, again, is under fire and the color is red. Two Roosters are water and the color is blue. The Tiger is metal and the color is white. So his power colors are a double dose of blue with a red-and-white complement.

My son David was born on August 1, 1972, at 7:15 P.M., PDT, so we would adjust it to standard time, 6:15 P.M. That makes him born in the Year of the Rat (green), the month of the Dragon (yellow), the Hour of the Rooster (blue/black), and the Minute of the Snake (yellow). His colors, green, yellow, and blue, are in sharp contrast to his sibling's and mother's predominant red.

Conceivably, you could have one power color. Say, for instance, you were born on August 15, 1964, at 7:00 A.M. That would be a quadruple Dragon, and yellow would be your power color.

In evaluating the elements, the fire element is concerned with relationships, while earth deals with power, identity, and finances. Metal rules the mental processes, while water has issues with our emotions and wood with our immune system and the desire to be autonomous and independent.

People with red as one of their power colors are going to deal with relationships, and learn from them. Red people need to learn how to walk the delicate tightrope of interaction and autonomy, how to compromise within a relationship and yet stay a defined human being in their own right.

When yellow is a power color, you are affected in the solar plexus. You seek personal identity and power. You are concerned with money issues and seek security. Finances occupy your mind.

White is the power color for the metal (air) element, and here you need to use your mental processes to think clearly and unclutter your life.

Blue and black are used interchangeably for the water element. If you have them as a power color, you are an emotional person who has deep reservoirs of feelings.

And, finally, green is the power color for the wood element. Wood is the element of independence, freedom, creativity, and the potential to be. With green as a power color, you need to live life to its fullest, and reach out to experience every aspect of life.

Now that you have discovered your power colors, do you like them? All of them, or just one or two? Do you really love them; do they really speak to you, or do you really not like some or all of them?

If you are pleased with your colors, and note that you have incorporated them into your environment, then you are pretty balanced. If you just love one or more of your colors, you are imbalanced in that area, but you are willing and open to working on healing those issues. If you really detest the color, never wear it, etc., you might look at meditating with the color and trying to incorporate it more into your life, because it says these are issues that you have suppressed or denied and you aren't ready to deal with as yet. Working with these undesirable colors and turning the negative into positive will create positive shifts and changes in your life.

To understand how the colors work in your life, let's do another visualization.

Situate yourself in a comfortable position, turn off the telephone and any extraneous noises; get in tune with your inner self.

Take some deep breaths, settle down and get into a comfortable position.

Once again, we are going to go to your secret place where truth prevails. You know exactly where to go; trust yourself. See a path ahead of you . . . leading down to your secret place . . . moving down the path one step at a time . . . each step taking you ten times deeper than before . . . moving down the path now . . . 10 . . . 9 . . . 8 . . . 7 . . . 6 . . . 5 . . . 4 . . . 3 . . . 2 . . . 1 . . .

Now, I'd like you to see yourself dressed all in red. . . . How does that feel? Do you like being dressed in this color? . . . Does it make you feel confident . . . or not? Do you feel aggressive? Assertive? Lovable? Amorous? or not? How do you feel wearing red? Is it a positive color for you? Below, please circle Yes or No and jot down your feelings about you and the color red.

Yes   No

_____
_____
_____
_____

Now, let that image dissolve, and see yourself dressed all in yellow. How does that feel? Do you like being dressed in yellow? Do you like standing out in a crowd like that? Or do you prefer more demure colors? Dressed in yellow, do you feel confident? Do you feel good about yourself? Is it a color you normally wear? Contrast these feelings with wearing an outfit in red. Which made you feel better, if one or the other did so. Is yellow a positive color for you? Below, please circle Yes or No and jot down your feelings about you and the color yellow.

Yes   No

_____
_____
_____
_____

Now, let that image dissolve, and see yourself dressed all in white. How does that feel? Do you like being dressed in white? Does it make you feel clean? Are you comfortable wearing white? Do you include white in your wardrobe? Contrast these feelings with wearing an outfit in red. . . . or yellow. Which made you feel better, if any of them did so.

Is white a positive color for you? Below, please circle Yes or No and jot down your feelings about you and the color white.

Yes   No

_____

_____

_____

_____

Now, let that image dissolve, and see yourself dressed all in blue. How does that feel? Do you like being dressed in blue? Do you feel you are an emotional person who gets subjectively involved with everyone in your life? Or do you feel that you are not in touch with your emotions? Either extreme could have you drawn to blue. Contrast these feelings with wearing an outfit in the other colors. Which made you feel better, if any of them did?

Is blue a positive color for you? Below, please circle Yes or No and jot down your feelings about you and the color blue.

Yes   No

_____

_____

_____

_____

Now, let that image dissolve, and see yourself dressed all in green. How does that feel? Do you like being dressed in green? Do you feel that you are free and independent to grow into your full potential? Or do you feel angry over being repressed and stifled from fulfilling your life's mission? How does wearing green differ, if at all, from wearing the other colors? Is green a positive color for you? Below, please circle

Yes or No and jot down your feelings about you and the color green.

Yes   No

_____

_____

_____

_____

Now, let that image dissolve, and remember your personal power colors. Visualize yourself in an outfit combining these colors. How do you like it? Do you resonate to all your power colors? Or just one or two of them? Which color do you like best? Which do you like least?

If there is a color you normally don't wear or have in your world at this time, let's look at the animals that represent that color and how they interact with the other animals of your power colors. Remember, the animals for the colors are:

Red:	Horse, Sheep, Boar, Dog
Yellow:	Dragon and Snake
White:	Tiger and Cat
Blue:	Rooster and Monkey
Green:	Ox and Rat

Open up on a scene with the animals that represent the color that is not included in your life. Let them reveal to you, in appearance and in posture, how healthy they are. Are they angry? Are they strong? Weak? How do they look to you?

Now, ask the animals from the other color(s) to move into the scene. Observe how they interact or don't interact with the animals of the excluded color. Are these animals excluded from the others as well? Why? Observe their interaction for a few moments and see what it reveals to you. . . . If it seems appropriate, dialog and work with them to see how you can resolve the issues between them and bring them back into harmony.

When you feel complete with this exercise, bring yourself back up 1 . . . 2 . . . 3 . . . 4 . . . 5 . . . 6 . . . 7 . . . 8 . . . 9 . . . 10 . . . fully awake, fully alert, fully back in the present time.

Working with your colors, you tuned in to some interesting insights on how they are symbolic in your life and how your animals can get you in touch with these elements of your being. Getting in touch with these colors allows you to see what needs to be worked on (if anything) . . . what's not being utilized for your health and well-being.

If you find you have a power color that is not being utilized in your life, you might deliberately buy some clothing with that color and wear it, and see how you feel about it. The more you can reach a place where every color is "okay"—does not produce an extreme emotion in either direction, good or bad, but is simply "okay, I like that color"—the more you will have integrated its emotions positively into your experience.

Healing Herbs and the Chinese Power Animals

Caroline Patrick—Herbalist, Artist, Feng Shui Consultant

Because the year, month, day, hour, and minute of birth relate to certain power animals in the Chinese system (which correlate with an organ/meridian), it becomes apparent that there are certain herbs, that would be beneficial to the health and well-being of individuals.

You take most of your emotions into the organ/meridian of the hour of your birth. Herbs that heal this organ can be helpful over a lifetime to keep your body healthy. The minute you are born is not so easy to correlate. You may not see evidence of any issue with this organ/meridian for years, but when you find out what it is, you can take steps early on to make sure nothing pops up in the future.

There are a variety of ways to use the power animals in relation to herbs and health:

1) Look at your power totem, the animal/organ for the year, month, hour, and minute of birth. This will give you an excellent array of herbs to help keep your body well.
2) Look at the animal/organs in "Chinese Power Animals and Illness." This is where you experience the most stress and herbs for these organs are an excellent combination.

Sometimes herbs clash. Take this book to your herbalist, Western or Chinese, and let them make up the perfect combination for you.

Look to these herbs when your body is expressing symptoms and/or emotions, as well as to your totem animals. Following are some recommendations for herbs that aid each organ.

The Rat

Major Organ: Gallbladder

Major herbs: nettle, mullein, turmeric, dandelion, red clover. Bupleurum is used by the Chinese for gallbladder issues, as well as for the liver.

Use dried nettle to sprinkle on food; use young shoots in salads, leaves cooked like spinach. Nettles are full of vitamins and minerals. They can also be made as a tea or tincture. Turmeric stimulates the gallbladder, while dandelion leaf reduces inflammation. It can be used as a tea, food, or tincture. In Chinese lore, bupleurum is reputed not only to detoxify, but to bring up deep emotions to be released. Red clover is used to correct bile.

The Ox

Major Organ: Liver

Major herbs: bupleurum, dandelion, milk thistle, eyebright, bilberry, horsetail, goldenseal, echinacea, garlic, red clover.

Dandelion root and leaf is an excellent herb used as a food, tea, or tincture to aid the liver. It is also a diuretic. For long-held anger that relates to liver, use milk thistle. It is also good for hepatitis; it is high in insulin for diabetics and raises the secretion of bile. Red clover is a blood cleanser that aids in the prevention of cancer.

Congested liver shows in the eyes. To clear the eyes, use eyebright, bilberry, horsetail, and goldenseal.

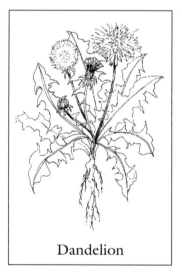

Dandelion

Echinacea is a viral and bacterial herb and goldenseal is used for infections. Goldenseal is a bitter anti-inflammatory, and bitter is the taste for the wood element. Garlic is also good for the liver. It has many, many benefits, among which is being a natural antibiotic.

The Tiger

Major Organ: Lungs

Major herbs: mullein, yarrow, coltsfoot, parsley, usnea, slippery elm, valerian, oatstraw, licorice, garlic.

Parsley is rich in vitamins A, B, and C. Mullein is good to relieve congestion for bronchial and asthmatic conditions, combined with yarrow for inflammations. Usnea tincture is an antibiotic for infections. Coltsfoot for coughs is a mucilaenocous, an herb that is slippery and smooth and aids in healing coughs and relieving the chest of phlegm. Make slippery elm into a gruel for dry cough. Valerian is an excellent herb to relieve tension and exhaustion. Try oatstraw for your nerves. Licorice root is a tonic for the adrenals and, of course, the ever-amazing garlic has antibiotic properties that are good for the Tiger.

The Cat

Major Organ: Large Intestine

Major herbs: artichoke, nettle, marshmallow root, anise, cascara sagrada, slippery elm.

Use nettle as a spring tonic, or cooked as a vegetable. Marshmallow root is good for mucous membranes. Anise in tea form is used as a stimulant and carminative to treat flatulence and colic. Add to laxative formulas to reduce cramping of the bowels. Cascara sagrada is a mild laxative without astringent (drying) effects. It will help restore tone and normal muscular activity to the lower bowel. Use as a tea or in capsules. Use slippery elm as a tea or gruel. It soothes, heals, and strengthens the digestive track for easier elimination.

The Dragon

Major Organ: Stomach

Major herbs: peppermint, dandelion, gingerroot, fennel, valerian, licorice root.

Peppermint tea increases bile flow, combats gas, heals stomach and liver. Dandelion root helps digestion; take a tincture 30 minutes before a meal. Gingerroot is good for digestion as a tonic or a tea. Fennel is a digestive healing tea. Valerian root is for stress. It calms the nerves, aids anxiety, PMS, insomnia, and gastrointestinal disorders. Marshmallow root soothes mucous membranes.

The Snake

Major Organ: Spleen/Pancreas

Major herbs: celery, red beets, apples, chicory, figs, dates, molasses, fennel, valerian, ginseng, astragalus, oatstraw, red raspberry, chickweed, echinacea, goldenseal, ginseng.

The Snake is often nervous, can suffer from a shortage of potassium sulfate found in celery, red beets, apples, chicory, figs, dates, molasses, fennel, savory, and valerian. Herbs grown in the high desert regions are of more benefit to the spleen and pancreas. They transform moisture in the body. Cooked foods of sweetness— yellow, orange, and brown foods such as corn, carrots, sweet potatoes, yellow squash, pumpkin, brown rice, millet, barley, onions, cabbage, and artichokes—are excellent for the Snake. Take chamomile tea as a bath or tea to relax. Red raspberry tea is soothing to the stomach. Chickweed is a blood cleanser that restores cells. Echinacea and goldenseal aid the stomanch, while ginseng is stimulating to all the systems. Astragalus is an immune-system booster.

The Horse

Major Organ: Heart

Major herbs: hawthorne, dandelion root and leaf, yarrow, chamomile, nettle.

Hawthorne is a tonic for the heart, regulates blood pressure, whether high or low. Dandelion is a diuretic and, interestingly, a cure for warts. Squeeze a leaf or flower of that milky looking juice, put on wart to dry. Wart will soon turn black and leave skin unmarked. You can cook the dandelion leaves and add yellow petals to muffins, salads, and pancakes. It has beta-carotene, which is full of vitamins and minerals to aid the heart. Chamomile is calming and relaxing for the heart muscles and healing for the tissues. Nettle helps to strengthen the heart.

Nettles

The Sheep

Major Organ: Small Intestine

Major herbs: nettle, barberry, yarrow, uva ursi usnea, oatstraw, astragalus, goldenseal.

Nettle is a spring fiber vegetable full of vitamins and minerals. It helps elimination. Use dry, sprinkled on foods. Barberry is a tonic, purgative, and antiseptic. It helps jaundice, complaints of digestion. Yarrow is an astringent; it heals inflamed tissues, internal and external.

Use uva ursi for urinary infections and usnea for general infections, as it is an antibiotic. Oatstraw heals nerves and stress. Astragalus root is good for the immune system. Cook strips of the root in soups, then discard. Goldenseal is an anti-inflammatory (bitter) herb to stimulate bile.

The Monkey

Major Organ: Urinary Bladder

Major herbs: asparagus, lemon balm, uva ursi, dandelion, milk thistle, red clover, vitamin C, yarrow.

Lemon Balm is a good tea for the digestive tract and is calming. Uva ursi is used for the bladder to kill bacteria. Dandelion is used as a high source of calcium. Comfrey is used for bones, restores bone loss.* Asparagus is a natural diuretic. Red clover purifies the blood and helps protect against cancer cells forming. Cranberry juice helps to stop a bladder infection that is just developing. Vitamin C is helpful in acidifying the urine and washing out bacteria. Yarrow is an astringent, antibacterial, and diuretic. Comfrey is used for bloody urine.

Red Clover

---

*Comfrey has become a controversial herb in recent years, but herbalists have used it for centuries. The problematic factor is found only in fresh young Comfrey. Most herbalists feel a tea of dried leaves is safe and beneficial, particularly in the knitting of bones . . . it is also called Knitbone. Consult your own herbalist or health professional to ascertain what the status is at the time you read this.

The Rooster

Major Organ: Kidneys

Major herbs: dandelion, nettle, comfrey, red beets, astragalus, ginger, ginkgo biloba, Korean ginseng, garlic.

The Rooster should eat eggs, cheese, kale, spinach, prunes, leeks, raisins, coconut, almonds, rye bread, and fish. Comfrey heals inside and out. It is often called knitbone. It has calcium, is a bone builder, is good for bone loss. Very good in ulceration of kidneys, stomach, and bowel, nettle and dandelion dried and sprinkled over food are both high in vitamins, minerals, and calcium. Dandelion is a blood cleanser for kidneys and nettle is a tonic for the kidneys. Astragalus is used for the immune system. Ginkgo biloba is good for fears. Korean ginseng is a warming blood tonic.

The Dog

Major Organ: Circulation-Sex (also the pericardium)

Major herbs: mullein, barley, hawthorne, ginkgo, ginger, eyebright, oatstraw, lavender, raspberry leaves, lemon balm.

The Dog needs a more vegetarian diet. Celery, apples, spinach, strawberries, coconut, figs, a few eggs, and some oily fish.

Hawthorne regulates blood pressure, Mullein soothes the lungs and mucous membranes. Ginkgo is good for circulation. Ginger is used to warm the body and good for circulation during colds and flus. Oatstraw is for the nerves; it heals and soothes. Lavender is calming, as are raspberry leaves. Lemon balm can be used as a calming diaphoretic for fevers.

The Boar

Major Organ: Triple Warmer (thyroid, thymus, metabolism)

Major herbs: sea vegetables, kelp, bilberry, meadowsweet, rosehips, lungwort, echinacea, Irish moss, alfalfa, parsley, poke root.

Sea vegetables and kelp are used for thyroid conditions. Use uva ursi for water retention, and fennel for adrenals. Bilberry is good for diarrhea, regulates glandular system. Meadowsweet has iron and magnesium. It is an astringent and promotes sweating. Rose-hips have vitamins C, A, B, and E. They are good for cough and chest problems. Lungwort is used for lungs, coughs, inflammation, and phlegm. Echinacea is for lymphatic purification, viral and bacterial infections. Poke root stimulates the thyroid gland, while chickweed tea cleanses fat from the blood.

The reason I have suggesed dandelion, nettle, and mullein repeatedly for many of the meridian imbalances is because I have found, over the years, that these plants are very compatible with people without any adverse effects. They are successfully used for several of the meridian imbalances, since these plants are powerhouses within themselves and very effective, yet mild.

As an herbalist, if I had to choose only one herb to take on a long journey, it would be dandelion. I was born in the Year of the Snake, Hour of the Ox, and Minute of the Cat. The health of my liver is of utmost importance to me. Dandelion has two particularly important functions: the formation of bile and removal of excess water from the body in edema conditions, resulting from liver problems.

The liver must be kept healthy in all the power animals, hence, dandelion is a perfect all-around tonic. Used as a tea or tincture, and in cooking (using the leaves and yellow petals), it removes toxins from the body.

Nettle would be my second choice as an important herb for preventive care. "Stinging nettle" is a perennial plant found all over the world. While harvesting this wonderful weed in Washington state, I was reminded several times by its attention-getting "stings." But, as my teacher would show the group, the antidote to any aggressive plant always grows close by. Yes, there was plantain waving its little stalk to show us its location. A small bruised leaf of the plantain would soothe the stinging finger immediately.

Used as an astringent, diuretic, and tonic, the young nettle leaves can be cooked as a pot herb. Full of vitamins and minerals, dried and crumbled nettle and dandelion can be spirinkled on salads, meats, and vegetables.

Nettle is wonderful for hayfever, stimulates the digestion, promotes milk flow in nursing mothers, and is a remedy for blood in the urine and urinary tract infections. Do not eat uncooked, old plants. Nettle is a perfect tonic for keeping healthy.

Mullein is a tall biennial plant. It grows in clearings, fields, and waste places from the Atlantic Coast west to South Dakota and Kansas. It is used as a tea for bronchitis, coughs, hoarseness, bronchial catarrh, and whooping cough, as well as for other respiratory problems.

In my family, there are members with asthma and bronchitis. Mullein is wonderful alone, but with nettle and yarrow it will help stop symptoms and give relief.

The herbs I have suggested in this chapter I grow and use daily for prevention of illness. Tincturing is my favorite way of preparing the plant for future use, since it will last indefinitely. You create tinctures by placing the herbs in alcohol; your herbalist can show you how.

Caroline Patrick is an herbalist, artist, and feng shui consultant. Skilled in every art medium, from watercolor to oil, she has created intuitive healing pictures for people for years. Caroline has over thirty years of teaching experience, including a ten-year instruction position with Cochise College in Southeastern Arizona. She has conducted workshops on art, herbs, and feng shui. Today, she brings her talent for art and color to feng shui, offering consultations and original art as healing "cures" for any area of the bagua. She does murals and paintings and has a studio in Benicia, California. Caroline is the cover artist and the author of this herb chapter, as well as creating the major artwork in this book. She may be reached at **Caroline@fengshuiartistry.com.**

Postures of the Meridians

In the course of a day, we assume different postures spontaneously. Sometimes we are known for the postures we take. Do you slouch? Do you fold your arms in front of you when others are speaking, as if you were rejecting that information so it can't enter your body? The postures we take compensate for any imbalance in a meridian/organ/power animal.

According to our four power animals, we will often find ourselves in the postures attributed to them, as some of our natural stances. Other times, our postures can be an indicator of what is currently out of balance in our bodies. When a Horse type crosses her arms in front of her, rejecting the information coming at her, she can either have the Snake/Spleen energy prominent elsewhere in her life, or it can be a momentary reaction to the party she's dealing with. Generally speaking, though, we've researched the

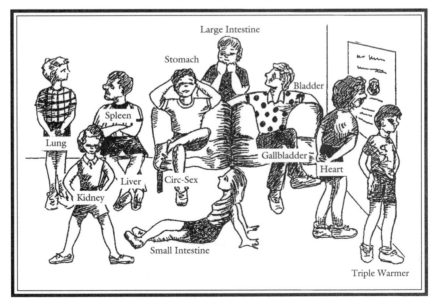

Figure 20. The Waiting Room.

material and found that the power animal will often use the posture attributed to the meridian more often than others.

The Rat will cross his legs, right ankle (or knee) on left knee when issues of betrayal or abandonment come up.

The Ox often sits with her left ankle over her right ankle when she's unhappy or perturbed, and may tap the foot to indicate she'd rather be somewhere else.

The Tiger will sedately clasp her hands in front of her, waiting patiently to be recognized, waiting for her turn, inwardly wondering why she must stand alongside the "star" when she is so much more delightful and should be in the spotlight.

The Cat will sit dejectedly, hands on chin, on the outside looking in, feeling insecure, not sure if he should make a move or not.

The Dragon puts his hands behind his head, in as much as to say "show me." He can use this posture when he feels disgusted by what he sees. After a meal, it can mean he's filled . . . finally.

The Snake crosses her arms in front of her in order to protect herself. It's also body language to say "I don't want to hear another perspective." The Snake needs to be right, you know.

The Horse crosses her hands behind her back and walks forward, or peers at a sign in front of her, seemingly nonchalant.

The Sheep closes up his stance and places the right ankle over the left ankle when he feels he's being discriminated against, or in some way victimized.

The Monkey spreads his arms along the back of a chair or sofa to show the expanse he covers, which indicates he's the one in charge.

The Rooster puts hands on hips and is the watchdog or whistle blower of the group. It's also a sign of sexual insecurity.

The Dog crosses his left ankle on the right ankle or knee, indicating a sexual inhibitedness—closing in, closing down, withdrawing.

The Boar, when pessimistic, slouches around with his hands in his pockets.

Sometimes the postures we take are involuntary reactions to what we've just experienced. For example, when I was taking the hypnotherapy course, there were about twenty of us in the introductory class. We were all right-brained people learning from a holistic perspective. It so happened that one woman who took the class had a best girlfriend who was drawn to take the class with her. This woman, however, was very left-brained. After about a day, she wanted more structure and more form, and something she could relate to tangibly. Being from a formal therapy, she confronted the teacher, who deftly asked the class how they felt about it. We "right-brainers" all stuck together and said we liked the format just the way it was.

It was interesting to watch the postures this woman then went into, one after another. First, she put her right ankle over her left, indicating she felt victimized by the group. Then she put her right knee over her left and crossed her legs, feeling abandoned by us.

As you watch TV, you can often detect, from the way people stand when they aren't the focal point of the script, what emotions/meridians are imbalanced. Those who stand with their hands clasped in front of them are experiencing some Tiger/Lung issues around their ego and being recognized or, conversely, ignored. Those who spread their arms across the back of the sofa are just waiting to interject their persona on the scene and take over.

When research was done on these postures, it was found that, by holding the posture and concentrating on the positive emotions of the meridian, it strengthens the muscles related to the meridian and, concurrently, strengthens the positive emotion, causing less necessity for holding the posture until it fades away.

So, if you find you are holding any of these postures, whether by the fact that you are reflecting your power animals of birth, or by current situations, when you notice it, repeat the positive emotion for a number of times while in that position.

The Rat	right ankle/knee on left knee	I am adored
The Ox	left ankle on right ankle	I am happy
The Tiger	hands crossed in front	I am recognized
The Cat	hands on chin	I am sacred
The Dragon	hands behind head	I am content
The Snake	arms crossed in front	I am confident

The Horse	hands crossed behind	I am loved
The Sheep	right ankle over left	I am equal
The Monkey	arms spread back of seat	I am faith
The Rooster	hands on hips	I am at peace
The Dog	left ankle on right	I am connected

As you go about your day, notice the postures you take and those with whom you interact. You'll be amazed to see how often you take a particular posture with a particular person. In some way, their energy is intimidating you and you are defensively using the posture to protect yourself. Repeat the affirmation silently and allow the positive to instill itself within you. Then, as you face this person from the positive energy, you will show them, by the lack of the defensive posture, that you are empowered in their presence, not disempowered.

Numerology and the Chinese Power Animals

Joe Ivory, Numerologist

Long ago, the ancients recognized that life seemed to move and progress in repeated cycles. They observed that the actual numbers contained within each year's designation (when reduced to a single digit through addition), i.e., $1935 = 1 + 9 + 3 + 5 = 18 = 1 + 8 = 9$, seemed to match qualities possessed by individuals born in those years. Through the use of the nine numerological number meanings, it became possible to compile a profile for that particular year/individual.

In like manner, the ancient oriental astrologers noticed that all earthly or mundane affairs and yearly events seemed to follow a similar repetitive sequence. They determined that people born in the same year seemed to possess similar character traits, characteristics that were identical to the nature and qualities possessed by the actual year.

In numerology, we use (9) numbers to identify traits of personality and character or human qualities of consciousness. Those qualities are:

1

Independence, determination, originality, willpower, pride, self-assurance, and individuality

2

Gentleness, tact, cooperation, diplomacy, sympathy, tenderness, forgiveness, affection, and love

3

Artistic expression, social, gregarious, talented, creative, communicative, caring, and spontaneity

4

Justice, responsibility, dependability, hard worker, organized, systematic, practical, and grounded

5

Freedom-loving, experiential, restless, curious, quick study, intellectual, analytical, restless, and clever

6

Caring, domestic, protective; a comforter, teacher, reformer, romantic, idealistic, and humanitarian

7

Scientific, intellectual, conservative, perfectionistic, introspective, pensive, spiritual, and meditative

8

Efficient, powerful, dominant, result-oriented, driven, hard-nosed, direct, a problem solver and seeker

9

Tolerant, charitable, understanding, self-sacrificing, artistic, psychic, poetic, dramatic, and generous

Applying these traits to the years and power animals, if you were born in 1934, the number is (8) ($1 + 9 + 3 + 4 = 17 = 1 + 7 = 8$). Your (8) would mean that you possess a strength of character that projects an air of authority. You like to take charge and have things well-organized around you.

If you were born in 1985, your number would be (5) ($1 + 9 + 8 + 5 = 23 = 2 + 3 = 5$). (5) indicates that you are a somewhat restless person who craves change and variety. You would be very uncomfortable in a regimented job and would need freedom to make your own decisions, even when unpopular.

If you were born in 1972, your number would be (1) ($1 + 9 + 7 + 2 = 19 = 1 + 9 = 10 = 1 + 0 = 1$). (1) indicates you want to be known distinctly as a unique and original innovator. You would be self-reliant and determined to make your mark and name in the world. You would allow no one to boss or direct you.

Considering the above, I reasoned the personality traits of each power-animal year might relate to numerological traits of the year's total. Not only was there a correlation, but an interesting pattern grouping began to appear. I discovered that the (12) animal signs fall into (3) groups of (4) animal signs. The first group of animals fell characteristically under the numbers (1, 4, and 7), the second group under the numbers (2, 5 and 8), and the third under the numbers (3, 6, and 9). I realized immediately that what had coalesced was known in numerology as the Mystic Cross. It is a classic number formation showing how certain numbers showing similar traits group together.

1 4 7 = 3 (The concord of initiative, knowledge, analysis)
2 5 8 = 6 (The concord of kindness, change, organization)
3 6 9 = 9 (The concord of love, beauty, service)

Putting the Mystic Cross to work as template and guide to further delineation of your Chinese power animal traits, we come up with the following character grids:

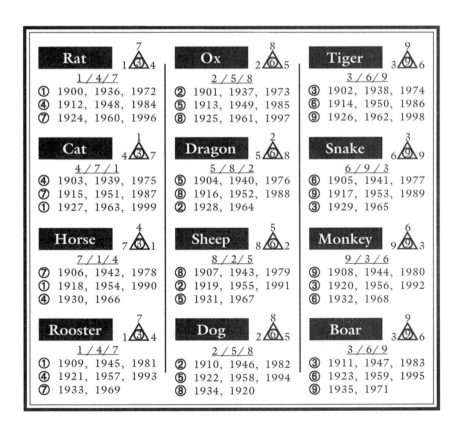

- 3 -

The Rat

① 1900, 1936, 1972 - Leaders in thought and action. Innovators, creative and expressive, accomplished planners, pace-setters.

④ 1912, 1948, 1984 - Good with detail, private, protective. Born adviser, diligent and hard-working. Problem solver, thrifty, collects things.

① 1924, 1960, 1996 - Outwardly cool, but sociable, intellectual. Observant, very private, analytical. Strong-minded, philosophical, logical, judgmental.

The Cat

④ 1903, 1939, 1975 - Strength of purpose, craves security, aloof and reserved. Hard-working, meticulous, cautious, scholarly, refined, virtuous.

⑦ 1915, 1951, 1987 - Observant, intellectual, aesthetic, spiritual. Very critical and secretive, conservative, pedantic, needs equilibrium, metaphysical.

① 1927, 1963, 1999 - Strong-willed, courageous, aggressive. Analytical, impatient, intuitive, charming, self-centered, competitive, confident.

The Horse

⑦ 1906, 1942, 1978 - Intolerant, altruistic, intellectual. Scholarly, brilliant, resists authority. Bold, sharp wit, charming, refined.

① 1918, 1954, 1990 - Brilliant, resourceful, stubborn, decisive. Emotionally private, impulsive, proud, restless, aggressive, rebellious.

④ 1930, 1966 - Hard-working, astute, technically creative. Strong-willed, leader, outspoken, methodical, fashion-conscious, skilled manager.

The Rooster

⑦ 1909, 1945, 1981 - Determined, animated, direct, alert. Idealistic, hates taking direction, bossy. Hard-worker, dignified, passionate.

① 1921, 1957, 1993 - Intellectual, aesthetic, analytical, detailed. Meticulous, regal presence, organized, skilled craftsman, hard worker.

④ 1933, 1969 - Conscientious, meticulous craftsman, efficient. Gourmet, avant garde, progressive, sociable, determined, success-oriented, perfectionist.

- 6 -

The Ox

② 1901, 1937, 1973 - A thinker, patient, hard-working, intuitive. Reliable, strong-willed, persistent, determined. A planner, an executive, cautious.

⑤ 1913, 1949, 1985 - Charismatic, impulsive, impatient. A planner, inspired, spiritual, attractive. A genius, inventive, outspoken, passionate, idealistic.

⑧ 1925, 1961, 1997 - Self-reliant, executive, tyrannical, pedantic. Very organized, methodical, experiential, restless. A leader, zealous, bold, honest.

The Dragon

⑤ 1904, 1940, 1976 - Energetic, dynamic, social, inspired, charming. Generous, elegant, fashion-conscious, magnetic, sentimental, romantic.

⑧ 1916, 1952, 1988 - An achiever, strong, tough, powerful. Ambitious, adventurous, dramatic, charismatic, assertive, decisive, controller.

② 1928, 1964 - Sensual, refined, scholarly, well-liked. Thoughtful, domestic, high curiosity, intuitive, passionate, soft touch, sentimental, dramatic.

The Sheep

⑧ 1907, 1943, 1979 - Combative, temperamental. A controller, manager, competitive, vengeful. Analyst, director, methodical, risk-taker, considerate.

② 1919, 1955, 1991 - Intuitive, sensitive emotionally, perceptive, charming. Sensual, loves attention, affectionate. Counselor, tenacious, quiet, strong.

⑤ 1931, 1967 - Emotional, passionate, wild and reactive. Charming, refined, appealing, inspirational, talented, spendthrift, impulsive, has temper.

The Dog

② 1910, 1946, 1982 - Artistic, aloof, private, aggressive, resolute, adviser. Gentle, analytical, intuitive, strong-minded, quiet, loyal, hates injustice.

⑤ 1922, 1958, 1994 - Passionate, emotional, enthusiastic, involved in life. A fighter, magnetic, desirable, entertaining, risk-taker, courageous, caring.

⑧ 1934, 1970 - Strong-minded, generous, inspirational, loyal, direct. A controller, resists change, sympathetic, critical, inspires confidence, sociable.

- 9 -

The Tiger

③ 1902, 1938, 1974 - Charismatic, dramatic, artistic. Restless, always searching, outspoken, revolutionary, tough. Altruistic, energetic, passionate.

⑥ 1914, 1950, 1986 - Charming, social, caretaker, artistic, musical. Counselor, reliable, magnetic, verbal, virtuous, hates injustice, natural teacher.

⑨ 1926, 1962, 1998 - Engergetic, humanitarian, philanthropic, sentimental, a healer. Born advisor, a powerhouse, action-oriented, optimistic, bon vivant.

The Snake

⑥ 1905, 1941, 1977 - Meticulous planner, imaginative, meditative. Emotional, psychic, counselor, adviser. Healer, youthful, generous, cautious.

⑨ 1917, 1953 1989 - Scholarly, deep-thinking, playful, brilliant. Competitive, loves power, strong-willed, avant garde, charming, ruthless, sexual, loves family.

③ 1929, 1965 - Artistic, talented, ambitious, sales-oriented, loves to please. Stylish, decisive, quick thinker, fashionable, communicative, social, optimistic.

The Monkey

⑨ 1908, 1944, 1980 - Dominating, forceful, hard-driving, broad-minded. Ambitious, energetic, imaginative, quick-minded. Driving, overindulgent, generous.

③ 1920, 1956, 1992 - Artistic, social, articulate, caring. Helpful, skillful, problem solver. Achiever, decisive, impulsive, visionary.

⑥ 1932, 1968 - Balanced, security-conscious, counselor. Healer, fashion-conscious, clever, social. A teacher, protective, sexy, sharp temper, hates injustice.

The Boar

③ 1911, 1947, 1983 - Energetic, a crusader, artistic, advisor. Extroverted, idealistic. A transformer, optimistic, a communicator, magnetic.

⑥ 1923, 1959, 1995 - Domestic, teacher, reformer. A comforter, protector, sentimental. Idealistic, kind-hearted, compassionate, homemaker.

⑨ 1935, 1971 - Intense, humanistic, artistic, communicator, introspective, caretaker. Loyal, self-preserving, sensitive, honorable. Meticulous, hard-working, passionate.

Born in January-February of Any Year

But what about those of you born in January and early February, when the power animal overlaps its principal year and extends slightly into the year following? In Chinese astrology, the tendencies are the same, but when adding numerology, we have to look at the new number involved. If you are a Monkey born during January of 1981, you will have a slightly different personality profile than the majority of Monkeys born in 1980 due to the number of the year 1981 (1 + 9 + 8 + 1 = 19 + 1 + 9 = 1). You will still have the basic traits given for the Monkey personality, but will blend them with traits gained from the influences of 1981. The chart below will delineate these added qualities.

The Rat

(3) 1900–1901   1936–1937   1972–1973
verbal skills, creative self-expression, a visionary zest for life.

(9) 1912–1913   1948–1949   1984–1985
emotional empathy, forgiving, warm and compassionate, altruistic.

(6) 1924–1925   1960–1961   1996–1997
caring, a counselor, teacher, facilitator for others, a truth-seeker.

The Cat (Rabbit)

(9) 1903–1904   1939–1940   1975–1976
humanistic, understanding, mystical, artistic, inspired, a visionary.

(6) 1915–1916   1951–1952   1987–1988
family oriented, responsible socially, cultured, charitable, a server.

(3) 1927–1928   1963–1964   1999–2000
fun-loving, animated, expansive, versatile, quick mind, ambitious.

The Horse

(6) 1906–1907   1942–1943   1978–1979
peacemaker, domestic, musical, honest and reliable, imaginative.

(3) 1918–1919   1954–1955   1990–1991
gregarious, charming, conversational, energetic, flirtatious, fun.

(9) 1930–1931   1966–1967
charismatic, universal in outlook, self-sacrificing, poetic.

The Rooster

(3) 1909–1910   1945–1946   1981–1982
demanding, detailed, versatile, aspiring, enduring, true friend.

⑨ **1921–1922   1957–1958   1993–1994**
psychic, aesthetic, generous, idealistic, dramatic, emotional.

⑥ **1933–1934   1969–1970**
sees beauty and justice, intelligent, gregarious, devoted to family.

The Ox

⑤ **1901–1902   1937–1938   1973–1974**
loves freedom, iconoclast; loves change, hates routine.

② **1913–1914   1949–1950   1985–1986**
retiring, self-conscious, artistic, peacemaker, team player.

⑧ **1925–1926   1961–1962   1997–1998**
wants success, power, control, authority; analyst, executive.

The Dragon

② **1904–1905   1940–1941   1976–1977**
compassionate, loyal, supportive; healer, good listener, orderly.

⑧ **1916–1917   1952–1953   1988–1989**
go-getter, drill-sergeant attitude, intolerant, aggressive, ruthless.

⑤ **1928–1929   1964–1965**
an analyst, curious, investigative, skilled technician, contemplative.

The Sheep

⑧ **1907–1908   1943–1944   1979–1980**
assertive, achiever, goal-setter, forceful, hard worker, efficient.

⑤ **1919–1920   1955–1956   1991–1992**
adventurous, experiential, technician, clever, witty, gambler.

② **1931–1932   1967–1968**
loyal, quiet, reflective, sensitive emotionally, easily hurt.

The Dog

⑤ **1910–1911   1946–1947   1982–1983**
impulsive, intelligent, imaginative, high strung, analyst, cautious.

② **1922–1923   1958–1959   1994–1995**
reserved, cautious, suspicious, practical, stress-prone, easily hurt.

⑧ **1934–1935   1970–1971**
serious, reserved, ambitious, tenacious, thorough, determined.

The Tiger

⑦ **1902–1903   1938–1939   1974–1975**
leader, thinker, introspective, contradictory tendencies, mystical.

④ **1914–1915   1950–1951   1986–1987**
organizer, hard worker, enthusiastic, efficient, pragmatic.

① **1926–1927   1962–1963   1998–1999**
positive, aggressive, original, unique style, self-assured.

The Snake

④ 1905–1906   1941–1942   1977–1978
serious, orderly, logical and rational, hard-working, methodical.

① 1917–1918   1953–1954   1989–1990
intelligent, capable, well-organized; precise, a leader, protagonist.

⑦ 1929–1930   1965–1966
imaginative, practical, analytical, logical, freedom-loving.

The Monkey

① 1908–1909   1944–1945   1980–1981
hard working, dignified, independent, decisive, self-reliant.

⑦ 1920–1921   1956–1957   1992–1993
leader, organized, mystical, innovator, investigative, elegant.

④ 1932–1933   1968–1969
fastidious, craftsman, efficient, disciplined; a planner, stable.

The Boar

⑦ 1911–1912   1947–1948   1983–1984
high strung, deep-feeling and thinking, affectionate, sympathetic.

④ 1923–1924   1959–1960   1995–1996
independent, refined, grounded, common sense, practical, patient.

① 1935–1936   1971–1972
self-directed, a path finder, inspired, idealistic, dynamic, confident.

Look at the chart on pages 307–309, to see if your January-February birthdate falls in the year of the animal in question or is symbolized by the one before.

Joe Ivory has been a career numerologist and astrologer since 1974. He has earnestly aided wisdom-seekers by supporting their spiritual advancement through clarificatioin of their soul's path and life purpose. He is a San Francisco Bay Area author, lecturer, and teacher on the subjects of tarot, numerology, and astrology. He joins Pam Powers on the website: www.acumind.com and can be reached at **lifeforce@aol.com.**

Appendices

Appendix A

The Power Animals and the Sun Signs

The power animals become animated aspects of our personalities as we begin to move from the year of the animal to see what other animals exist within us. The next step is the month or sign of an animal.

Within the sections delineating the different animals, I state, after the celebrities who were born in the year of the animal archetype, "Those born in the Month of (the Dog, Boar, Cat, etc.) . . . are generally (Aquarians, Pisces, Cancerians)." Because the Chinese calendar is not quite in sync with the astrology calendar, those born on the cusps may find they reflect the animal next to the one assigned.

It is commonly agreed that the Chinese lunar calendar and its animals coincide generally with the Western astrology Sun signs.

In this book, the animals are assigned to different signs than you may have read elsewhere. I've seen at least three different versions, and mine is different from the previous ones.

In making this correlation from the Sun signs to the animals, I used the meridians and their emotions as they related to the animals on the Time of Day Wheel as the criteria and found that this worked out best. If I had my druthers and could move the animals around as I pleased, I would make a few adjustments. But, we have an astrology wheel that has been handed down through the centuries that works. And, we have a Time of Day Wheel with the meridians and the animals, which has come down through time, and so we need to have them work together. Because there are different animals attributed to the Sun signs in other books, I felt the need to take a few pages and address the reasons why I chose the system I did.

Aries—the Rat

It has been written that, when the Chinese animals were called by the Buddha, the Rat came first, and Aries is the first sign. The Rat is very subjective and acts on his anger. Arians are known for their need to be first, also for their tempers and stamping their feet and demanding their own way as the baby of the zodiac might. They are hotheaded at times.

Taurus—the Ox

Well, the Ox fits here very well, as a surrogate for the Taurean bull. They are both very solid, sturdy. They till the soil and are one with Earth. They move slowly, but make steady progress. The meridian is the Liver, and the Ox may never take the yoke from around his neck and so feels repressed.

Gemini—the Tiger

While the elements of astrology and the elements of the meridians don't coincide on the wheels, with the Tiger, the Lung meridian is in the metal or air element, and so is Gemini an air sign. The Tiger roars, much like the lion, and needs a lot of lung power to do it. He is one of the powers of the jungle and the Lung meridian deals with ego and pride . . . and lung power.

Cancer—the Cat

The independent Cat may not seem like a true animal for the Cancerian sign, but we have all sorts of cats: alley cats, outdoor cats, and house cats. We have cats that always stay home and are never allowed outdoors. And, we should remember that, no matter how far he goes, the Cat will always find his way home. The Cat maintains his independence whatever path he's put on. The Large Intestine is the meridian and the emotions have to do with self-esteem, self-love, guilt, feeling clean about oneself . . . and developing self-love. Cancer meets the criteria of these symbols and emotions.

Leo—the Dragon

Ah! The roar of the Leo lion or the fire-breathing Dragon . . . not much difference here. The Leo personality is larger than life, and so is the Dragon. Leo loves theater and make believe and the

Dragon is a mythical character. The Stomach is the meridian for the Dragon, and Leo never wants to feel deprived, but always seeks to live greater and grander than us all. The Stomach meridian speaks to identity and the roles we take on in life, much as the Leo acts out roles on stage or in film.

Virgo—the Snake

The Snake has a tongue that lashes out, and Virgos are often criticized for having a vituperative tongue. Virgo is a mutable sign, which means it is fluid and moves with the energy flow. The snake moves by slithering along. The Spleen is the meridian for the Snake, and there is a perfectionism about the emotions of the Spleen. The Snake hates to be wrong, always has to be right, and has to have the last word. Virgos work so hard to make sure they do everything right and are shattered when they discover they haven't covered all the bases, or have interpreted wrongly.

Libra—the Horse

Librans seek to join with another and belong in a twosome. The primary emotion for the Heart meridian and its animal, the Horse, is to belong. The Heart resonates to touch and being touched, to truly belong and love. Love is a primary motivation for the Horse. The Heart meridian is in the fire element and this element is generally considered to deal with relationships.

Scorpio—the Sheep

Of all the animals, this coupling seems to be the one that doesn't work. The Sheep . . . in relation to Scorpio? We can force a square peg into a round hole and say that Pluto/Scorpio energy deals with the masses, and the Sheep runs with the herd . . . that it is important that humanity in general doesn't fall into a herd mentality and get swept away with any one concept. There is a saying, "like a sheep to slaughter," and certainly "slaughter" is a Scorpio word. It can also be attributed to the "poor me" aspect of the water sign personality that can be employed by Scorpios . . . as long as it works for them. If it doesn't, then they can fall back on intimidation. The meridian is the Small Intestine, which deals with victim or victor and certainly the Scorpio energy can be intense and seeks to dominate and be victorious.

Sagittarius—the Monkey

The Monkey personality creates a form of reality he can live with. He really doesn't want anyone to challenge it. Sagittarians, too, tend to get hold of a dogma to which they ascribe. A dogma tends to override anything unlike itself, and the Monkey person override's signals from the body in order to maintain his truth. The Bladder is the meridian that has to do with control vs. faith in a higher source. Sagittarius is generally considered the home of organized religion, and religion believes in duty.

Capricorn—the Rooster

The Rooster decides that we shall wake up when the Sun comes up and cock-a-doodle-doos to make sure we do, just as Capicorns like to control their world and set the rules and regulations for the rest of us. Saturn and Capricorn rule the bones and skeletal system, and so does the Rooster and the Kidney meridian rule bones, teeth, and the skeletal structure.

Aquarius—the Dog

The Dog is a friendly animal and, like the Aquarian, can be open to all who treat him right. But the Aquarian also has an iconoclastic side, and retreats from humanity. He loves humanity as a whole, but may not like them on a one-to-one basis. So, too, the Dog can be open and guileless as a puppy, or get territorial and bark loudly and create a boundary through which no one is allowed unless invited. The Circulation-Sex meridian rules here, inclining people to be reserved, cautious, and shy, with sexual-intimacy issues at times. Aquarians are known to love everyone, but be awkward in one-to-one relationships.

Pisces—the Boar

Pisces has been called the collective garbage can of the universe, encompassing all of the other eleven signs. Pisceans are known to have deep depressions that are hard to pull out of. The Boar deals with hope and hopelessness, and can fall into a bog of despair. He needs to rise to the heights of spirituality and light, and not stay in the darkness.

As you can see, the correlation from the meridians to the signs works pretty accurately this way. I've tried to work the meridian emotions with the other Sun sign–animal systems that are in print, but they don't resonate as this system does.

If I were God and could move the wheels around, I'd tend to switch Virgo and Scorpio. I'd assign the Snake to Scorpio and the Sheep to Virgo. Certainly, the Snake has aspects of the Scorpio inclination to bide its time and get even, striking when the time is right. Scorpions don't like rejection and will wait to get even. It's a form of not being in the right.

We could also lay claim to Scorpio for the Monkey. In traditional astrology, the Bladder is a Scorpio organ, and certainly the Monkey is in control and will override anything in its way that it doesn't agree with.

But, in fact, we could probably write a sound argument for the animals reflecting most of Pluto's tendencies, since Scorpio/Pluto rule the masses and are a motivational part of us all. My feeling with the Sheep being assigned to Scorpio in this system is that it's simply a matter of understanding the Sheep and it's psychological motivations more deeply. Certainly, Pluto is the planet of the masses, and our collective evolution and growth, and the Sheep would represent the herd or the collective consciousness that is in constant evolution and growth.

Appendix B

The Years of the Chinese Power Animals

Rat
1900 • 1912 • 1924 • 1936 • 1948 • 1960 • 1972 • 1984 • 1996

Ox
1901 • 1913 • 1925 • 1937 • 1949 • 1961 • 1973 • 1985 • 1997

Tiger
1902 • 1914 • 1926 • 1938 • 1950 • 1962 • 1974 • 1986 • 1998

Cat
1903 • 1915 • 1927 • 1939 • 1951 • 1963 • 1975 • 1987 • 1999

Dragon
1904 • 1916 • 1928 • 1940 • 1952 • 1964 • 1976 • 1988 • 2000

Snake
1905 • 1917 • 1929 • 1941 • 1953 • 1965 • 1977 • 1989 • 2001

Horse
1906 • 1918 • 1930 • 1942 • 1954 • 1966 • 1978 • 1990 • 2002

Sheep
1907 • 1919 • 1931 • 1943 • 1955 • 1967 • 1979 • 1991 • 2003

Monkey
1908 • 1920 • 1932 • 1944 • 1956 • 1968 • 1980 • 1992 • 2004

Rooster
1909 • 1921 • 1933 • 1945 • 1957 • 1969 • 1981 • 1993 • 2005

Dog
1910 • 1922 • 1934 • 1946 • 1958 • 1970 • 1982 • 1994 • 2006

Boar
1911 • 1923 • 1935 • 1947 • 1959 • 1971 • 1983 • 1995 • 2007

Chinese Power Animals by Year

1900	January 31, 1900	February 19, 1901	Rat
1901	February 19, 1901	February 8, 1902	Ox
1902	February 8, 1902	January 29, 1903	Tiger
1903	January 29, 1903	February 16, 1904	Cat
1904	February 16, 1904	February 4, 1905	Dragon
1905	February 4, 1905	January 25, 1906	Snake
1906	January 25, 1906	February 13, 1907	Horse
1907	February 13, 1907	February 2, 1908	Sheep
1908	February 2, 1908	January 22, 1909	Monkey
1909	January 22, 1909	February 10, 1910	Rooster
1910	February 10, 1910	January 30, 1911	Dog
1911	January 30, 1911	February 18, 1912	Boar
1912	February 18, 1912	February 6, 1913	Rat
1913	February 6, 1913	January 26, 1914	Ox
1914	January 26, 1914	February 14, 1915	Tiger
1915	February 14, 1915	February 3, 1916	Cat
1916	February 3, 1916	January 23, 1917	Dragon
1917	January 23, 1917	February 11, 1918	Snake
1918	February 11, 1918	February 1, 1919	Horse
1919	February 1, 1919	February 20, 1920	Sheep
1920	February 20, 1920	February 8, 1921	Monkey
1921	February 8, 1921	January 28, 1922	Rooster
1922	January 28, 1922	February 16, 1923	Dog
1923	February 16, 1923	February 5, 1924	Boar
1924	February 5, 1924	January 25, 1925	Rat
1925	January 25, 1925	February 13, 1926	Ox
1926	February 13, 1926	February 2, 1927	Tiger
1927	February 2, 1927	January 23, 1928	Cat
1928	January 23, 1928	February 10, 1929	Dragon
1929	February 10, 1929	January 30, 1930	Snake
1930	January 30, 1930	February 17, 1931	Horse
1931	February 17, 1931	February 6, 1932	Sheep
1932	February 6, 1932	January 26, 1933	Monkey
1933	January 26, 1933	February 14, 1934	Rooster
1934	February 14, 1934	February 4, 1935	Dog
1935	February 4, 1935	January 24, 1936	Boar
1936	January 24, 1936	February 11, 1937	Rat
1937	February 11, 1937	January 31, 1938	Ox
1938	January 31, 1938	February 19, 1939	Tiger

Chinese Power Animals by the Year *(continued)*

1939	February 19, 1939	February 8, 1940	Cat
1940	February 8, 1940	January 27, 1941	Dragon
1941	January 27, 1941	February 15, 1942	Snake
1942	February 15, 1942	February 5, 1943	Horse
1943	February 5, 1943	January 25, 1944	Sheep
1944	January 25, 1944	February 13, 1945	Monkey
1945	February 13, 1945	February 2, 1946	Rooster
1946	February 2, 1946	January 22, 1947	Dog
1947	January 22, 1947	February 10, 1948	Boar
1948	February 10, 1948	January 29, 1949	Rat
1949	January 29, 1949	February 17, 1950	Ox
1950	February 17, 1950	February 6, 1951	Tiger
1951	February 6, 1951	January 27, 1952	Cat
1952	January 27, 1952	February 14, 1953	Dragon
1953	February 14, 1953	February 3, 1954	Snake
1954	February 3, 1954	January 24, 1955	Horse
1955	January 24, 1955	February 12, 1956	Sheep
1956	February 12, 1956	January 31, 1957	Monkey
1957	January 31, 1957	February 16, 1958	Rooster
1958	February 16, 1958	February 8, 1959	Dog
1959	February 8, 1959	January 28, 1960	Boar
1960	January 28, 1960	February 15, 1961	Rat
1961	February 15, 1961	February 5, 1962	Ox
1962	February 5, 1962	January 25, 1963	Tiger
1963	January 25, 1963	February 13, 1964	Cat
1964	February 13, 1964	February 2, 1965	Dragon
1965	February 21, 1965	January 21, 1966	Snake
1966	January 21, 1966	February 9, 1967	Horse
1967	February 9, 1967	January 29, 1968	Sheep
1968	January 29, 1968	February 16, 1969	Monkey
1969	February 17, 1969	February 5, 1970	Rooster
1970	February 6, 1970	January 26, 1971	Dog
1971	January 27, 1971	February 14, 1972	Boar
1972	February 15, 1972	February 2, 1973	Rat
1973	February 3, 1973	January 22, 1974	Ox
1974	January 23, 1974	February 10, 1975	Tiger
1975	February 11, 1975	January 30, 1976	Cat
1976	January 31, 1976	February 17, 1977	Dragon
1977	February 18, 1977	February 6, 1978	Snake

Chinese Power Animals by the Year *(continued)*

1978	February 7, 1978	January 27, 1979	Horse
1979	January 28, 1979	February 15, 1980	Sheep
1980	February 16, 1980	February 4, 1981	Monkey
1981	February 5, 1981	January 24, 1982	Rooster
1982	January 25, 1982	February 12, 1983	Dog
1983	February 13, 1983	February 1, 1984	Boar
1984	February 2, 1984	February 19, 1985	Rat
1985	February 20, 1985	February 8, 1986	Ox
1986	February 9, 1986	January 28, 1987	Tiger
1987	January 29, 1987	February 16, 1988	Cat
1988	February 17, 1988	February 5, 1989	Dragon
1989	February 6, 1989	January 26, 1990	Snake
1990	January 27, 1990	February 14, 1991	Horse
1991	February 15, 1991	February 3, 1992	Sheep
1992	February 4, 1992	January 22, 1993	Monkey
1993	January 23, 1993	February 9, 1994	Rooster
1994	February 10, 1994	January 30, 1995	Dog
1995	January 31, 1995	February 18, 1996	Boar
1996	February 19, 1996	February 6, 1997	Rat
1997	February 7, 1997	January 27, 1998	Ox
1998	January 28, 1998	February 15, 1999	Tiger
1999	February 16, 1999	February 4, 2000	Cat

Appendix C

The Minutes of the Chinese Power Animals*

A.M.

12:00**	Horse	4:00	Monkey	8:00	Dog		
12:10	Sheep	4:10	Rooster	8:10	Boar		
12:20	Monkey	4:20	Dog	8:20	Rat		
12:30	Rooster	4:30	Boar	8:30	Ox		
12:40	Dog	4:40	Rat	8:40	Tiger		
12:50	Boar	4:50	Ox	8:50	Cat		
1:00	Ox	5:00	Cat	9:00	Snake		
1:10	Tiger	5:10	Dragon	9:10	Horse		
1:20	Cat	5:20	Snake	9:20	Sheep		
1:30	Dragon	5:30	Horse	9:30	Monkey		
1:40	Snake	5:40	Sheep	9:40	Rooster		
1:50	Horse	5:50	Monkey	9:50	Dog		
2:00	Sheep	6:00	Rooster	10:00	Boar		
2:10	Monkey	6:10	Dog	10:10	Rat		
2:20	Rooster	6:20	Boar	10:20	Ox		
2:30	Dog	6:30	Rat	10:30	Tiger		
2:40	Boar	6:40	Ox	10:40	Cat		
2:50	Rat	6:50	Tiger	10:50	Dragon		
3:00	Tiger	7:00	Dragon	11:00	Horse		
3:10	Cat	7:10	Snake	11:10	Sheep		
3:20	Dragon	7:20	Horse	11:20	Monkey		
3:30	Snake	7:30	Sheep	11:30	Rooster		
3:40	Horse	7:40	Monkey	11:40	Dog		
3:50	Sheep	7:50	Rooster	11:50	Boar		

*Chart made by author.
**Example: 11:00 P.M.—Rat, Rat is from 11 P.M. through 11:09 P.M.

P.M.

12:00	Rat	4:00	Tiger	8:00	Dragon
12:10	Ox	4:10	Cat	8:10	Snake
12:20	Tiger	4:20	Dragon	8:20	Horse
12:30	Cat	4:30	Snake	8:30	Sheep
12:40	Dragon	4:40	Horse	8:40	Monkey
12:50	Snake	4:50	Sheep	8:50	Rooster
1:00	Sheep	5:00	Rooster	9:00	Boar
1:10	Monkey	5:10	Dog	9:10	Rat
1:20	Rooster	5:20	Boar	9:20	Ox
1:30	Dog	5:30	Rat	9:30	Tiger
1:40	Boar	5:40	Ox	9:40	Cat
1:50	Rat	5:50	Tiger	9:50	Dragon
2:00	Ox	6:00	Cat	10:00	Snake
2:10	Tiger	6:10	Dragon	10:10	Horse
2:20	Cat	6:20	Snake	10:20	Sheep
2:30	Dragon	6:30	Horse	10:30	Monkey
2:40	Snake	6:40	Sheep	10:40	Rooster
2:50	Horse	6:50	Monkey	10:50	Dog
3:00	Monkey	7:00	Dog	11:00	Rat
3:10	Rooster	7:10	Boar	11:10	Ox
3:20	Dog	7:20	Rat	11:20	Tiger
3:30	Boar	7:30	Ox	11:30	Cat
3:40	Rat	7:40	Tiger	11:40	Dragon
3:50	Ox	7:50	Cat	11:50	Snake

Bibliography

Arrien, Angeles. *The Tarot Handbook*. Sonoma, CA: Arcus Publishing, 1987.

Bass, Maureen. *Soul Food*. Napa, CA: Valhalla Press, 1996.

Bauer, Cathryn. *Acupressure for Everybody*. New York: Henry Holt & Co., 1991.

Beijing College of Traditional Chinese Medicine. *Essentials of Chinese Acupuncture*. Beijing: Foreign Language Press, 1980.

Biokinesiology Institute. *Muscle Testing*. Shady Cove, OR: 1982.

Bradshaw, John. *Healing the Shame that Binds You*. Deerfield Beach, FL: Health Communications, 1988.

Campbell, Don. *Music & Miracles*. Wheaton, IL: Quest Books, 1992.

_____. *Music Physician*. Wheaton, IL: Quest Books, 1991.

Chia, Mantak. *Fusion of the 5 Elements I*. Huntington, NY: Healing Tao Books, 1989.

Clogstorm-Willmott, Jonathan. *Western Astrology & Chinese Medicine*. Rochester, VT: Destiny Books, 1985.

Connelly, Dianne M. *Traditional Acupuncture: The Law of the Five Elements*. Columbia, MD: Center for Traditional Acupuncture, 1979.

Course in Miracles. Huntington Station, NY: Coleman Graphics, 1975.

Crawford, E. A. *Chinese Elemental Astrology*. New York: Signet, 1990.

Diamond, John, M.D. *Life Energy*. New York: Paragon House, 1985.

Epstein, Gerald, M.D. *Healing Visualizations*. New York: Bantam Books, 1989.

Falder, Stephen. *Tao of Medicine*. Rochester, VT: Healing Arts Press, 1980.

Fanning, Patrick. *Visualization for Change*. New York: New Harbinger Publishers, 1988.

Fast, Julius. *Body Language*. New York: Pocket Books, 1970.

Fillmore, Charles. *Twelve Powers of Man*. Unity Village, MO: Unity Books, 1930.

Firebrace, Peter. *Acupuncture, How it Works.* Los Angeles: Keats, 1994.

Fratkin, Jake Paul. *Chinese Classics.* Boulder, CO: Shya Publishers, 1990.

Gach, Michael Reed. *Acu-Yoga.* New York: Japan Publications, 1981.

Galadrial, Pamela. *We Never Left the Garden.* S. Lake Tahoe, CA: Mount Tallac Press, 1998.

Gendlin, Eugene T. *Focusing.* New York: Bantam Books, 1978.

Gordon, Marilyn. *Healing is Remembering Who You Are.* Oakland, CA: Wise Word Publishers, 1991.

Haas, Elson M. *Staying Healthy with the Seasons.* Berkeley, CA: Celestial Arts, 1981.

Hadly, Josie. *Hypnosis for Change.* New York: New Harbinger, 1989.

Kaptchuk, Ted, J. *The Web that Has No Weaver.* New York: Congdon & Weed, 1993.

Kavanaugh, Philip, M.D. *Magnificent Addiction.* Lower Lake, CA: Asian Publishers, 1992.

Kenyon, M.D., Julian. *Acupressure Techniques.* Rochester, VT: Healing Arts Press, 1988.

Lau, Kwan. *Secrets of Chinese Astrology.* New York: Tengu Books, 1994.

Lau, Theodora. *Chinese Horoscope Guide to Relationships.* New York: Doubleday, 1995.

_____. *The Handbook of Chinese Horoscopes.* New York: Harper & Row 1979.

Levitt, Susan. *Taoist Astrology.* Rochester, VT: Destiny Books, 1997.

Maciocia, Giovanni. *Foundations of Chinese Medicine.* Philadelphia, PA: Churchill Livingstone, 1989.

Manaka, Yoshio, M.D. *Layman's Guide to Acupuncture.* New York: John Weatherhill, Inc., 1972.

Mann, Felix, M.D. *Acupuncture.* New York: Vintage Books, 1973.

Matsumoto, Kiiko. *Five Elements & Ten Stems.* St. Paul, MN: Paradigm Publishers, 1983.

Moen, Larry. *Guided Imagery.* Los Angeles, CA: United States Publishers, 1992.

Mole, Peter. *Acupuncture.* Boston: Element Books, 1992.

Moss, Louis. *Acupuncture and You*. Secaucus, NJ: Citadel Press, 1964.

Ni, Maoshing. *Yellow Emperor's Classic of Medicine*. Boston: Shambala, 1995.

Olson, Stuart Alve. *Cultivating the Chi*. St. Paul, MN: Dragon Door Publishers, 1992.

Ponder, Catherine. *Healing Secrets of the Ages*. Marina Del Ray, CA: De Vorss, 1967.

Reid, Lori. *Chinese Horoscopes*. New York: Sterling Publishers, 1992.

Rochlitz, Steven. *Why Do Music Conductors Live Into Their 90's*. Mahopac, NY: Human Ecology Balancing Sciences, 1993.

Seem, Mark. *Acupuncture Energetics*. Rochester, VT: Healing Arts Press, 1987.

_____. *Acupuncture Imaging*. Rochester, VT: Healing Arts Press, 1990.

Shanghai College of Traditional Medicine. *Acupuncture, A Complete Text*. Seattle, WA: Eastland Press, 1981.

Somerville, Neil. *Chinese Love Signs*. London: Aquarian, 1995.

Teeguarden, Ron. *Chinese Tonic Herbs*. New York: Japan Publishers, 1985.

Teeguarden, Iona Marsaa. *Joy of Feeling*. New York: Japan Publishers, 1987.

Thie, John. *Touch for Health*. Marina Del Ray, CA: De Vorss, 1973.

Walters, Derek. *Chinese Astrology*. London: Aquarian Press, 1987.

_____. *Chinese Love Signs*. Torrance, CA: Heian Int'l, 1997.

White, Suzanne. *The New Astrology*. New York: St Martin's Press, 1986.

Index

Pamela Leigh Powers is an astrologer, certified clinical hypnotherapist, Reiki Master Teacher, and Applied Kinesiology teacher through Energetic Life Balancing. She is a hypnotherapist re-certification teacher for A. C. H. E. and teacher of holistic health principles including the relationship between the five-element theory and guided visualization. Recently, she added the  DNA Activations technique to her skills. She continues to do astrology readings, as well as voice and body readings based on this work.

In 1988, she published a holistic newspaper in the San Francisco Bay Area, a 16-page tabloid, 20 editions. During that time, she interviewed many holistic healers and decided to learn Touch for Health (TFM). Astrology and TFH were the basis on which this whole new concept was established. When healers started talking about the emotions related to the different organs of the body, she applied it to the hypnotherapy process. She calls her work, "Body-Mind Synergetics"—using the principles of acupuncture to guide visualization, so the mind can do what the needles do. She lives in Vallejo, California with her family.

Her website can be found under **www.acumind.com** and she can be reached by email at: **plp@acumind.com**